What Must I Do To Be Saved?

James R. Anderson

WHAT MUST I DO TO BE SAVED?
Copyright © 2011 by James R. Anderson
All rights reserved.

All Scripture quotes are taken from the King James Version of the Bible

Cover Design & Interior Layout: Anderson Christian Foundation at jamesranderson22@yahoo.com

Printed in the United States of America
U.S. Printing History

Second Edition: October 2014

*To my wonderful Savior, Jesus,
whose great pathway to salvation,
and promise that we can know for sure
when we have eternal life (I John 5:13),
became ever more clear to me as I worked on
and studied the Bible verses
contained in this book.*

NOTES

NOTES

NOTES

NOTES

NOTES

NOTES

NOTES

NOTES

INTRODUCTION

In this book we will journey through the New Testament of the Bible, stopping to discuss the verses that tell us how we might gain eternal life in heaven. There are literally hundreds of such verses.

The Bible tells us that when we die we will spend eternity in either paradise (John 3:16; Revelation 21) or torment (Matthew 25:46). If we search the Bible with an open mind and heart, we will discover what God says about how to gain eternal life in heaven. If not, maybe we are relying upon what friends, family, or churches have told us. Is this wise? Or should we investigate for ourselves? If you were buying a car or a home, would you rely upon what you were told or would you check it out for yourself? Eternity is much more important than earthly matters. Let's look at what God says, verse by verse, to see how what we might think compares with what the Bible says. Remember, God promises that if we seek Him, we will find Him (I Chronicles 28:9; II Chronicles 15:2; Proverbs 8:17).

First, let us spend a moment considering whether the Bible is true and inspired by God as it declares in II Timothy 3:16, or whether it is a collection of fairy tales, as some would contend. If the Bible is not true, such a search is without any value. But if the Bible is true, and God *does* tell us in the Bible how to gain eternal life in heaven and avoid eternal torment, then this is the most important search that any of us will ever conduct.

There are many proofs that the Bible is true, but let me mention a few. At the center of the Bible is Jesus, and the key question here is whether or not He rose from the dead as the Bible says. If He did, I think this would prove the Bible is true, don't you? Will you be writing out today's date at any time? For instance, 2014 means 2014 years from the birth of Jesus. Something important must have happened back then to establish our dating system. And do you notice a difference between the Christian countries of the world and the countries that have been plagued by false religion? If not, I suggest you turn on your television news this evening and you may notice some differences. Then let us consider the disciples. All but one of the remaining eleven died a martyr's death for teaching that Jesus was God. These men knew whether Jesus rose from the dead or not because they were there. Did they die a martyr's death to protect a lie? If so, for what conceivable reason? Next, let's consider what may be the greatest outside proof of the Bible's truth, and then we'll begin to look at verses that tell us how to gain God's great gift of eternal life in paradise.

Let's consider prophecy. Most of the false religions and cults of the world do not even attempt to prophesy, and those that do invariably get it wrong. I challenge you to find an exception. However, the Bible contains hundreds of prophecies fulfilled to the letter. Dr. J. Barton Payne has compiled an exhaustive listing of all 1817 prophecies contained in the Bible. They are all contained in his published book, *Encyclopedia of Biblical Prophecy*. This great book is a complete guide to the Bible's predictions and their fulfillment. I can guarantee that you will not find another religion or philosophy, anywhere, that will match this record—yes, the Bible came from God!

For example, thousands of years ago it was predicted that Jerusalem would be destroyed and the Jews would be exiled, scattered, persecuted, and again be drawn to Israel to re-create their nation (which occurred in 1948). The Bible also foretold that as we approach the end of time, Israel—a tiny nation no bigger than most of our states—would become the center of world history. And if you don't believe that incredible prophecy is being fulfilled before your very eyes, just pick up and read any newspaper any day of the week.

I think we should worry a lot less about today's maddening political situation, which God will deal with in His time, and a lot more about where you and I will spend eternity. The Bible, for example, has a lot to say about what will happen in the Middle East in the coming years, but more importantly, it has much more to say about where you and I will spend eternity. Let's see what the Bible says.

And she shall bring forth a son, and thou shalt call his name JESUS: for he shall save his people from their sins (Matthew 1:21).

This verse tells us very simply that it is Jesus Who will save us from our sins. When we are saved from our sins, we go to heaven. Please note that the verse does not say that we must be a good person to go heaven. The verse does not say that we must do good deeds to go to heaven. The verse does not say that we must attend church to go to heaven. The verse does not say that our pastor, priest, or church will save us from our sins. The verse does not say that a religious ritual will save us from our sins. The verse **DOES** say that Jesus will save us from our sins. Yes, praise God, gaining eternal life in heaven is this simple—if we will simply believe and trust in Jesus, as our Savior, then He will save us all from our sins. Then, out of gratitude, we will desire to do the good things that please God. This message is repeated, in different ways, throughout the Bible. For many people, this is too simple and our suspicious, cynical minds tell us there must be more to it. Today, there is a lot added to this message, isn't there? Each week, let's see if we can follow the pathway to heaven, based upon what God says.

Blessed are the poor in spirit, for theirs is the kingdom of heaven. Blessed are the pure in heart, for they shall see God. Blessed are they which are persecuted for righteousness' sake, for theirs is the kingdom of heaven. For I say unto you, that except your righteousness shall exceed the righteousness of the scribes and Pharisees, ye shall in no case enter into the kingdom of heaven. Be ye therefore perfect, even as your Father which is in heaven is perfect (Matthew 5:3,8, 10, 20, 48).

Normally, we would take a verse or two at a time, but these five verses are all found in Jesus' Sermon on the Mount, which is a difficult message. It leads to one inescapable conclusion, so we must consider the whole message. The first three verses give us clues, but not precise instructions, on how we might gain eternal life in heaven. The first verse tells us that we must be poor in spirit. I take this to mean that we must not trust in ourselves, our accomplishments, or any of our goodness to gain eternal life in heaven. The second verse tells us that we must be "pure" in heart, **BUT** who can claim to be "pure"? The third verse tells us that if we are persecuted for righteousness' sake, we have the kingdom of heaven. But we cannot control whether or not we are persecuted in this fashion. And how can we sinners be righteous? There are clues here, but not precise instructions.

But then it gets bad. In the fourth verse, we are told that if our righteousness does not exceed the righteousness of the scribes and Pharisees, we will not see heaven. No people, probably ever, had more religious zeal than the Pharisees. They piled hundreds of laws and rituals on top of the Ten Commandments, and we can't even keep those ten. For example, they hired people to come and light their stoves on the Sabbath so that they would not violate the Sabbath. Their lives were one religious work and ritual after another. There is almost no one today who would meet their standards. And then it gets even worse. In the last verse, after showing us in much of chapter five how impossible it is to keep even the commandments, Jesus tells us we must be **PERFECT!**

Now, what hope is there for me? There must be another way besides my own works, righteousness, rules, and rituals. And yes, praise God, there is! Let's see if we can find it.

> *Enter ye in at the strait gate, for wide is the gate, and broad is the way, that leadeth to destruction, and many there be which go in thereat. Because strait is the gate, and narrow is the way, which leadeth unto life, and few there be that find it. Beware of false prophets, which come to you in sheep's clothing, but inwardly they are ravening wolves (Matthew 7:13–15).*

Do you have certain thoughts in mind as to how to gain eternal life in heaven based upon what almost everyone else is thinking, saying, or doing? If so, such beliefs should be examined more closely. Jesus, in these verses, is telling us that the way to heaven is not the way it seems everyone else is following. Furthermore, Jesus tells us that there will be those who say they are speaking for the Lord when really they are not.

The way that seems right is the wrong way and if some people who pretend to speak for God really don't, then what is a person to do? The answer is obvious. We must get our answers from God Himself—in the Bible! So far, we've been learning from Jesus about the wrong way, traps, and deceptions. I encourage you to follow along in your own Bible to make sure that I do not miss important passages and so that you will gain insight from important teachings we do not cover. The Bereans were **commended** (not rebuked) by the great apostle Paul for double checking even his own teachings (Acts 17:11). Likewise, we should always double check the Bible teachings of anyone, especially on the important matter of eternal life.

There are many verses that tell us specifically how to gain eternal life in heaven, but first, it seems, we must do some searching.

Not every one that saith unto me, Lord, Lord, shall enter into the kingdom of heaven; but he that doeth the will of my Father which is in heaven. Many will say to me in that day, Lord, Lord, have we not prophesied in thy name? and in thy name have cast out devils? and in thy name done many wonderful works? And then will I profess unto them, I never knew you; depart from me, ye that work iniquity (Matthew 7: 21–23).

The Matthew verses seem to give us clues as to how we might gain eternal life in heaven, but they do not tell us so explicitly. In some New Testament books, like John and Romans as we shall see, there is literally one verse after another that tells us explicitly how we might gain eternal life in heaven. Yet, in Matthew, it appears that God is giving us things to consider before showing us the pathway more clearly.

In these verses, we are told that it is not everyone who *says* he is a Christian who shall enter heaven for eternity, but it is rather the one who "doeth the will" of God. But what does this mean? Can anyone or does anyone *always* do the will of God? Or even most of the time? We shall learn in upcoming verses that the first thing any of us must do, before we can even begin to please God, is to come to God—and that is only through Jesus Christ (John 14:6). When we repent of not having trusted in Jesus alone, we gain eternal life in heaven by thus doing the will of God. We also, then, live by faith and become just (through Jesus) in the eyes of God (Hebrews 10:36–39). This is not because there is any good in us without Christ (Mark 10:18), but because the goodness of Christ is attributed to us by virtue of our faith in Him (Philippians 3:9). The Savior of the world becomes our Savior only when we transfer our trust to Him and Him alone!

And, behold, they brought to him a man sick of the palsy, lying on a bed; and Jesus seeing their faith said unto the sick of the palsy; Son, be of good cheer; thy sins be forgiven thee (Matthew 9:2).

In this verse, finally, we begin to see more clearly how we might gain eternal life in heaven. There are several key points here. First, when our sins are forgiven, we have eternal life in heaven (Mark 4:11–12; Acts 13:37–39; Colossians 1:13–14). Why would Jesus forgive our sins and how do we come to have our sins forgiven? Is it by good works, attending the right church, or following rules and rituals? No, the answer we see in this verse, and repeatedly in hundreds of verses throughout the New Testament, is the word *faith* and synonyms such as *belief* and *trust*. That faith, belief, or trust must always be in the One to Whom it was directed in this verse—Jesus Christ.

One more relevant question is raised by this verse. There are many today who pretend to forgive our sins, perhaps in the name of Jesus. But can they really do so? The story is told of an old Scottish woman who lay dying. Her neighbors, not knowing her religious background, sent for the priest. When he came, he announced he was there to give her absolution. When she asked the meaning of the word, he said he was there to forgive her sins. She asked to see his hands and, puzzled, he complied. Upon examining his hands, she announced, "You, sir, are an imposter. The One Who forgives my sins has nail prints in His hands."

Many churches, pastors, and priests today pretend to forgive sins. If you believe that, that means you have a Savior other than Jesus or in addition to Jesus, do you not? Maybe that is just fine with your church, pastor, or priest. But do you really want to trust in that church, pastor, or priest to carry you across that great divide when life is over? When Jesus announced His authority to forgive sins, He felt compelled to prove His authority by healing the sick (Matthew 9:6). Can the One Who forgives your sins do likewise? Let's save our trust for the One we know has the power to forgive sins, and Who will carry us across Jordan to heaven when our life on this earth is over—if only we will **trust** in **Him alone**!

And (Jesus) said, Verily I say unto you, except ye be converted and become as little children, ye shall not enter into the kingdom of heaven (Matthew 18:3).

This verse tells us that we must "become as little children" in order to enter into the kingdom of heaven. Here again, unlike verses we shall examine in the future, we have a verse that gives us a clue as to how we might gain eternal life in heaven, but it does not tell us directly.

What is it that a child almost always has in greater measure than an adult? Is it intelligence? Strength? Is it a lifetime of good works or rituals? No, the one thing that a child will invariably have in greater measure than an adult is trust. We adults, over time, become hardened and cynical because we know that everything on this earth, to one degree or another, at one time or another, will prove unworthy of our trust. But that is not so with Jesus. Other verses tell us that we gain eternal life in heaven by believing and trusting in Jesus alone. The Bible tells us that gaining eternal life in heaven is just that simple!

Jesus said unto him, If thou wilt be perfect, go and sell that thou hast, and give to the poor, and thou shalt have treasure in heaven; and come and follow me (Matthew 19:21).

In this intriguing incident, the rich, young ruler came to Jesus and asked him, "What good thing shall I do, that I may have eternal life?" (Matthew 19:16). Jesus thereupon told him to keep the commandments, thus directly challenging the ruler's preconception that he had to do some "good thing" to gain eternal life in heaven. Raising the stakes further, the young ruler had the audacity to tell Jesus that he had kept all the commandments. Evidently, the young man was quite pleased with himself, as one who trusts in self and works will be. However, Jesus called his bluff and told him to sell everything he had and give it to the poor. This demonstrated to the rich, young ruler, when he would not comply, that he hadn't kept all the commandments. In fact, he had violated the very first and greatest commandment: "Thou shalt have no other gods before me" (Exodus 20:3).

Did Jesus really mean that we have to keep all, or even certain, commandments to gain eternal life in heaven? Or was He showing the rich, young ruler, and us, that there must be another way to heaven other than by works, like keeping the commandments? I believe it is obvious that it is the latter, because if not, there will be no one in heaven except Jesus. Other verses will show us that Jesus died on the cross to pay the penalty for the sins that each of us inevitably commit. By trusting in Jesus and His great sacrifice, we will gain the eternal life that we cannot gain for ourselves. Therefore, as we are commanded in Romans 4:3–7 and elsewhere, let us not follow the example of the rich, young ruler in trying to work our way to heaven. Let us simply trust in Jesus Who paid the price for our sins, giving us eternal life in heaven!

MATTHEW 19

And every one that hath forsaken houses, or brethren, or sisters, or father, or mother, or wife, or children, or lands, for my name's sake, shall receive

an hundredfold, and shall inherit everlasting life (Matthew 19:29).

Jesus tells us in this verse that if we forsake earthly things "for my name's sake" we will receive earthly blessings plus "everlasting life." Standing alone, this verse could be taken to mean that if we forsake things on this earth, we can thereby earn everlasting life. However, we know from other more explicit verses that eternal life in heaven is a gift, not a reward. When a seemingly odd verse in the Bible seems to both conflict and coincide with a multitude of other verses, always interpret the vague verse so it coincides with the other verses. God's Word does not contradict itself. We thus learn in Ephesians 2:8–9, and many other verses throughout the Bible, that we gain eternal life in heaven by trusting in Jesus alone, Who died on the cross to pay the penalty in full for our sins. Knowing that Jesus has saved us, we should be grateful and thankful to Him and do the good things that please Him (Luke 17:17–19).

Let's say, for example, a friend had saved my life and became crippled in the process. There would be no way that I could ever repay him for his great gift, and I should not pretend that I could; it would only insult him and his great sacrifice. However, I certainly would not want to hurt such a friend, and I hope I would be good to him. I would be grateful for his sacrifice and friendship. In the same fashion, we should do good things to please our Savior—follow His commandments, attend a Bible-based church, and tell others about Him. We are saved despite who we are, not because of who we are. We must try each day, in word and deed, to better give thanks to our Savior for His great gift.

MATTHEW 26

And the disciples did as Jesus had appointed them; and they made ready the passover. For this is

my blood of the new testament, which is shed for many for the remission of sins (Matthew 26:19, 28).

Just before Jesus died on the cross, He took part in the Passover remembrance with His disciples. He told them that His blood would be shed for the forgiveness of our sins. There are at least two items of significance here.

First, there's a great deal of symmetry throughout the entire Bible, and we see it again here. God had finally had His fill of Pharaoh and his refusal to let the Israelites go. Despite the many miracles that Moses performed in God's power in front of Pharaoh, God set the stage for one final calamity that would break the will of Pharaoh and free the Israelites—the death angel was sent throughout Egypt, killing every first born. This should be a reminder that God is not patient forever. However, God told the Israelites that the death angel would pass over every house on which the occupants smeared the blood of a lamb, without blemish, on their doorposts. Every house that trusted God's promise, and was covered with this blood, was saved from death. Can you see this event pointing to Jesus' blood sacrifice to save us from death and eternal suffering?

It is no coincidence that Jesus died on the cross at the time of the Passover. Jesus is the perfect "lamb" promised by God. His blood covers our sins, if we simply trust God's promise (Colossians 1:13–14). When our sins are covered, we are righteous and without sin in God's eyes and, thus, gain God's gift of eternal life in heaven, for which we should always praise God!

MATTHEW 27

And, behold, the veil of the temple was rent in twain from the top to the bottom; and the earth did quake, and the rocks rent; And the graves were opened; and many bodies of the saints which slept arose, And came out of the graves after his resurrection, and went into the holy city, and

appeared unto many. Now when the centurion, and they that were with him, watching Jesus, saw the earthquake, and these things that were done, they feared greatly, saying, Truly this was the Son of God (Matthew 27:51–54).

These verses do not deal directly with how to gain eternal life in heaven, but they are nonetheless very important. The incredible supernatural events that occurred when Jesus died caused even this centurion to recognize that this was the Son of God Who was being crucified. The fact that the veil of the temple was torn in two at the time of the crucifixion is very significant. This all came at the very time Jesus died on the cross. Jesus' death occurred at the very moment (3 p.m.) that the Jewish priests in Jerusalem were sacrificing the lamb (the Tamyid sacrifice), the symbol of Jesus' death on the cross. God often uses analogies in the Bible to teach us the most important spiritual truths.

Prior to Jesus' death on the cross, God had established that people could approach God only through His appointed representatives from the Levite tribe of the Israelites. At the time of Christ, this system had degenerated to the point where the Pharisees, with their man-made system of rules, rituals, and regulations, had become the self-appointed gatekeepers to heaven. Although they were very religious, they loved the praise and worship of men more than obedience to God (John 12:43). Jesus condemned them for causing the people to worship themselves rather than helping people find their way to God (Matthew 23).

The torn veil, which previously separated man from God, tells us that we now can and should approach God directly through our Savior Jesus Christ (Hebrews 4:14–16). We do not need and should not follow intermediaries who insist that they are the intermediary to heaven. Since Jesus' death on the cross, there is only one mediator between God and man, and that is Jesus (I Timothy 2:5). There is no person, living or dead, and no rites, rituals, or ceremonies, regardless of their originator, that can save us. Jesus is the only One. God is no respecter of persons, as Peter himself declared (Acts 10:34). Let us, therefore, place our trust in the only true mediator, Jesus Christ.

MARK 2

When Jesus saw their faith, he said unto the sick of the palsy, Son, thy sins be forgiven thee (Mark 2:5).

As we have learned previously, when one's sins are forgiven, one has gained eternal life in heaven (Colossians 1:13–14). God's great gift of eternal life in heaven, as we again see in this verse, is gained by "faith." And when one believes, this is a gift of "eternal" life and not "temporary" life (John 3:16). Thus, one is not saved by faith and then unsaved by works. Salvation is forever from the moment of faith. How much faith is enough? When ALL of one's faith, however small, is in Jesus and nothing else, that is enough.

Why must we have all sins forgiven in order to gain eternal life in heaven? In our human way of thinking, we hear of people who have done things that seem much worse than our sins. Then we think that maybe we don't really need to do something about our sin. But let's consider James 2:10. This verse tells us that if we were able to keep the whole Law and commit just one little sin, this would be the same as if we were guilty of every sin. In other words, that little white lie we tell is just as serious in God's eyes as murder. It is not that murder is acceptable—it is that God is so holy that He cannot tolerate even one little sin. Do we really want to come before God without having called upon Jesus to forgive our sins? Let us trust in Jesus alone and His great sacrifice on the cross for our sins. In doing so, we will gain His great gift of eternal life in heaven!

> *He that believeth and is baptized shall be saved; but he that believeth not shall be damned (Mark 16:16).*

This verse, which appears to say that one must believe *and* be baptized to be saved, seemingly stands in contradiction to the hundreds of other verses in the Bible that tell us that belief alone in Jesus, and His sacrifice for our sins, will save us. In resolving the seeming contradiction, one should assume that the multitude of verses are correct, and interpret the odd verse accordingly, not the reverse. Furthermore, when there is an interpretation that renders all the verses non-contradictory, this is the interpretation that is correct. In this instance, such an interpretation is that belief alone saves, and baptism adds nothing to salvation. Why is baptism then mentioned in conjunction with salvation? We know it is very important and we also know that the Bible commands all who have believed to be baptized to show the world they are Christians. One who believes and is not baptized is thus disobeying God, but he is still saved, as the multitude of other verses tells us.

What, then, do we make of the prevalent practice of baptizing babies? There are many things we don't know about this practice, but there is one thing we do know—it is not found in the Bible. We don't know who instituted the practice and we don't know when it began, although it was probably one or two hundred years after the time of Christ. In the Bible, all people who were baptized had previously believed and were thus saved by the time they were baptized. This verse clearly tells us that baptism without belief does not save. A baby cannot believe.

Is there any harm in believing or causing others to believe that they are saved by a ritual—baptism as a baby—they don't even remember? The practice is not condemned in the Bible because it did not even exist at the time the Bible was written. However, there were Jews who apparently believed that salvation came by both belief in Jesus and another infant ritual, circumcision. John Calvin concluded that infant baptism saves because of its similarity to circumcision. But the Bible tells us that if one were trusting in his circumcision that "Christ shall profit you nothing," and this *partial* trust in Jesus was essentially worthless (Galatians 5:1–6). With Jesus, it is all or nothing. He will not share His throne with rituals, authorities, or institutions. It is trust in Jesus alone that will save us!

LUKE 7

And he said to the woman, Thy faith has saved thee; go in peace (Luke 7:50).

In Luke 7, we learn that Jesus has come to a Pharisee's home for dinner. A woman, a known sinner, brought Jesus a gift and kissed His feet. The Pharisees prided themselves on keeping the commandments, rules, and rituals. This Pharisee was indignant that Jesus would associate with this known sinner. We don't know if the Pharisee ever came to trust in Jesus, but we do know that the sinner did, and it was her "faith" that saved her. Jesus forgave all her sins and saved her.

Perhaps you might think, *There is too much wrong with my life now. When I am a little better, I will come to Jesus and trust in Him.* Or maybe we are a little like the Pharisee and trust in our own goodness, works, and rituals instead of trusting in Jesus and His sacrifice. Jesus wants us to come as we are. Until we trust in Jesus, we will never get better. No matter how seemingly good or bad we might be, we must, now, turn from the ways we think are best, which in fact lead to hell (Proverbs 14:12), and trust in Jesus. We will then gain God's great gift of eternal life in heaven.

LUKE 8

Those by the way side are they that hear; then cometh the devil, and taketh away the word out of

their hearts, lest they should believe and be saved (Luke 8:12).

Can it be plainer than this? We are told by Jesus Himself in this parable that if we "believe," then we are "saved." Jesus tells us in this verse, and repeatedly throughout the Bible, that if we will simply believe in Him, and the blood He shed at Calvary as the sacrifice for our sins, we have then gained eternal life in heaven. But how can this be? How can it be this simple? And how can we come to believe?

The Bible tells us that we gain faith as we read and study the Bible (Romans 10:17). That is why the devil tries to keep us away from the Bible, as we see in this verse. Don't we see a lot of activity from the devil and his helpers today to keep people away from the Bible? The devil tries to convince us to trust in all kinds of things for our salvation, good and bad, rather than trust in Jesus. But God promises that if we seek Him, we will find Him (I Chronicles 28:9; II Chronicles 15:2). That means don't blindly accept things told you by whoever has your ear at the moment. Each week, if you humbly and prayerfully ask God to show you the meaning of the verses we study, you are seeking God. He promises that you will find Him and His Holy Spirit will give you the power to believe and, thus, gain eternal life in heaven.

LUKE 18

And Jesus said unto him, receive thy sight; thy faith hath saved thee (Luke 18:42).

There are many instances in the New Testament where Jesus heals people, physically and spiritually. In all such cases, it is the "faith" of the person resting in Jesus that healed him. When a person is healed spiritually, he is saved for eternity. Jesus did many good things while He was here on earth, including feeding the hungry, healing the sick, and performing miracles. Jesus did not do these things as an end in themselves—to make people's lives n this earth a little better. Jesus did these things to prove that He ad the power to forgive sins (Matthew 9:6). He did these things o that the people would believe and trust in Him and thereby ain eternal life in heaven. Let's consider priorities for a moment.

Let's say that some person or organization was so owerful that it could make the life of everyone on earth perfect —no more hunger, homelessness, discrimination, or war. And hat would be a wonderful thing! Now, let's say there are five illion people on earth and each lives an average of eighty years. This would be 560 billion man-years (80 x 7 billion). So, for xample, when you die, you will live another 560 billion years. Then when 560 billion years have passed, eternity has just begun nd you will live many trillion more years. The 560 billion man-ears would be an example of the cumulative number of years ved by everyone alive on this earth at this time. Of course, 560 illion does not compare with eternity, but I'm just using this xtreme number as an example to help illustrate the length of ternity. I would say that where you, and others, spend eternity is nuch more important than the condition of your life on this arth, wouldn't you?

LUKE 19

And Jesus said unto him, This day is salvation ome to this house, forsomuch as he also is a son of Abraham. For the Son of man is come to seek and to save that which was lost (Luke 19:9–10).

These verses, as with most of the salvation verses in Luke, give us clues as to how to gain eternal life in heaven, but are ot nearly as explicit as other verses.

In this story of Zacchaeus, we know that Jesus saved Zacchaeus. We also know that Jesus said He came to save those who were "lost." We further know that Zacchaeus came seeking esus, even going so far as to climb up into a tree to search Him ut. Can you imagine the sight of this little man climbing up into a tree to see Jesus? Are you seeking Jesus that fervently? Would you go this far? Jesus is not on earth today, but you can find Him, just as Zacchaeus did, in the pages of your Bible.

Let's note a couple of things here. First, Zacchaeus did not come through the religious leaders of his day, the Pharisees, to gain eternal life in heaven. He did not use intermediaries; he came directly to Jesus. God promises that if we diligently seek Him, we will find Him (I Chronicles 28:9; II Chronicles 15:2). Just as promised, when he sought God (through Jesus), Zacchaeus found God and eternal life in heaven to boot!

Second, Jesus evidently looked into Zacchaeus' heart and mind and realized that Zacchaeus knew he was "lost" and needed a Savior. Jesus will only save those who already know they are "lost," not those who think they are good enough by virtue of their works, rules, or rituals (Matthew 9:11–13). Let us consider the lesson of Zacchaeus. Let us come directly to Jesus, trusting only in Him, knowing that we are lost sinners and need a Savior. He will save us! According to God and His Word, it is just that simple!

LUKE 23

And he said unto Jesus, Lord, remember me when thou comest into thy kingdom. And Jesus said unto him, Verily I say unto thee, today shalt thou be with me in paradise (Luke 23:42–43).

As Jesus hung on the cross, crucified between two thieves, one of the thieves doubted and tested Him and is no doubt in hell today. The other thief believed in Jesus and simply said to him, "Jesus, Lord, remember me when thou comest into thy kingdom." You see Jesus' response above.

There are at least a couple of items to consider here. First, Jesus was on that cross because the religious leaders of His day put Him there. Why? One big reason was that these religious leaders had brainwashed the people to the point where they holeheartedly trusted in their leaders, rules, and rituals to get to eaven. These leaders saw Jesus as competition. I suspect that for ie last two thousand years they have been thinking that they hould have put their trust in Jesus instead of in their system. 'he fact is that anytime Jesus is preached, there will be pposition. This was true two thousand years ago and it is true day.

Second, do you think that you need to be baptized in rder to be saved? Do you think that you need to spend time in urgatory to pay God back for your sins? Do you think you need o be a good person to get to heaven? Do you think that you eed to know and abide by religious rituals or attend the right hurch to go to heaven? Apparently, Jesus doesn't think so. Jesus id not require any of those man-made preconditions. This thief vas no doubt a very bad person, or he would not have been on he cross. Yet, his belief in Jesus alone saved him **THAT VERY)AY**. And that, fellow seeker, is exactly what will save you and ne—nothing more and nothing less!

JOHN 1

But as many as received him, to them gave he ower to become the sons of God, even to them that elieve on his name (John 1:12).

O ur search for the pathway to eternal life in heaven has taken us now to the gospel of John. If a person has limited time n which to search the Bible for verses on eternal life, there are robably no better books to search than John and Romans.

We receive Jesus when we "believe," as this verse tells us. Vhat we "believe" is what Jesus, as recorded in the Bible, tells us bout Himself and what He did for us. Jesus came to earth from leaven—where He had lived and will live for eternity—to suffer ind die on the cross in order to pay the penalty for our sins Revelation 1:5, 8, 18).

God is both love (I John 4:8) and just (Exodus 34:7). If God were only love, everyone would be saved, and if He were only just, no one would be saved. Like the judge who must punish wrongdoers, even if the wrongdoer is someone he likes, God must punish sin. We could not possibly do enough good works or religious rituals to atone for our sins. So God sent Jesus to suffer and die for our sins, and thus pay the penalty once and for all. This would be like a judge who sentenced a man to prison and then sent his own son to serve the sentence; no earthly judge would do this, but God did.

Eternal life in heaven is thus a gift (Romans 6:23; Ephesians 2:8–9) because there is nothing that we can do or should try to do to earn it. If we did, we would only be insulting Jesus by pretending that His great sacrifice was not sufficient. When we stop believing in our own works, goodness, rules, rituals, ceremonies, and any other thing, and place our entire belief and trust in Jesus and His finished work on the cross, we become a son of God, and will have gained eternal life in heaven!

JOHN 1

The next day John seeth Jesus coming unto him, and saith, Behold the Lamb of God, which taketh away the sin of the world (John 1:29).

When God killed the firstborn son throughout Egypt, each Israelite who had enough faith to obey God and take the blood of an unblemished lamb and smear it on the doorposts of his house, was protected by God from death (Exodus 12). This was also the beginning of the Jewish Passover. With the Passover, God, for reasons of His own, established that the Israelites should periodically sacrifice an unblemished lamb for their sins. This unblemished lamb was a symbol of the perfect Lamb to come, our Savior, Jesus Christ. The Israelite who trusted in this sacrifice, and the coming Savior it portrayed, would have his sins covered (forgiven by God). When Jesus died on the cross (not

oincidentally at Passover time), He became the ultimate sacrifice
or the sins of all who would believe in Him and accept His great
ift (Hebrews 10:1–14; I Corinthians 5:7). When Jesus died on
he cross, trust was transferred from the imperfect symbol
Passover lamb) to the perfect sacrificial Lamb (Jesus).

Much of the Old Testament predicts what would then
ccur in the New Testament. We know that there is a penalty for
in. We know that blood is required as a sacrifice for sin. We also
now that in the Old Testament, the repeated periodic sacrifice
f a lamb would cover the sins of the people. The Bible also tells
s that when Jesus came, we would gain eternal life in heaven by
rusting in His blood sacrifice for our sins. The relationship of
hese two sacrifices would be like a mortgage on a house. If you
nake a payment on that mortgage each month, the lender is
atisfied, but only for a month. But if someone comes along and
ays off the entire mortgage, the lender is satisfied forever. The
Old Testament lamb sacrifice satisfied God only for a time. When
esus sacrificed Himself on the cross, His blood would cover our
ins forever, but we must believe and trust in Him. That would be
ke paying off the mortgage forever. Jesus paid a great price for
ur sins! Will you set aside pride, tradition, or anything else and
humbly accept His great gift?

JOHN 3

Jesus answered and said unto him, Verily,
verily, I say unto thee, except a man be born again,
he cannot see the kingdom of God (John 3:3).

This verse tells us that a person must be "born again" to enter
heaven. Some denominations call it "regeneration."
Nicodemus asked, how does one become "born again"? The
verses following John 3:3 tell us it has to do with the Holy Spirit.
Again, we come to the question, how does one become "born
again"? This one verse has perhaps generated more controversy
and soul searching among Christians than any other verse in the

Bible. In the verses we shall study next week, Jesus clearly tells us how each of us might become "born again." The verses we shall study next are, I believe, the best and most clearly stated in the Bible about gaining eternal life in heaven. So, rather than attempting to deal with this difficult verse, let's allow Jesus, in the next verse, to clearly answer the question: "What must I do to be saved?" If you don't want to wait, feel free to read ahead!

JOHN 3

And as Moses lifted up the serpent in the wilderness, even so must the Son of man be lifted up. That whosoever believeth in him should not perish, but have eternal life. For God so loved the world, that he gave his only begotten Son, that whosoever believeth in him should not perish, but have everlasting life (John 3:14–16).

The Bible is a supernatural book that is difficult to understand without first being saved (I Corinthians 2:14). After one is saved, it all begins to make sense. The Bible tells us how to find God and be saved, if we would only read the Bible (I Chronicles 28:9; II Chronicles 15:2). As to how one is saved, I believe that no book in the Bible explains it better than John. The third chapter of John is the center of that great book and the sixteenth verse is the center of that chapter. John 3:16 has been called "the Bible in a verse." Let us look at it.

Jesus tells us that if we simply "believe" in Him and His blood sacrifice, then at that moment of belief, we have gained eternal life. One might think that his faith is not great enough. In this regard, Jesus gives us an example from the Old Testament that would point to Jesus' death on the cross. When the Israelites left Egypt and were in the desert, they sinned against God. God sent serpents that bit them; they became sick and many were dying. But then God miraculously intervened and told Moses to put a likeness of a serpent upon a pole, raise it up, and every

Israelite who looked at that serpent on the pole would live (Numbers 21:8–9). In other words, if an Israelite had just enough faith to look at that serpent on the pole, as God commanded, he would live. Of course, if he refused, he would die.

This great example from the Old Testament, according to Jesus Himself, shows us how simple it is to gain eternal life. If we would simply look to Jesus on the cross, our now risen Savior, whose suffering and blood paid the price for our sins, and place all of our trust in Him for eternal life, we have, at the moment of trust, gained eternal life. We are "born again." It is simply a matter of obeying and trusting God and setting aside everything else. If a sick Israelite had decided to trust in something other than God's remedy, the serpent on the pole, I doubt he would have been healed. Do you really want to place your trust in something other than Jesus for your eternal life? When we have just enough faith, however little it may be, and cast aside everything else and trust in Jesus alone, that amount of faith is sufficient. Praise God!

JOHN 3

For God sent not his Son into the world to condemn the world; but that the world through him might be saved. He that believeth on him is not condemned, but he that believeth not is condemned already, because he hath not believed in the name of the only begotten Son of God (John 3:17–18).

God is telling us that if we will simply believe and trust in Jesus, we will have eternal life in heaven but that if we do not believe in Him, we will have eternal life in hell. This is because Jesus (God) came to this earth primarily to die on the cross to pay the penalty for our sins. If we do not believe or trust in that great sacrifice, or decide that we will do it our own way, we are lost.

It is a good thing to obey the commandments, help others, attend church, and be baptized to show that we are Christians. We should also take communion to remember Jesus and His sacrifice. We should do these things out of gratitude and remembrance for what Jesus has done for us. If we start to think that any of these things will save us, then we are trusting in self, fellow man, and his devices, and not entirely on Jesus. Is this where you want to be on Judgment Day?

God has provided everything that we need in Jesus and His sacrifice. Therefore, let us, as the Bible commands us, believe and trust in Jesus to gain eternal life. And out of gratitude, we will do the good things that He wants us to do.

JOHN 3

He that believeth on the Son hath everlasting life; and he that believeth not the Son shall not see life; but the wrath of God abideth on him (John 3:36).

There is really nothing anyone can add to this verse. It clearly tells us how we gain eternal life, but it also speaks on the consequences of not believing and trusting in Jesus for eternal life. Yet, there has been a lot added to God's simple plan of believing and trusting in Jesus alone to gain eternal life. Why is that?

I think that it is our natural inclination to believe that we are really not so bad after all. Our experience in this world is that there is very little, if anything, that comes to us absolutely free with no strings attached. It is our natural inclination to trust in ourselves and our rituals instead of Jesus. It is hard for us to believe that it is Jesus alone. Yet, the Bible tells us so.

Feeding off our natural thoughts and suspicions, which are really rebellion against God, there are those who are only too happy to lead us down that path for their own personal gain. If an individual or institution can cause you to believe that there are special rites, rituals, or confessions that will save you, in whole or in partnership with Jesus, then that individual or institution has a powerful grip over you. Is your pastor, priest, or church pointing you toward the Savior or toward themselves?

JOHN 4

And many more believed because of his own word; And said unto the woman, Now we believe, not because of thy saying, for we have heard him ourselves, and know that this is indeed the Christ, the Saviour of the world (John 4: 41–42).

In these verses, we learn that Jesus is the Savior of the world and many believed in Him. Every person in the world who believes in Jesus, at the moment of belief, is saved, just as these people were two thousand years ago.

This situation and these verses arise out of Jesus' encounter with the Samaritan woman at the well in Samaria. The entire situation was most unusual. Jesus was a Jew and most Jews would have nothing to do with the Samaritans. The Samaritans were a mixed race, but partly Jewish, and they held to part of the Jewish religion but it was mixed with idolatry. The woman whom Jesus met at the well had been married five times and was no doubt regarded, and rightly so, as a sinner. But when she met Jesus, she believed and was instantly saved. There are many lessons here.

We may be tempted to think that we are too sinful to come to Jesus and have Him accept us. We think that when we get a little better, then we will come to Jesus. This is a lie from the devil, and one of his most useful tools. In God's eyes, none of us, however seemingly good, is better than anyone else, however seemingly bad (James 2:10). In fact, paradoxically, many times those who are seemingly the most sinful are closer to salvation than those who are seemingly good and religious, because a sinner knows he needs a Savior (Matthew 9:11–13). The seemingly good person may think his works and religion are enough.

Jesus shows us that being saved transcends one's religion. The Jews and Samaritans were as far apart religiously as any of the denominations are today. But when the Samaritan woman trusted Jesus, she was saved. Whether we are saved or not does not depend upon which church we attend, how many religious rites or rituals we have undertaken, or how many good works we have done. The Pharisees were the most religious people of their day, but Jesus harshly condemned them. It is not that it is bad to keep the commandments or be a religious person—what is bad is to trust one's religion, its rituals, or its leaders instead of Jesus. Our salvation depends exclusively upon whether we have believed in Jesus only!

JOHN 5

For the Father judgeth no man, but hath committed all judgment unto the Son; That all men should honour the Son, even as they honour the Father. He that honoureth not the Son honoureth not the Father which hath sent him. Verily, verily, I say unto you, He that heareth my word, and believeth on him that sent me, hath everlasting life, and shall not come into condemnation; but is passed from death unto life (John 5: 22–24).

These verses make clear that we are to honor both God the Father and God the Son (Jesus). If we do not honor Jesus, regardless of what we may think or say, we do not honor God. God the Father sent Jesus to save us from our sins, and to be the sacrifice for sin in our place. When we so believe, we are saved.

Why would God condemn us, as this verse tells us, simply for not believing? But if we reject that simple plan of salvation that was so costly to God, don't we deserve what we shall surely receive? When we reject Jesus as Savior, we give ourselves over to our own judgment. Why would anyone do so? Let us reject all the tricks and enticements of the devil and all his helpers, and simply believe and thereby gain God's great gift of eternal life

JOHN 6

> ***And shall come forth; they that have done good, unto the resurrection of life; and they that have done evil, unto the resurrection of damnation (John 5:29).***

This verse seems to indicate that we gain eternal life by good works, which is directly contrary to all the other verses that we have been studying, including the immediately preceding verses (John 5:22–24). These other verses all clearly tell us that eternal life comes by faith and not by works (Ephesians 2:8–9). We know that eternal life is a gift and that it cannot be earned or deserved through good works (Romans 6:23). We further know that all have done evil (Romans 3:23) and that no one is good in themselves (Matthew 19:17). It is the blood that Jesus shed on the cross (and our trusting this sacrifice) that cleanses us from sin and washes away the evil that each of us commits (I John 1:7). By believing and trusting in Jesus and His shed blood that covers our sins, we thereby gain the righteousness that we could never gain by our own works (I John 4:15–17). In fact, until we trust in Jesus, all our own righteousness is to God as "filthy rags," no matter how seemingly good our good works may be (Isaiah 64:6; Luke 18:9–14). How then do we explain this verse?

It is like the biblical story of Cain and Abel. Both brought a sacrifice to God and both seemingly did a "good work" (Genesis 4:1–5). Cain's sacrifice was seemingly acceptable, but he did not do it God's way.

After we have believed and trusted in Jesus for eternal life in heaven, His blood covers our evil sin and His righteousness allows us to do good works (fruit), which God will then accept (John 15:1–8). In this verse, this is the "good" that God desires from us, but the "evil" of rejecting Jesus is the one evil that His blood cannot cover. Let us, therefore, believe and trust in Jesus and thus do the good that will be acceptable to God, solely out of gratitude to God for the great **GIFT** that He has given us!

JOHN 5

And the Father himself, which hath sent me, hath borne witness of me. Ye have neither heard his voice at any time, nor seen his shape. And ye have not his word abiding in you; for whom he hath sent, him ye believe not. Search the scriptures; for in them ye think ye have eternal life; and they are they which testify of me. And ye will not come to me, that ye might have life. I receive not honour from men. But I know you, that ye have not the love of God in you. I am come in my Father's name, and ye receive me not; if another shall come in his own name, him ye will receive. How can ye believe, which receive honour one of another, and seek not the honour that cometh from God only? (John 5:37–44).

We learn several things in these verses. First, we learn the extreme importance of searching the Bible for ourselves. God tells us clearly that if we seek Him (by diligently searching His Word, the Bible) we will find Him (II Chronicles 15:2; Proverbs 8:17; James 4:8). These verses in John reiterate and show us that we find God, and consequently the way to eternal life in heaven, by searching His Word and not by exclusively listening to men, even religious leaders or authorities. When the Pharisees—the religious leaders of their day who knew the Bible inside and out—used their religious rules, rites, and rituals to draw men to themselves instead of Jesus, do you think the same thing could happen today, whether innocently or purposefully? The great apostle Paul commended, not condemned, his flock for searching their Bibles to be certain that what he was telling them was true and from God. If the great Paul, as recorded in the Bible, required this, should not you do the same? (Acts 17:10–13). Are the religious leaders you trust happy or displeased when you question, from the Bible, what they say?

Second, Jesus tells us that the great danger from religious systems, churches, and leaders is that they will start seeking honor from people, instead of from God, and will then slowly but surely begin to teach doctrines that will cause people to honor themselves instead of Jesus alone. It happened in Jesus' day and it can and does happen today. Churches and religious leaders can do tremendous good when they turn people to Jesus, and they can do tremendous harm when they turn people toward themselves, their institution, or rituals. No church is perfect and no religious leader or man is perfect, but some are better than others. The standard is whether they are pointing us toward Jesus or not. In any event, let each of us, individually, as these verses instruct us, seek truth through the Bible. And then, if you so believe, trust in Jesus alone and thereby gain life eternally in heaven with Jesus.

JOHN 6

Jesus answered them and said, Verily, verily, I say unto you, ye seek me, not because ye saw the miracles, but because ye did eat of the loaves, and were filled. Labor not for the meat which perisheth, but for that meat which endureth unto everlasting life, which the Son of man shall give unto you; for him hath God the Father sealed. Then said they unto him, What shall we do, that we might work the works of God? Jesus answered and said unto them, this is the work of God, that ye believe on him whom he hath sent (John 6:26–29).

Jesus perceives and tells the crowd following Him that they are seeking Him not because of the great miracles that He had just performed, but rather because Jesus could create bread and they liked to eat the bread. Jesus tells the people not to be so concerned with food but rather to seek eternal life. But sadly, the crowd was more concerned with their next meal than seeking eternal life with Jesus. Do we see the same today? It is important to have food, but isn't it more important to know where one will spend eternity?

The crowd, though, did ask Jesus what work they could do that would please God. Jesus tells the crowd the work that is most pleasing to God and the foundation of all else that is pleasing to God—one must believe in Jesus Christ. Please note that Jesus did not say to keep the commandments, to do good deeds, to be baptized, to take communion, or to do any one of many things, that in and of themselves are good. Jesus told them the one thing that we all must do for any of the other good things to please God—believe in Jesus Christ! At the moment we transfer our trust from other things, even good things, to Jesus alone, we have gained the everlasting life that Jesus talks about in these verses. We then receive this great gift for which Jesus paid.

JOHN 6

They said therefore unto him, what sign shewest thou then, that we may see, and believe thee? What dost thou work? Our fathers did eat manna in the desert; as it is written, He gave them bread from heaven to eat. Then Jesus said unto them, Verily, verily, I say unto you, Moses gave you not that bread from heaven; but my Father giveth you the true bread from heaven. For the bread of God is he which cometh down from heaven, and giveth life unto the world. Then said they unto him, Lord, evermore give us this bread. And Jesus said unto them, I am the Bread of Life; he that cometh to me shall never hunger; and he that believeth on me shall never thirst (John 6:30–35).

Jesus has just told the crowd that is following Him that they must believe in Him to gain everlasting life. These verses begin with the crowd, incredibly, asking Jesus what sign He will give them that they might believe. This is an incredible demand because just the previous day Jesus had taken five barley loaves, two small fish, and had literally created such a feast from it that five thousand saw the miracle, ate their fill, and there were still twelve baskets of food left over. The crowd even said it was a miracle, but evidently the next day they felt they needed to see another one. Do you think that if only you could see a miracle from God that you would believe? It seems that this didn't work for this crowd when Jesus was there in the flesh. God's Word, the Bible, tells us all we need to know to believe, if we will only read it with an open mind and searching heart. The Bible tells us repeatedly, as do these verses, that if we will simply believe in Jesus, and trust His blood sacrifice on the cross at Calvary to cover our sins, that at the moment of belief, He will give us eternal life. But we must accept that gift, not seek to do it our own way by trusting in other things besides Jesus.

Please notice also in these verses that Jesus talks of Himself as the "Bread of God" and the "Bread of Life." Saying this, Jesus obviously does not mean that He is a loaf of bread. He is speaking figuratively. Some may read the Bible always literally and some always figuratively, but it seems best to read it with common sense, and let it speak for itself. Just as eating earthly bread gives us physical life, trusting in the "Bread of Life," Jesus, gives us eternal life. This is interesting and instructive because in other places in the Bible Jesus, who often speaks in parables, tells us that we should take communion as the wine or grape is His blood and the bread or wafer is His body. Some insist that this means the wine and bread that you drink and eat at communion are literally the blood and body of Jesus, while others state that Jesus was speaking figuratively and that the wine and bread are important symbols of Jesus' sacrifice for us on the cross. The problem with taking the communion verses literally is that, first, we are obviously not drinking real blood nor eating real flesh. At communion, any scientific analysis of the elements would tell us this. Second, insisting that we are drinking blood and eating flesh at communion seems to then lead to giving salvation powers to these elements and those who administer them. These verses that we have just studied, I believe, are in support of the figurative interpretation. However we view these verses, let us trust in Jesus alone to gain His great gift of eternal life, but always remember the great cost to our Savior!

JOHN 6

All that the Father giveth me shall come to me; and him that cometh to me I will in no wise cast out (John 6:37).

This verse tells us that when we come to Jesus, He will accept us as we are, He will not cast us out, and we can live with Him in heaven. But notice that condition—first we must come. Why would anyone come to the Savior, Jesus? The answer is that one must know he needs a Savior before he will come to the Savior.

Do we think that we are pretty good, at least in comparison to those we see around us? If so, we will never come to the Savior. Do we think that our religious rules, rituals, and regulations will save us? If so, like the Pharisees, we will never come to the Savior. Jesus told us that until we realize we are sick (sinful), we will never realize our need for a Savior (Matthew 9:12). I suggest we read Matthew chapters 5, 6, and 7 to refresh our memories as to how easy it is to sin. Then, after we realize how much we sin, let us further realize that a holy God cannot tolerate even one little sin (James 2:10).

The God of the Bible is not a big jolly twenty-first-century pluralistic Santa Claus, and this is the God each of us will face on Judgment Day. The God of the Bible appears to be very different than the god that many have constructed within their own minds. Since the world is winking at sin today, we think God does too. But God still hates sin. God doesn't change (Malachi 3:6). And if we will admit it, each of us has a real problem with sin (Jeremiah 17:9). We greatly need healing by the Great Physician. Like the doctor who wants to help us, but cannot do so until we come, Jesus is always watching and waiting—praise God for our great Savior!

JOHN 6

And this is the will of him that sent me, that every one which seeth the Son, and believeth on him, may have everlasting life: and I will raise him up at the last day. The Jews then murmured at him, because he said, I am the bread which came down from heaven (John 6:40–41).

Aren't these two verses interesting? First, Jesus tells us, as He does repeatedly throughout the Bible, that if we will simply believe in Him, we *have* everlasting life. Do you see any other preconditions, qualifications, rules, rituals or anything else required, other than belief? I don't.

But just as interesting as Jesus' clear simple statement of how we might gain eternal life is the reaction of the Jews. When Jesus figuratively calls Himself the "Bread of Life," they are disgusted. Why? Because, like many today, they had built their own system of rules, rituals, and regulations, administered by the religious leaders of their day. Through this religious system, people could supposedly gain eternal life, and many had been fooled into believing it. Jesus came and told them the truth, and instead of believing in Jesus, they became angry. Do we fault them? What if Jesus came around today and told each of us salvation is by Jesus alone, and not the rules, rituals, and regulations in which we might be trusting for eternal life. How would we react?

Let us lay aside the pride of our religion or anything else that may be keeping us from the Savior and believe and trust in

Jesus alone, and thereby gain the great gift of eternal life, which Jesus purchased for us with His blood.

JOHN 6

Verily, verily, I say unto you, He that believeth on me hath everlasting life. I am that bread of life. Your fathers did eat manna in the wilderness, and are dead. This is the bread which cometh down from heaven, that a man may eat thereof, and not die. I am the living bread which came down from heaven; if any man eat of this bread, he shall live for ever; and the bread that I will give is my flesh, which I will give for the life of the world. The Jews therefore strove among themselves, saying, How can this man give us his flesh to eat? Then Jesus said unto them, Verily, verily, I say unto you, except ye eat the flesh of the Son of man, and drink his blood, ye have no life in you. Whoso eateth my flesh, and drinketh my blood, hath eternal life; and I will raise him up at the last day. For my flesh is meat indeed, and my blood is drink indeed. He that eateth my flesh, and drinketh my blood, dwelleth in me, and I in him. As the living Father hath sent me, and I live by the Father; so he that eateth me, even he shall live by me. This is that bread which came down from heaven; not as your fathers did eat manna, and are dead, he that eateth of this bread shall live for ever (John 6:47–58).

This passage begins with the verse telling us that if we believe in Jesus, we have everlasting life. Yet, what these verses specifically also tell us, in Jesus' own words, is that Jesus is the Bread of Life and that if we "eat the flesh of Jesus" and "drink His blood," we have eternal life. What does this mean? Does it mean that if we could find some remnants of Jesus' flesh and blood and would eat and drink these remnants, that thereby we would gain eternal life? Or does it mean that men on this earth can create Jesus' flesh and blood, like at communion?

If we start with the simple principle of translating difficult Bible verses so as to coincide with other verses dealing with the same subject, the answer becomes obvious. Jesus tells us repeatedly throughout the Bible that if we believe in Him and nothing else, we will gain eternal life in heaven. If we interpret these above verses figuratively, and not literally, all verses, including these, agree. Paradoxically, the theologians who are most likely to interpret the Bible figuratively, like a big book of fairy tales, are also the most likely to interpret these obviously figurative verses in literal fashion. When Jesus tells us He is a door (John 10:9), this does not mean that we will find Him hanging on hinges. When He tells us that He is the vine (John 15:1), this does not mean that we will find Him growing in a garden. He is obviously speaking figuratively. We thus learn that just as earthly bread gives us physical life, Jesus could be compared to bread in the sense that He gives us eternal life. We simply need to believe in Him, that His flesh was pierced at Calvary, and that His shed blood covers our sins. Why did this have to happen? Because God demands a penalty for sin and nothing we could do would pay for that. Jesus paid that price on our behalf with His holy blood. If today we pretend that someone on this earth can create Jesus' flesh and blood and trust in it instead of Jesus' shed blood, we are trusting in the wrong thing. Jesus alone will save us. Let's praise God for His great gift!

JOHN 7

It is the spirit that quickeneth; the flesh profiteth nothing; the words that I speak unto you, they are spirit, and they are life (John 6:63).

Jesus here tells us that His words are life—eternal life. How can this be? Jesus' words are the words of God, because Jesus was man, but He was also God. The Bible itself is the complete Word of God. But how can words be eternal life?

The Bible tells us that faith comes by hearing and hearing by the Word of God (i.e. the Bible) (Romans 10:17). We know from the many other verses we have been reviewing that it is "faith" that gains us eternal life. So as you ask, "How do I gain faith?" the answer is, "By searching the Bible." It is my desire that you take nothing that I am telling you, except the Bible verses I am quoting, at face value, but rather that you will pull out your own Bibles and read the verses I am quoting with the commentary I am giving. Be sure to read the verses before and after the quoted ones I present so that you will form your own conclusions to the truthfulness of my commentary. You should do this with anyone who tells you anything about what God says or what the Bible says because this is exactly what God indicates we should do (Acts 17:11). Those who double checked what even the great apostle Paul taught were not rebuked but commended. I suggest further that you circle in your own Bible the verses that tell us how we might gain eternal life. As you do this, you are seeking God and when we seek God, He promises that we will find Him. As the Bible tells us, faith comes by searching the Bible and it is by faith that we gain God's great gift of eternal life in heaven.

JOHN 7

He that believeth on me, as the scripture hath said, out of his belly shall flow rivers of living water. But this spake he of the Spirit, which they that believe on him should receive for the Holy Ghost was not yet given; because that Jesus was not yet glorified (John 7:38–39).

Once again, Jesus tells us that if we believe in Him, good things will happen. We will receive the Holy Spirit to dwell within us, guide us, and reveal truths to us, specifically the truths contained in the Bible. We also gain eternal life as we have already seen in many verses. Some people say that they will not believe in Jesus until they understand all or great portions of the Bible. Unfortunately, these people will die lost, because a person will never understand much of the Bible until one believes (I Corinthians 2:14). The reason is that the Holy Spirit, which indwells in all believers since the time of Jesus' resurrection, only dwells within us *after* we believe. And it is only with the help of the Holy Spirit that much of the Bible, and even life itself, begins to make sense (I Corinthians 2:10–13).

Each of us is given enough faith, however small, to believe in Jesus. But all our faith, however small, must be in Jesus, as opposed to other things like works, rites, rituals, etc. After we believe in Jesus, the Holy Spirit comes to live within us. Day by day, we will begin to understand the Bible better because the Holy Spirit helps us. The Holy Spirit then enables us so that the fruit of good works, or as these verses say "rivers of living water," flow from us. Once again, it all begins with belief.

JOHN 8

I said therefore unto you, that ye shall die in your sins, for if ye believe not that I am he, ye shall die in your sins (John 8:24).

The context for this verse is that, once again, Jesus is battling with the Pharisees. The Pharisees were the religious leaders of His day and knew the Bible of that day (the Old Testament) better than anyone. Many parts of the Old Testament, including Isaiah 53 and Psalms 22, clearly identified Jesus. Yet, they not only did not recognize Jesus as the Savior, they were so outraged by Jesus that they eventually killed Him. Why? Because while they pretended to direct the people to God, and to be a conduit between the people and God, they were actually, slowly but surely, causing the people to worship themselves instead of God. And they loved the praise of men more than the praise of God (John 12:43). If these religious phonies had truly been directing the people to God, instead seeing Jesus as a rival, they would have been directing their people to Him and to Him alone. The Pharisees were circumcising babies and performing other rituals that they believed would save the person. But Jesus didn't need any help saving people then, and He doesn't need any help today. Jesus is all we need!

A person, religious leader or not, who will direct people to any work, rite, or ritual outside of Jesus, is walking down the same road as the Pharisees. There is no Savior besides Jesus (Isaiah 43:11), and God will not share His glory with any person, regardless of who it may be (Isaiah 42:8). Let's not make the same mistake as the Pharisees and their many followers. Let's trust in Jesus, and Him alone, so that we will "believe" in Jesus and not die in our sins, and not miss God's great gift of eternal life.

JOHN 10

I am the door; by me if any man enter in, he shall be saved, and shall go in and out, and find pasture (John 10:9).

In this verse, Jesus tells us He is "the door" and if anyone enters in by Him that person will be "saved." Jesus is not telling us that we will find Him in a cabinet shop hanging on hinges; He is speaking figuratively. There has been, I believe, much mischief caused in Christendom over the years by taking verses that are obviously figurative and pretending that they are literal.

Jesus talks about us eating His body and drinking His blood at communion, when we are obviously drinking grape juice or wine and eating crackers or bread. A theology has developed that certain churches, and their pastors or priests, can actually turn grape juice or wine into blood and bread or crackers into flesh. This is simply not true. If one were to chemically analyze the elements, one would learn that they are grape juice and crackers before the ceremony and they are grape juice and crackers after the ceremony. There is no one, except Jesus, who can turn water into wine, nor wine into blood for that matter. So, who is one to believe and who or what is one to trust for eternal life? The answer, as God tells us repeatedly in the Bible, is Jesus alone! Any "door" but Jesus is the wrong one. This verse, and many others, tell us that if we go through Jesus, and Him alone, we shall be saved.

JOHN 10

The thief cometh not, but for to steal, and to kill, and to destroy; I am come that they might have life, and that they might have it more abundantly (John 10:10).

Once again, Jesus tells us that through Him we might have "life." As we have been learning through the many verses that we have studied, when we believe in Jesus, we have gained eternal life. In fact, even trusting in Jesus in addition to good works is not good enough. As the great apostle Paul tells us in Galatians 5, some who believed in Jesus to save them also trusted in the ritual of their day, circumcision, to save them. To these people, Paul said that Jesus would "profit them nothing."

The problem in trusting in Jesus' plus rituals is that we are saying that Jesus alone is not fully sufficient. The amount of trust we put in the work or the ritual is the amount we do not trust Jesus. I would not want to be in that position, considering everything the Bible is telling us on this subject.

This may seem innocent enough but Jesus warns us that just as He comes to give life, there are thieves out there who come to "steal, kill, and to destroy." A thief does not go around announcing what he is up to. In fact, the best thieves are often quite clever at disguising who they are and what they are up to. One clue to spotting a thief is that their trickeries always benefit themselves in some fashion. There is only one Savior and His name Jesus Christ. Let's trust in Jesus alone and gain God's great gift of eternal life in heaven.

<hr>

JOHN 10

> *But ye believe not, because ye are not of my sheep, as I said unto you. My sheep hear my voice, and I know them, and they follow me. And I give unto them eternal life; and they shall never perish, neither shall any man pluck them out of my hand. My Father, which gave them me, is greater than all; and no man is able to pluck them out of my Father's hand. I and my Father are one (John 10:26–30).*

We learn several important truths in these verses. First, Jesus is telling those who did not believe were not His sheep because they did not hear His voice. Jesus is thus telling us that if we believe in Him, we are His sheep and we have eternal life. In other words, Jesus is telling us that gaining eternal life is as simple as believing and trusting in Him.

Second, believing in Jesus begins with hearing His "voice." Today, the "voice" of Jesus is found in the Bible. The important truth we see here is that when Jesus gives us eternal life, we will "never" perish (eternal life, not temporary life), and we shall never lose it. Some may say we do good works to retain our salvation. The fact of the matter is that none of us can keep the commandments. This verse, like John 3:16 and many others, tells us that Jesus, and not His agents, gives us eternal life. And once we have eternal life, we shall "never" perish. We do not gain eternal life by faith and then lose it by insufficient works (Ephesians 2:8–9). God's great gift, when received by faith, lasts forever!

Jesus said unto her, I am the resurrection, and the life, he that believeth in me, though he were dead, yet shall he live (John 11:25).

L et's say that you were contacted by someone you knew had all kinds of credit problems and judgments against him. Let's say that Mr. Bad Credit told you that if you were to give him your car, tomorrow he would give you $1,000,000. Would you give him your car? On the other hand, let's say that a person you knew to be Microsoft billionaire, Bill Gates, promised to give you $1,000,000 tomorrow if you gave him your car today. Would you do it? The issue, of course, is credibility.

In these verses, Jesus tells us that he is the **RESURRECTION AND THE LIFE,** and that if we believe in Him, we will live even after we die. In other words, if we believe in Jesus, as simple as that may seem, we shall gain eternal life. But can we believe Him? Jesus reminds us that He was resurrected from the dead. Some say that all religions are the same, but I don't think it would be wise to believe Buddha's promises, because he is dead and rotting in a grave. Those who believed in Lenin, the god of many humanists, were disappointed. Lenin now lies in a glass cage like a stuffed bird, inadvertently reminding his followers of how human and fallible he was. But of all the religions, Jesus alone rose from the dead because He was God—the real God! When God Himself promises us something, we can count on it!

He that loveth his life shall lose it; and he that hateth his life in this world shall keep it unto life eternal (John 12:25).

This verse presents quite a contrast to today's humanist teaching that "you must love yourself" or "you must love yourself before you can love others." There is nothing new, though, in the "self-esteem" line of thinking. The devil has been head over heels in love with himself since he was booted out of heaven, and he spends a lot of time trying to convince us that "love yourself" is a good principle. All this is actually called pride and it is a sin. Just as it got the devil evicted from heaven, this one sin of pride probably keeps more people out of heaven than any other (Psalm 10:4).

Pride is what causes us to think that our good works will be good enough to be accepted by God. Pride is what causes us to think that our system of rules and rituals or our denomination is the best or only one. Pride is what keeps us from coming to Jesus with the humility of a little child and acknowledging that we can't do it on our own, and we can't do it with our works, rites, rules, and rituals. Pride is what keeps us from simply placing our trust in Jesus and His finished sacrifice on the cross for our sins and eternal life.

Thus, this verse tells us that when we hate our lives in this world, and its system, in comparison to what Jesus alone offers, and when we then place our belief and trust in Him alone, then we have gained God's great gift of eternal life. May we lay aside pride and thus gain eternal life!

JOHN 12

And I, if I be lifted up from the earth, will draw all men unto me (John 12:32).

This is not a clear salvation verse, but it does give us an important truth from which we can find eternal life. When Jesus speaks of being "lifted up," He is speaking of being crucified on the cross. Jesus tells us that this "will draw all men" to Himself.

It is said that the world divides at the cross and that is certainly true. For believers, the cross tells of how our Savior suffered and died to pay the penalty for sin that He knew we could not pay. He knew we could not do enough good works to gain eternal life, so He paid the price of sins in full for us. Yet, while the believer accordingly cherishes the cross as a reminder of what Jesus did for us, it is also evident that there are many unbelievers who hate the cross and what it symbolizes. The devil, who knows that Jesus is real, has many helpers today and he is directing their efforts, whether they know it or not. Perhaps the only things that are not tolerated in America today are Jesus, the Bible, and the cross. In their own peculiar way, unbelievers are another proof of the Bible, because no one hates or dedicates their time to eliminating something that doesn't exist or something that is nothing more than a fairy tale. You don't see anyone trying to eliminate or marginalize Santa Claus, do you?

I suggest reading this verse in conjunction with John 3:14–16 which, I believe, are the greatest verses in the Bible and the greatest declaration by God to us of just how much our salvation cost and how simple it is for us to gain that great gift of eternal life. It is man, not God, who complicates gaining eternal life, and it is always for the "complicator's" benefit. In the third chapter of John, Jesus tells us that if we simply look to Him and His sacrifice on the cross, believing and trusting in Jesus alone, having eliminated all other objects of our trust, that in that instant we shall gain eternal life. Praise God for this great and costly gift!

JOHN 12

But though he had done so many miracles before them, yet they believed not on him (John 12:37).

This verse does not deal with how we might be saved, but we know from the many other verses we have been studying that we are saved by trusting and believing in Jesus, His death on the cross, His resurrection, and His shed blood as the covering for all our sins, past, present, and future. So, when this verse tells us that these people "believed not," it means they sealed their fate for eternity.

I have heard people say that if there is a God, He could certainly do some miracle and when they saw the miracle, they would believe in God and Jesus. This verse clearly tells us that this is not the case. This verse tells us that Jesus did many miracles before these people and they "believed not on him." You may wonder how this could possibly be. The devil can blind the minds, eyes, and hearts of men. Do you remember how in John 6:13–14, Jesus took a little bit of food and miraculously turned it into so much food that five thousand people were fed? Do you remember how the people then praised Jesus? Then, incredibly, the very next day these people, perhaps the very same people, demanded that Jesus perform a miracle so that they could "believe." Astounding!

I personally think that if Jesus showed up in Times Square tomorrow and started performing miracles on national television, that not many more people would trust in Him than do now. God has given us a Bible to tell us all about Himself and Jesus. There are hundreds of predictions in the Bible that were fulfilled to the letter. We see the world around us that God created and it is just simply preposterous to think that our world created itself and everything else from nothing. People today have everything they need to believe. The key question is, will you?

JOHN 12

I am come a light into the world, that whosoever believeth on me should not abide in darkness (John 12:46).

48

I n this verse, Jesus tells us that He is a light in the world and that if we believe in Jesus, we will not abide in darkness. As we look around today, we see a lot of darkness, don't we? We see darkness in many relationships between men, in politics, in false religions, and in many other things. In Jesus alone, we see constant and eternal light, healing, and inspiration.

This verse tells us that when we believe, we can live this life in the light. Many other verses that we have studied tell us that when we believe, we also gain the gift of eternal life from God. But as with any gift, if we elect not to receive God's gift of eternal life, we will not have it. We receive this gift by believing and trusting in Jesus alone, as the Bible tells us in many, many verses. Considering how feeble, false, and bad all the alternatives are, I think that this is the least we can do, don't you? Do you know of any better place for your belief and trust?

JOHN 12

Nevertheless among the chief rulers also many believed on him; but because of the Pharisees they did not confess him, lest they should be put out of the synagogue. For they loved the praise of men more than the praise of God (John 12: 42–43).

W e know from the many other verses we have been studying that when a person believes in Jesus, that person is then saved. These two verses tell us that many of the religious rulers of Jesus' day believed in Jesus, but would not confess Him because it would offend other religious leaders.

In Jesus' day, like today, there were evidently religious leaders who believed in Jesus and other religious leaders who did not. Even among the religious leaders who believed in Jesus, there were those who did not confess Him too loudly or even at all, as "they loved the praise of men more than the praise of God." Maybe they didn't want to be seen as Jesus freaks or radicals.

Isn't this sad, and even frightening? There are religious leaders who are not only *not* saved, but also actively oppose Jesus and people's efforts to confess Jesus and teach about Jesus. This clearly demonstrates how important it is that you pull out your own Bible to review anything that you are taught about salvation, the Lord Jesus, or anything about the Bible itself. If someone told you how to spend your money, I'm sure you would do a little independent thinking and research before following that advice. Your soul is a lot more important than your money. You can, of course, let your religious leaders do your thinking for you on spiritual matters. Your religious leaders, whoever they may be, are perhaps okay with that, but is it really wise?

Lastly, what about these cowardly religious leaders who believed in Jesus but would not publicly confess or preach Him because they were more concerned with impressing unbelieving anti-Jesus Pharisees, than the Lord Himself? Since we know that they were saved by believing, they are in heaven today, but just barely (I Corinthians 3:13–15). Don't you think that they experience great sorrow when thinking of those who were perhaps lost because of their cowardly testimony? Others, like Joseph and Nicodemus, eventually did come forward. Praise God for religious leaders who are not ashamed to preach Jesus—theirs is the most important job on earth. Let us believe in the Lord Jesus Christ, and thereby gain eternal life, and then tell others the best we can about our great Savior!

JOHN 14

Jesus saith unto him, I am the way, the truth, and the life, no man cometh unto the Father, but by me (John 14:6).

Today we live in a pluralistic age, which means that many people think that one belief is as good as another, and one religion is as good as another, and so forth. People believe this because they are taught this in the public school and in many other social settings. They seldom stop to think about whether it is true or not. Let's say you want to take an airplane to New York and the plane is scheduled to leave at 2:00 p.m. and, in fact, it leaves at 2:00 p.m., but you think that it leaves at 4:00 p.m. Your belief is not really as good as that of the person who correctly believes that it leaves at 2:00 p.m., is it? Not all beliefs and ideas are equally valid, nor are all religious beliefs. Please notice that the one and only thing that those who preach tolerance (pluralism) most loudly will never tolerate is Christianity. I think that deep down they too know that Christianity is transcending truth.

This verse clearly tells us that no one gets to heaven (comes to God) without going through Jesus. This means, as many other verses have taught us, that we are to believe and trust in Jesus alone, and in His shed blood as the covering for all our sins. If you believe this, you are saved! If not, you are not. Man, and false religion, may seek to add or subtract many things from this simple truth, but it is God, not man, who is the gatekeeper to heaven. When we come to the gatekeeper of heaven, God Himself, wouldn't it be wonderful if we could say, "I seek to enter in simply because I have believed and trusted in Jesus Christ, just as you, God, told me to do!"

JOHN 17

And this is life eternal, that they might know thee the only true God, and Jesus Christ, whom thou hast sent (John 17:3).

Jesus is telling us that we have eternal life when we know God and Jesus Christ, whom God sent to earth. Before we can know Jesus, though, we must believe in Him. If we do not believe in Jesus, or think that He is a fairy tale, we will never come to know Him.

Sometimes people might say that they will not believe in Jesus until they understand the Bible. In fact, they have it backwards. They will never understand the Bible until they believe in Jesus (I Corinthians 2:14). God gives each of us just enough faith so that we can place that faith in Jesus alone for eternal life, if we so choose (John 3:16). Then, once we believe in Jesus, God sends the Holy Spirit to dwell within us to teach us things of the Bible, to understand the Bible, and to know God and Jesus (I Corinthians 2: 9–14). Thus, we come to know Jesus as we gain eternal life by believing and trusting in Him alone!

JOHN 20

But these are written, that ye might believe that Jesus is the Christ, the Son of God; and that believing ye might have life through his name (John 20:31).

In this verse, Jesus tells us that the things that are written in the Bible are there so that we might "believe" and thus have "life" through Jesus. This is one more verse that clearly teaches that we gain life, meaning eternal life in heaven with Jesus, by simply believing in Him.

Some may say that they don't believe or can't believe because they don't have faith or that there is nothing after death. Others might have faith in their church to take them to heaven, others might have faith in some person to take them to heaven, and yet others might have faith in their good works, religion, rules, or rituals to take them to heaven. The Bible, though, clearly teaches that while some of these things might be good and others bad, it is only faith in Jesus alone that will take us to heaven. The Bible simply does not teach that faith in something else, either alone or with Jesus, will take us to heaven. If such were so, how could the hundreds of verses like this one be explained? And if the devil were trying to trick us into trusting things outside of Jesus, do you think he would make it obvious? Faith in these other things, or even faith in Jesus plus these other things, is simply not good enough. Faith in Jesus plus something else is simply telling Jesus that He is not sufficient.

If you are trying to build your faith, this verse tells us that reading and studying the Bible is the key. Other verses tell us directly that faith comes by reading and studying the Bible (Romans 10:17). God Himself promises that when we seek Him with an open and searching mind and heart, we will find Him! (Jeremiah 29:13; Proverbs 8:17). If you want to gain eternal life and know that you have eternal life (I John 5:13), take your Bible and begin reading. Start with John or Romans, maybe a chapter a day, and pray that God will teach you from the verses you read. You will become a believer and, praise God, the doubts about your eternal future will vanish!

ACTS 1

For John truly baptized with water; but ye shall be baptized with the Holy Ghost not many days hence (Acts 1:5).

This is not a direct salvation verse, but since some believe and teach that Jesus alone is not sufficient, and that one must also be baptized by a pastor or priest in order to be saved, this is an important verse. The failure to distinguish between water baptism and baptism by the Holy Spirit is the source of much erroneous teaching—baptism by water will save you. That is completely incorrect. Water baptism by a pastor or priest is simply a public ceremony showing others that you have trusted Jesus as your personal Lord and Savior. The Bible teaches that when we repent of our unbelief and place our trust and belief in Jesus for eternal life, we are then baptized with the Holy Ghost, meaning that the Holy Spirit comes to live within each believer to guide each believer to greater truth (Acts 11:16–18; John 14:16–26). The Holy Spirit, which lives within each believer, is thus the reason that Christians do not need or seek human spiritual bosses to tell them what to believe and what not to believe (I John 2:27). It is belief in Jesus that will save us from our sins (Acts 16:31; I John 1:8)

> **And it shall come to pass, that whosoever shall call on the name of the Lord shall be saved (Acts 2:21).**

There are three important truths in this verse. The first is that "whosoever" shall call on the Lord and be saved. The verse does not say that we must be good enough or do enough good works. In fact, the Bible tells us that if we are trusting in our own righteousness and good works, instead of Jesus or in addition to Jesus, we are not saved (Ephesians 2:8–9). The second thing the verse tells us is that we don't have to have perfect faith or the faith of a Daniel—our faith in Jesus must simply be great enough to "call upon" Jesus and then we are saved. **BUT** please note that the verse does not tell us that we must call upon Jesus in addition to other things. Lastly, God is telling us that when we call upon the Lord, we "**SHALL** be saved," not that we *might* be saved or *may* be saved. And He's not saying that we will be saved if we do enough good works or if we keep from sinning after we are saved. No, praise God, this verse tells us that whosoever shall call upon the name of the Lord **SHALL** be saved!

> **Neither is there salvation in any other, for there is none other name under heaven given among men, whereby we must be saved (Acts 4:12).**

Referring to Jesus, we once again see that salvation is through Jesus and Him alone. What is especially interesting is the context. Peter and John were teaching in Jerusalem. They taught that you are saved by believing in Jesus, Who died and rose from the dead to pay the penalty for our sins. Acts 4 tells us that the religious leaders of the day were present, and they listened and saw these men perform miracles in Jesus' name. By their silence, ney appeared to agree that Jesus rose from the dead. What did ney do? It would appear that the logical thing to do would be to elieve and be saved. But, no, they tried to silence Peter and John. Vhy? Their religious system was more important to them than ne truth, leading people to salvation, and even, evidently, being ived themselves. Let us not make the prideful mistake of the harisees and the Sadducees. Let each of us, regardless of our ackgrounds, in simple faith, call upon that One name whereby e must be saved—Jesus.

ACTS 5

And believers were the more added to the .ord, multitudes both of men and women (Acts 5:14).

I n this verse, we are taught that "believers" were "added to the Lord." When we are "added to the Lord," we are saved. Their elief—nothing more, and nothing less—saved them.

Salvation is a gift. Let's say that you gave someone a gift hat cost you dearly—let's say, many thousands of dollars. Then, t's say that the recipient of your gift took some change out of is pocket, handed it to you, and said, "Now we are even." How vould you feel? You would feel just as God feels when we try, vith our paltry, feeble, and insufficient good works, to earn alvation, which cost Jesus Christ His suffering and blood on the ross. Salvation isn't a gift if we think and believe we have earned :. And if it isn't a gift, we don't have it. May each of us, with verlasting thanksgiving to our great Savior, **BELIEVE** and hereby accept His great gift of eternal life!

ACTS 5

The God of our fathers raised up Jesus, whom je slew and hanged on a tree. Him hath God exalted vith his right hand to be a Prince and a Saviour, for o give repentance to Israel, and forgiveness of sins.

And we are his witnesses of these things; and so is also the Holy Ghost, whom God hath given to them that obey him (Acts 5:30–32).

These verses tell us that Jesus was crucified, and thus became our Savior. When we repent of unbelief, we receive forgiveness of our sins. God then gives us the Holy Ghost to live within us when we obey God by trusting in Jesus. We see in this chapter how this simple message, which is repeated throughout the Bible hundreds of times, affects different people in different ways. Please notice that the apostles, like Peter here, always pointed to Jesus and not themselves. Upon hearing this gospel message, some believed and trusted in Jesus and were saved for all eternity. The Holy Ghost then came to live within them to better guide them to spiritual truths. But others, including many religious leaders, became furious and tried to harm or kill these simple messengers.

Likewise, many today become furious when Bible truths are taught. They often do everything they can to rid the Bible and its messengers from our society. They ridicule or hinder those who would bring this life-changing and life-giving message to others. But their actions betray them. Deep down, they too know the Bible is true. If the Bible were a falsehood, would anyone waste his time attacking it? Does anyone attack or become furious at Santa Claus or the Easter bunny? Whenever Jesus is taught or preached, there are powerful spiritual forces at work. The actions of both the followers and the detractors of Jesus point to the truth of the Bible.

ACTS 8

And as they went on their way, they came unto a certain water and the eunuch said, See, here is water; what doth hinder me to be baptized? And Philip said, If thou believest with all thine heart,

thou mayest. And he answered and said, I believe that Jesus Christ is the Son of God (Acts 8:36–37).

There is a line of thinking today that if one is baptized, without believing, that such a baptism will save a person. But these verses teach us that we may not be baptized unless we have first believed. All cases of water baptism in the Bible are of those individuals who believed and were thus saved by the time they were baptized. Their baptism was merely a way of choosing to identify with Christ and showing the world that they were a Christian, as God tells believers to do. Jesus wants us to publicly identify as one of His followers. Thus, we should be baptized *after* we have believed.

ACTS 10

To him give all the prophets witness, that through his name whosoever believeth in him shall receive remission of sins (Acts 10:43).

This verse tells us that whoever believes in Jesus Christ "shall" receive forgiveness of his or her sins. We have learned previously that when our sins are forgiven, God sees us as righteous and we can then live in heaven with Him forever. This verse does not say that when we believe, our sins are forgiven until the next time we sin. This verse does teach us that all our sins—past, present, and future—are forgiven forever when we believe in Jesus Christ.

How can this be? The Bible tells us that Jesus was the perfect Lamb of God, who willingly sacrificed Himself in our place, to pay the penalty for our sins. When we believe in Him and His great sacrifice, then His sacrifice is credited to us and all our sins are forgiven forever. But doesn't this mean that we could be saved and then go out and sin whenever we please? Yes, but the Bible indicates that our lives may well be shortened if we choose to do this (I Corinthians 11:29–31). Much more importantly, the Bible tells us in the next two verses, Acts 10:44–

45, that when we are saved, the Holy Ghost comes upon us as Christians. When we have the Holy Ghost, we have the power to resist sin, as we did not before (Romans 8:1–15). A believer will desire to do good and not evil, Matthew 7:16, out of gratitude for what Jesus did for us.

Lastly, the next few verses tell us that we do not become baptized in order to receive the Holy Spirit—we are taught that we are baptized after we have believed and thus after we have received the Holy Spirit (Acts 10:43–48).

Then remembered I the word of the Lord, how that he said, John indeed baptized with water; but ye shall be baptized with the Holy Ghost. Forasmuch then as God gave them the like gift as he did unto us, who believed on the Lord Jesus Christ; what was I, that I could withstand God? (Acts 11: 16–17).

In verses Acts 11:1–17, we are taught that the religious authorities of Peter's day "contended" with Peter. They evidently believed that we are saved by circumcision, an infant ritual similar to infant baptism (Acts 11:2–3). They also believed, as Peter did until the Lord showed him otherwise, that the ritual of avoiding certain food was of some spiritual merit (Acts 11:7–10).

Peter then makes two important points. First, in verse 16, he tells those who believe that they will be "baptized" with the Holy Spirit. Upon believing, and being saved, the Christian receives the Holy Spirit, who guides him into truth and away from sin. There has been much confusion within the Christian community by virtue of the failure to distinguish between water baptism and baptism by the Holy Spirit when we see the word *baptized* in the Bible. In verse 17, Peter makes clear that we receive the gift of the Holy Spirit—proof of our salvation (Ephesians 1:13–15; Romans 8:16)—by "believing" in the Lord Jesus Christ

When they heard these things, they held their peace, and glorified God, saying, Then hath God also to the Gentiles granted repentance unto life (Acts 11:18).

There are at least two important things that we learn in this verse. The verse just prior to this verse tells us that God gave the GIFT to those who "believed" in the Lord Jesus Christ. We learn in that verse, once again, that salvation is a "gift" and it comes by belief in Jesus Christ alone. This verse tells us that "life," meaning eternal life, is given by "repentance." Does this verse mean that some gain eternal life by "belief" and others gain eternal life by "repentance," or does it mean that these two seemingly different paths to eternal life are really the same? Since we know that the Bible does not contradict itself, we know that when "repentance" is used in conjunction with salvation, it means repenting of not previously believing and trusting in Jesus Christ alone for eternal life. Thus, the two verses mean the same thing and reinforce each other.

The second great truth here is that salvation is opened to the Gentiles, and is not exclusively for the Jews. We do know that the Jews are God's chosen people and that we who are Gentiles are always to treat them and bless them as such, if we desire God's blessing and not His curse (Genesis 12:2–4). Yet, a Gentile living just prior to God extending salvation to the Gentiles might have thought God to be unfair. All this would demonstrate is that such people, like us today, would not have known God's ultimate plan, which is always best. May each of us allow God to be the judge of what is fair. May each of us then act upon the knowledge that God has chosen to reveal to each of us today and, by believing and trusting in Jesus Christ, gain His great gift of eternal life!

And the hand of the Lord was with them; and a great number believed, and turned unto the Lord. Then tidings of these things came unto the ears of the church which was in Jerusalem and they sent forth Barnabas, that he should go as far as Antioch. Who, when he came, and had seen the grace of God, was glad, and exhorted them all, that with purpose of heart they would cleave unto the Lord. For he was a good man, and full of the Holy Ghost and of faith and much people was added unto the Lord (Acts 11:21–24).

These verses tell us, once again, that many "believed," "turned unto the Lord," and "were added unto the Lord," meaning they were saved. As we go through verses telling us how we might be saved, do you see one word repeating itself? Is that word "believe"? Now, let me ask you a question. When you die and you stand before God, if He asks why He should let you into heaven, what would you say? Would you tell Him of your good works? Would you tell Him that you attend a church? Would you tell Him of the various sacraments, rituals, or rites in which you participated? Or would you have the one answer that He is looking for: "because I have believed in your Son, the Lord Jesus Christ, and have accepted His blood sacrifice as paying the penalty and as the covering for all my sins—nothing more and nothing less."

Many are trying all the man-made ways to work themselves to God. But a sinful man can never work his way into the presence of a Holy God, not even with religious works and rituals. If you don't believe that, please search your Bible and see what God says. It is God, not my church or yours, Who determines who goes to heaven. Salvation is a gift from God and we must humble ourselves to accept that gift and thereby gain eternal life. If God has made salvation a gift, who are we to try to earn it? As these verses tell us, once this gift has occurred, let us do what we can to tell others the good news of this great gift!

***

ACTS 13

Be it known unto you therefore, men and brethren, that through this man is preached unto you the forgiveness of sins. And by him all that believe are justified from all things, from which ye could not be justified by the law of Moses (Acts 13:38–39).

We are told by God, through His Bible, that "through this man," meaning Jesus, we have forgiveness of sins and we are "justified." What does justified mean? There is a little saying that helps us remember what it means: "just as if I'd never sinned." By believing in Jesus and the price He paid for our sins on the cross, we can be covered with Jesus' righteousness, and God no longer sees our sins (I John 1:7). We then have the perfect holiness that we need to meet God and go to heaven.

How can this be? It is like needing a medical operation you cannot afford. A very kind and very wealthy man takes pity on you and goes with you to the hospital. He is instantly recognized; his credit is good all over town. He tells the cashier that from now on you get all the treatment you need, and your new friend will pay for it. The hospital does not care who pays— you are now covered. Here is another ending. Let's say you get prideful at this point and say that you won't accept charity from anyone—you are going to do it your own way. Happy ending?

Let's not get prideful with God; Jesus paid the price. All we need to do, praise God, is accept His great gift.

And when the Gentiles heard this, they were glad, and glorified the word of the Lord and as many as were ordained to eternal life believed (Acts 13:48).

The context here is that the Jewish leaders and many of the Jewish people had rejected Jesus as their Savior, and Paul and the other apostles were now commanded by God to bring the message of salvation by belief in Jesus Christ to the Gentiles (people other than Jews). In this verse, once again, we see how simple it is to gain eternal life. We are taught that those who "believed" received eternal life. This was so simple that the Jewish religious leaders were filled with envy, and they stirred up opposition to Paul and Barnabas who preached this salvation message (Acts 13:45, 50). Why would these Jewish leaders behave in this childish fashion? Why would they not simply believe to gain eternal life? Because they had brainwashed the people into believing that salvation came by a series of works, rites, and rituals they performed. The simple message of believing in Jesus and thus gaining eternal life threatened to destroy their whole religious system. Then they, the Jewish leaders, would no longer have the admiration and worship of the people. These unfortunate religious leaders (and their poor followers) are in hell today because the devil caused them to be fearful of losing their religious system and filled them with anger and envy. What's the lesson here? Do not let anything, including religion, friends, tradition, pride, anger, envy, or anything else keep you from trusting in Jesus alone and thereby gaining eternal life! Maybe your religion tells you something different. If these religious leaders could come back to earth today and speak truthfully, they would tell you that not trusting Jesus is the greatest mistake you will ever make!

> ***Confirming the souls of the disciples, and exhorting them to continue in the faith, and that we must through much tribulation enter into the kingdom of God. And when they had ordained them elders in every church, and had prayed with fasting, they commended them to the Lord, on whom they believed (Acts 14:22–23).***

Once again, in these verses, we see that we enter into the "kingdom of God," meaning heaven, by "faith." As these two verses also tell us, this faith must be in the "Lord," or Jesus. Yes, God tells us in His Bible that gaining eternal life is just that simple—when we believe and trust in Jesus, we gain eternal life. And if God says it, who are we to contradict God?

But these verses also tell us that there may well be "tribulation" as a result of our belief. If we read the surrounding verses (and you should always pull out your own Bible and read the surrounding verses to make sure that you are not given something out of context), we see that the great apostle Paul was greatly persecuted for bringing this simple message of salvation by faith. How did Paul react? Did he whine about being mistreated for trying to do good? Did he feel sorry for himself? Did he get discouraged and quit? No, he kept on preaching the simple gospel message with more vigor than ever. And the devil himself, who certainly wanted to see Paul silenced, could not harm him, because God was protecting him.

When you place your trust in Jesus, and gain eternal life, you'll know that there is nothing more important in the whole world. As you further gain faith by reading and studying the Bible (Romans 10:17) you will want to tell others. You will probably be persecuted because of this. But the devil himself cannot harm you until God determines that your time on this earth is over. As long as your focus is on Jesus, all will be well and you will have not only heaven, but also a great peace in the midst of trouble

(Romans 5:1). Isn't it ironic that today people are marching and protesting and searching everywhere for peace that never seems to come, and it is there simply for the asking?

And put no difference between us and them, purifying their hearts by faith (Acts 15:9).

In this verse, God tells us that our hearts can be "purified," meaning that in God's eyes, our hearts will become as if we had no sin. This is great news because when we become as if we have no sin, despite the fact that we indeed are sorry sinners, then we can come into God's presence and have eternal life with Him in heaven.

But the question is, how may we "purify" our hearts? You might be able to think of many different ways that people are trying to do this today, but the Bible tells us there is only one way —"by faith"—meaning faith in Jesus alone (John 14:6). These verses are also telling us that in God's great plan and wisdom, salvation was now opened to the Gentiles (the "us" being the Jews and the "them" being the Gentiles), and thank God for this! Many think today that God is unfair because of this or that. This simply proves that we are not as smart as God, and we don't see the whole picture. God loves all of us and we see it again in this verse. The key question is not whether or not God is fair. God offers eternal life to each and every one of us as His own son, Jesus, paid the great price for our sins on the cross at Calvary. The key question is what we will do about this—will we accept it or not? If so, we will then desire to do good works to please Him out of gratitude for His great gift of eternal life.

And certain men which came down from Judea taught the brethren, and said, except ye be

circumcised after the manner of Moses, ye cannot be saved. . . . But there rose up certain of the sect of the Pharisees which believed, saying, that it was needful to circumcise them, and to command them to keep the law of Moses. . . . Now therefore why tempt ye God, to put a yoke upon the neck of the disciples, which neither our fathers nor we were able to bear? But we believe that through the grace of the Lord Jesus Christ we shall be saved, even as they (Acts 15:1, 5, 10–11).

Circumcision was a ritual prevalent at the time the New Testament of the Bible was written. It was very similar to infant baptism, which is a man-made tradition that did not come to be practiced until long after the New Testament was written. There were those who taught that a person could be saved by having a religious ritual, circumcision, performed upon him as an infant and/or that one could not be saved without it. The Bible nowhere addresses the subject of infant baptism, pro or con, because the practice did not arise until one or two hundred years after the Bible was written. However, as we see here, circumcision and the doctrine of salvation by works, which often accompanies salvation by ritual teachings, is roundly condemned.

We are told here that trying to get to heaven through man-made rituals and good works is a "yoke" that none of us are able to bear. I don't know why God, in His love and goodness, chose to sacrifice His Son, Jesus, to pay the penalty on the cross for our sins, but I do know that I am eternally grateful He did!

ACTS 16

And brought them out, and said, Sirs, what must I do to be saved? And they said, Believe on the Lord Jesus Christ and thou shalt be saved, and thy house (Acts 16:30–31).

This is one of many great verses in the Bible that tells us in all its power and simplicity how you, me, and everyone else on this earth might be saved. Please notice the key word: **BELIEVE!** And, fellow seeker, please note that God is telling us that we "shall" be saved when we "believe," not *might* be saved or *almost certainly* be saved. The verse also does not say that if we believe and do this certain ritual, do good works, or lead a good life that we will be saved. This verse tells us in all authority that we are saved when we "believe on the Lord Jesus Christ," period! This is the greatest news in the world. There is nothing on earth of more value and I believe that each of us should spend the rest of our days thanking and praising God for this great gift that He has given us through Jesus Christ, our Lord and Savior!

You may ask, "What if I don't believe? How can I believe?" In the Bible, God tells us that we gain faith by hearing and reading the Bible. We should read the Bible and attend a Bible-teaching church. God promises that if we seek Him diligently with an open mind, we shall find Him (I Chronicles 28:9; Proverbs 8:17; James 4:8; Jeremiah 29:13). This is one gift well worth searching for!

ACTS 17

And Paul, as his manner was, went in unto them, and three sabbath days reasoned with them out of the scriptures, opening and alleging, that Christ must needs have suffered, and risen again from the dead; and that this Jesus, whom I preach unto you, is Christ. And some of them believed and consorted with Paul and Silas; and of the devout Greeks a great multitude, and of the chief women not a few. But the Jews which believed not, moved with envy, took unto them certain lewd fellows of the baser sort, and gathered a company, and set all the city on an uproar, and assaulted the house of Jason,

and sought to bring them out to the people (Acts 17:2–5).

The great apostle Paul preached Jesus Christ as our crucified and risen Savior, and some "believed." We know from the many other verses we have studied that when a person believes in Jesus as his or her Savior that, at that moment, that person is saved for all eternity. This simple message is the message that Paul, Peter, John, and all the other great Christians of ages past, and even Jesus Himself, taught as the way to heaven and as the only way to heaven (John 14:6). Much has been added to and much has been subtracted from this simple but powerful message over the centuries, which is still the only way to heaven.

But please note that Paul and other believers were violently opposed by nonbelievers. The actions of these nonbelievers also prove the power and truth of the Bible's Christ-centered message. What difference should it make to these nonbelievers whether someone else believed in Jesus? Why was it so important to them that the name of Jesus be removed from their presence? Why is it so important to so many today that the name of Jesus be removed from their presence? Does anyone waste their time fighting against things that are obviously false? But just watch the reaction whenever Jesus is mentioned. I think, deep down, everyone knows that there is something different about Jesus. By making Him your Savior, you need never fear Him again!

ACTS 17

And the times of this ignorance God winked at; but now commandeth all men every where to repent. Because he hath appointed a day, in the which he will judge the world in righteousness by that man whom he hath ordained; whereof he hath given assurance unto all men, in that he hath raised him from the dead. And when they heard of the

resurrection of the dead, some mocked and others said, we will hear thee again of this matter (Acts 17:30–32).

The scene of these verses is the great apostle Paul on Mars hill at Athens debating and preaching to the Athenians. The Athenians, like Americans today, worshipped many gods. Paul delivered God's message to the Athenians that they, like we today, are commanded to repent of their unbelief in Jesus. God raised Jesus from the dead and this should prove to us that Jesus is our Savior, just as God tells us. If Jesus were not raised from the dead, how do you explain all the historical accounts of it? How do you explain the apostles dying martyr's deaths for simply trying to teach others about Jesus? Would they have done this if it were all a lie?

But what about you? Are you like these Athenian intellectuals? Have you fallen for today's adult fairy tale called evolution? Take a look around you. Do you really think that all of this came about by chance from nothing? Have you, like the Athenians, rejected God, and Jesus as Savior, because self is god? Or is it some other little god? Have you found a religion that serves you better than Jesus? If so, I plead with you to search for the truth of this matter with a more open and searching mind. As Paul tells the Athenians, there is a "day appointed" in which we will stand before a judge who knows everything. On that day, I pray that each of us might have the right answer to that question: "Why should God let you into heaven?"

ACTS 26

To open their eyes, and to turn them from darkness to light, and from the power of Satan unto God, that they may receive forgiveness of sins, and inheritance among them which are sanctified by faith that is in me (Acts 26:18).

The apostle Paul is recounting the words that Jesus Himself spoke to Paul. Jesus tells us, through Paul, that we receive forgiveness of our sins and inheritance of eternal life in heaven by "faith" in Jesus. The word *sanctify* means "to make free from sin." As this verse teaches, when we are made free from sin we are saved and we are saved by "faith" in Jesus.

Do you sometimes think that this is too simple? Or that Jesus could never save someone who has committed the sins that you have committed? Paul was a Pharisee, and as such had built up an entire system of good works, rules, and rituals by which he thought that he might gain eternal life. Yet, when Jesus appeared to him, on the Damascus road, he saw in an instant how wrong he had been. It is "faith" in Jesus alone that saves. Paul had also participated in some great sins, including the murder of Christians. Whether we think of Paul as a misdirected religious zealot or a great sinner—and he was both—God saved him at the moment of "faith." If God could save Paul, don't you think that he can save you and me when we turn to Jesus in simple, trusting faith? We will never get to God through religious zealotry, rites, rules, or rituals. Let's do it God's way—**FAITH IN JESUS!**

ACTS 26

That Christ should suffer, and that he should be the first that should rise from the dead, and should shew light unto the people, and to the Gentiles. King Agrippa, believest thou the prophets? I know that thou believest. Then Agrippa said unto Paul, almost thou persuadest me to be a Christian (Acts 26:23, 27–28).

The setting for these verses is that the religious leaders of Paul's day had once again caused Paul to be arrested on false trumped-up charges, and he was now being tried before King Agrippa. The religious leaders of Jesus' day were always opposed to the preaching of salvation by faith in Jesus alone. This is because such preaching conflicted with their system of salvation by works, rites, rules, and rituals, which caused the people to worship their system of religion, and themselves incidentally, instead of Jesus.

King Agrippa observed all this and "almost" became a believer. Why did King Agrippa not become a believer, at least at this time? Was it because of position? If King Agrippa came to trust in Jesus, instead of Caesar, could he have continued to be king? Could it have been vanity? Was King Agrippa ashamed to have his subjects and friends know that he had become a believer in Jesus? It could have been these things or any of a hundred other things. Yet, if King Agrippa never came to believe in Jesus, you can be assured that he now knows he made the biggest mistake of his life at this moment, when God's Holy Spirit was working upon him, and he refused to believe. How about you?

ACTS 28

And when they had appointed him a day, there came many to him into his lodging; to whom he expounded and testified the kingdom of God, persuading them concerning Jesus, both out of the law of Moses, and out of the prophets, from morning till evening. Be it known therefore unto you, that the salvation of God is sent unto the Gentiles, and that they will hear it (Acts 28:23, 28).

The apostle Paul was brought as a prisoner to Rome to stand trial before Caesar. Paul had been converted from believing in the religious system of his day with its rites, rules, and rituals, to believing and trusting in Jesus for eternal life. Everywhere that Paul went, in all circumstances, he now taught people to believe in Jesus alone to thereby gain eternal life.

These verses tell us that Paul taught the people who came to him that even the Law of Moses (the Ten Commandments) and the prophets (who are recorded in the Old Testament) were inting the way to Jesus. For example, the fifty-third chapter of aiah and the twenty-second chapter of Psalms point clearly to sus. Still, the religious experts of that day, the Pharisees, could t see that Jesus was the Savior and the fulfillment of the Old stament. This situation is just as true today when many ligious leaders trust in their own churches, devices, rules, and uals instead of Jesus alone, even though today we also have the ew Testament to point even more clearly to Jesus as the way to ernal life.

It seems that man has a natural inclination to trust in ings, symbols, or institutions that point to Jesus, but that are t Jesus. These people and things, when functioning as tended, should point to Jesus and never replace Jesus as the vior. Trusting in any of these things, instead of Jesus alone, ould be like eating a picture of beef steak instead of the beef eak itself—it will never replace the real thing!

ROMANS 1

Concerning his Son Jesus Christ our Lord hich was made of the seed of David according to he flesh; And declared to be the Son of God with ower, according to the spirit of holiness, by the esurrection from the dead. By whom we have eceived grace and apostleship, for obedience to the ith among all nations, for his name (Romans 1:3–).

here are many books in the New Testament that are loaded with verses that tell us how to gain eternal life. John and omans may be among the best of these books. I suggest that ou do one additional thing that I promise will benefit you piritually in a great manner, much more than just reading this ommentary. I know this because the Bible promises this—if you eek God, you will find him. I suggest that you go to the book of hn and then to the book of Romans and start reading until you find a verse that tells you how to gain eternal life. When you find that verse, circle it in your Bible and then pray over and study it, asking God to teach you the meaning of the verse. If you find just one verse a day, I think you will soon find that you are communicating with God in a serious fashion.

These verses tell us that we receive "grace" through Jesus Christ, Who rose from the dead. We know that Jesus died on the cross to pay the penalty for our sins. Eternal life is thus a "gift" because someone else, Jesus, paid the price so that we might gain eternal life. As simple as it may seem, and it is, when we simply believe and trust in Jesus and His blood sacrifice for our sins, at that very moment we have gained eternal life forever. What is "grace"? It is simply explained in this little mnemonic: God's Riches At Christ's Expense—GRACE!

ROMANS 1

For I am not ashamed of the gospel of Christ, for it is the power of God unto salvation to every one that believeth; to the Jew first, and also to the Greek. For therein is the righteousness of God revealed from faith to faith as it is written, The just shall live by faith (Romans 1:16–17).

The "gospel of Christ" is the simple message that tells us how we might gain eternal life. In order to be with God in heaven, our sins must be dealt with. A penalty must be paid for our sins because God does not only love, but He is also just (Exodus 34:7). God is like the kind judge who dislikes punishing people; yet, He must do so because sin, like crime, demands a penalty. None of our good works is sufficient to pay the price of sin against a holy God. So what does God do? The "gospel of Christ" tells us that God, in the greatest act of love in the universe, sent his own Son, Jesus, to suffer and die on the cross and pay the penalty for our sins in our place. This would be like a judge sentencing a criminal to prison and then sending his own son to pay the penalty. The blood that Jesus shed on the cross paid the price for our sins (Romans 5:8–9; Ephesians 1:7; I Peter 1:18–19). As with any gift, we do not have eternal life until we accept the gift, and we accept this gift by trusting in Jesus and His great sacrifice.

Let us never believe that we can earn this great gift of eternal life through our feeble works or doings but rather, by childlike faith, simply accept God's great gift. Also, let us never be ashamed of this great gospel.

ROMANS 3

Therefore by the deeds of the law there shall no flesh be justified in his sight, for by the law is the knowledge of sin. But now the righteousness of God without the law is manifested, being witnessed by the law and the prophets; Even the righteousness of God which is by faith of Jesus Christ unto all and upon all them that believe, for there is no difference (Romans 3:20–22).

These verses tell us that none of us will be justified by the "law," which means either doing good deeds or refraining from bad deeds. In order to live in heaven with a holy God, we must become without sin. I think each of us knows that we sin far too often, and these verses tell us that because of our sins we cannot be "justified," no matter how good we might think we are relative to someone else. It doesn't sound very good for any of us, does it?

But, praise God, there is another way to heaven. If we will stop trusting in our own good deeds, which will never be good enough, these verses tell us that we can gain the "righteousness of God." We can do this "by faith of Jesus Christ," which is available to all who believe. In other words, if we will simply believe in Jesus Christ and His great sacrifice for our sins, we are then "justified" and we have then gained the "righteousness" that we could never earn for ourselves. May we ever be grateful to Jesus for His great gift!

Even the righteousness of God which is by faith of Jesus Christ unto all and upon all them that believe; for there is no difference (Romans 3:22).

All of us inherently know that we must obtain some degree of goodness to be in heaven with God when we die, instead of hell for eternity. But have you ever asked yourself, "How good must I be to get to heaven? How little must I sin? How many good deeds must I do?" The answer to the question of how good you must be to get to heaven is actually in the Bible. In the Sermon on the Mount, in Matthew chapters five through seven, Jesus shows us how easy it is for each of us to sin and how many sins we actually commit, even if we might think that we are pretty good compared to somebody else. After reading the Sermon on the Mount, I don't see how any of us could think that we are good enough to get to heaven. Jesus then makes it even worse. In Matthew 5:48, Jesus tells us that we must be "perfect" to get to heaven. In other words, we must become as "righteous" as God. You may be thinking now that there is no hope, and you are right. That is, if are trying to be *good enough*. But, praise God, there is another way!

In this verse, we are told that by "faith" in Jesus Christ, we gain the "righteousness of God," which is just what we need to gain eternal life in heaven. There is no difference between any of us, no matter how good or how bad we may think we might be. The pathway to heaven is not works or other man-made devices, but rather faith in Jesus Christ alone and His finished work on the cross at Calvary.

For all have sinned, and come short of the glory of God; Being justified freely by his grace through the redemption that is in Christ Jesus (Romans 3:23–24).

These verses tell us that every single one of us has sinned. We live in an "anything goes" society, and perhaps we have constructed in our own mind a false god that winks at sin, just as society today winks at sin. If this should be your line of thinking, you really should review the Old Testament and remind yourself of how seriously God takes sin. This God, the real God, also tells us that He never changes (Malachi 3:6). God takes sin just as seriously today as He did then. Furthermore, the great judgments of God upon sin are not confined to the Old Testament. As time draws to a close, the greatest judgments the world has ever seen will be delivered by God, once and for all, against sin and the devil. A review of the book of Revelation should convince anyone that God is still very serious about sin, even if many of us may think otherwise.

Then, we read that each and every one of us has sinned. Some may think, *My sins are more acceptable than the sins of some other really bad people.* If we think like that, we must consider James 2:10, which tells us that one sin is no different than any other in God's eyes. In other words, that little white lie you or I might tell is the same as murder. It is not that murder is okay—it is that God is so holy that any sin is equally offensive to Him. Considering all this, what hope is there for any of us?

The hope, and a great one it is, is justification (just as if I'd never sinned) through Jesus Christ. Jesus died on the cross to pay the penalty for our sins. If we will simply trust in Jesus and His sacrifice, His blood covers our sins, and we have "redemption" by God's "grace" through Jesus Christ. This is a gift from Jesus. If we try to earn it with our paltry works, we insult God and do not gain the gift. You can't buy a gift. Yes, praise God, gaining eternal life is just that simple—trust in Jesus alone, add nothing!

Whom God hath set forth to be a propitiation through faith in his blood, to declare his righteousness for the remission of sins that are past, through the forbearance of God (Romans 3:25).

The third chapter of Romans, like many other chapters in Romans and John, is a road map to heaven. But a road map is useless unless it is consulted. Let's say, for example, that you are driving to Los Angeles. Let's say that someone who had never been to Los Angeles told you the roadways to take. But you also had a roadmap to Los Angeles drawn by someone who had been there and back, and it was the direct opposite of what you had just been told. What set of directions would you follow? So, too, with the matter of going to heaven. When what you are told conflicts with what God tells us in the Bible about the route to heaven, which do you believe?

This verse refers specifically to Jesus, Who is directly mentioned in the previous verse. We are told by God as directly as possible that when we have "faith" in Jesus' blood (as the complete sufficient covering for our sins), then we have "his righteousness" (or Jesus' righteousness) for the remission or covering of our sins. The Bible tells us that a price had to be paid for our sins. Regardless of what we or anyone else may think, all our good works, etc. are not sufficient to pay that price. Jesus had to die on the cross so that His blood would pay the price for and cover our sins. When we "believe" and accept that gift, all our sins—past, present, and future—are covered under Jesus' blood, just as this verse declares, and we thereby gain eternal life. Praise God for this greatest gift ever!

> ***To declare, I say, at this time his righteousness
> that he might be just, and the justifier of him which
> believeth in Jesus (Romans 3:26).***

P aul is speaking of Jesus and "his righteousness." The Bible
tells us that Jesus is part of God (Father; Son, Jesus; and
Holy Spirit) and also became fully man when He was on this
earth. He came to earth to suffer and die on the cross and rise
again from the dead to pay, with His blood, the penalty for our
sins. The Bible tells us that of all the people who ever lived on
earth, only Jesus was without sin and therefore "just," meaning
sinless.

The Bible contains a lot of symmetry, and much of the
Old Testament is a picture of the New Testament. In the Old
Testament, before Jesus came, the Israelites sacrificed a spotless
lamb for their sins, but they had to keep doing so, because the
sacrifice was not totally perfect nor was it sufficient. It was only a
symbol, like baptism or communion. When Jesus came, He was
the perfect "lamb" of God, and Jesus' blood sacrifice on the
cross did satisfy God and pay the penalty for all sins for all time.
This could be explained like a mortgage on which you make
payments each month. The lamb sacrifice would be like a
monthly payment, which would satisfy the lender, but only for a
month. The sacrifice of Jesus would be like paying the mortgage
in full, which would satisfy the lender for all time.

This verse tells us that gaining eternal life is not about our
righteousness (which will never be good enough) but rather it is
all about Jesus' righteousness and that Jesus is the "justifier" of
whoever "believeth" in Him. The word *justify* means "just as if I'd
never sinned." We gain this justified condition not because of
anything that we have ever done or ever could do. If we think
this, we tell Jesus that we don't need His sacrifice, and we have
made a serious, prideful mistake. But when we humbly come to
Jesus, admitting that nothing we ever have done or ever could do

would be good enough, and simply "believe in Jesus," we have gained God's great gift of eternal life. Isn't it comforting to know that our eternal life does not depend upon ourselves and what we DO but rather upon Jesus and what he has DONE?

Therefore we conclude that a man is justified by faith without the deeds of the law (Romans 3:28).

God tells us clearly in this verse that we become justified in God's eyes by "faith" and not by "deeds of the law." As we have learned in other verses, our faith must be in Jesus and in His blood that He shed on the cross to completely cover our sins.

In our natural way of thinking, this is not possible because it is too easy. It is difficult for us to believe that God Himself (Jesus) paid the price for our sins. We think that we have to work for eternal life by obeying the Law (the Ten Commandments) and by making up ceremonies and rituals that we perform to earn our way to heaven. But God tells us that this way, even though it seems to us to be the right way, is the wrong way (Proverbs 14:12). Working our way to heaven by doing good deeds, trying hard not to sin, or performing rituals would be like the man whose father wants to gift him with a million dollars and in fact has a cashier's check for a million dollars waiting for him, if only the son would come and accept it. Yet the son, who needs the money badly, refuses to do so, attempts to earn the money on his own, and is never able to do so. Maybe the son or someone in his family had a health need that the million dollars could cure. Wouldn't that be a tragic situation? But wouldn't it even be more tragic if we pridefully refuse to simply believe in Jesus and refuse to accept His shed blood as a covering for our sins, while trying to work our way to heaven on our own? Wouldn't we then be telling Jesus that His sacrifice was not good enough, but our efforts *are* good enough? This would be the greatest tragedy of all!

> *Seeing it is one God, which shall justify the circumcision by faith, and uncircumcision through faith (Romans 3:30).*

You may recall that the Jewish people had a ritual of circumcising their babies. This practice was very similar to infant baptism and John Calvin and others have even declared that infant baptism saves people because of its similarity to circumcision.

However, here we see that God justifies (or saves) us whether or not we are circumcised and that it is by "faith" that we are saved. Another truth conveyed here is that both uncircumcised people (Gentiles) and circumcised people (Jews) get saved in the same way—by "faith."

Some may say that if we don't need to earn our salvation, then this is too easy or too good to be true. But it was not easy for Jesus Who had to suffer and die on the cross and shed His blood to pay the penalty for our sins.

But doesn't the Bible tell us we should avoid sin and do good works? Of course. We can never pay, with our own feeble efforts, the great price that Jesus paid for us; we can only believe and accept His great gift. Then, once we have believed, and thereby gained eternal life, we desire to obey God (and His Commandments) out of gratitude for what God has done for us. If someone gives you a great gift, don't you desire to please that person, not out of drudgery but out of a heart full of gratitude? You certainly wouldn't desire to hurt such a person, would you? Yes, a person should, of course, try to obey the Commandments, do good deeds, attend church to learn more about God, and many other things, but, thank God, our salvation does not depend upon our feeble and often insufficient efforts. Our salvation is already secured by the all-sufficient sacrifice of Jesus —may we only accept it. Praise God!

For if Abraham were justified by works, he hath whereof to glory; but not before God. For what saith the scripture? Abraham believed God, and it was counted unto him for righteousness (Romans 4:2–3).

The Bible tells us that Abraham did many great works. In fact, Abraham was called the father of God's chosen people. Abraham obeyed God in leaving his home and moving to a land where he was a stranger. He was willing to sacrifice his beloved son, Isaac, when and if God told him to do so. When it became evident that Abraham and his nephew, Lot, could not continue tending herds together, Abraham unselfishly offered Lot the best land. There are many other stories in the Bible of how Abraham lived a godly life and obeyed God. Yet, did the great works of Abraham save him? These verses tell us the answer is no. If Abraham's great works could not save him, then your works will not save you. We know that Abraham is saved, but how did he become saved?

The key word is "believed." Abraham was saved the same way we are—through "belief" in God and His promises, specifically "belief" in our Savior, Jesus Christ. When we believe that Jesus' shed blood is sufficient to cover our sins, we are counted righteous, not by any work that we have done or could ever possibly do, but rather because of Jesus' righteousness. God then sees us as righteous (Acts 20:28; I Peter 1:18–19; Hebrews 9:14). Yes, you and I are dead in sin, and there is nothing we can do to earn our way to heaven. But, praise God, when we believe and accept God's great gift, we have gained eternal life.

> ***Now to him that worketh is the reward not reckoned of grace, but of debt. But to him that worketh not, but believeth on him that justifieth the ungodly, his faith is counted for righteousness (Romans 4:4–5).***

There are two ways to get to heaven. One way is by being good enough. How many good deeds must we do? How few times must we sin before we have sinned too much? Or maybe if we only commit little sins, and not big sins, we will be okay, right? Let's see what the Bible says. The Bible tells us that any sin, even that little white lie, is the same in God's eyes as a major sin, like murder (James 2:10). It is not that murder is acceptable—it is that all sin, even seemingly little sin, is terribly offensive to a holy God. You might think, *What if I do many good things and only sin a few times? How good must I be to get to heaven?* God answers that one too in Matthew 5:48. If we are to get to heaven by being good enough, we must be "PERFECT." Do you think that you can get to heaven by being good enough? I don't. There is another way.

The first part of these verses tell us, if we are going to get to heaven by being good enough and through our works, we will only work ourselves further and further into debt. But if we believe, our "faith" is counted for righteousness. In other words, when we believe and trust in Jesus and His great sacrifice on the cross for our sins, then Jesus' blood covers all our sins (Acts 20:28; I Peter 1:18–19; Hebrews 9:14). God then sees us, because of Jesus' sacrifice and our faith in Jesus alone, as righteous. Jesus' sacrifice was sufficient to pay the price for our sins and satisfy God. But if part of our faith is in Jesus and part in self or something else, then I guess we are telling Jesus that He and His blood sacrifice alone is not sufficient, right?

Our salvation, praise God, does not depend upon what we may **DO**; it depends upon what Jesus has **DONE**. Praise God that all of our trust may and should be in an all-sufficient Jesus, and may none of our trust be in a very insufficient self.

ROMANS 4

Even as David also describeth the blessedness of the man, unto whom God imputeth righteousness without works, Saying, Blessed are they whose iniquities are forgiven, and whose sins are covered. Blessed is the man to whom the Lord will not impute sin. Cometh this blessedness then upon the circumcision only, or upon the uncircumcision also? For we say that faith was reckoned to Abraham for righteousness. How was it then reckoned? When he was in circumcision, or in uncircumcision? Not in circumcision, but in uncircumcision. And he received the sign of circumcision, a seal of the righteousness of the faith which he had yet being uncircumcised that he might be the father of all them that believe, though they be not circumcised; that righteousness might be imputed unto them also. And the father of circumcision to them who are not of the circumcision only, but who also walk in the steps of that faith of our father Abraham, which he had being yet uncircumcised. For the promise, that he should be the heir of the world, was not to Abraham, or to his seed, through the law, but through the righteousness of faith (Romans 4:6–13).

Instead of one verse, I've compiled many verses together, because each builds upon the other, but they all deliver one central, common, powerful message. We are saved by faith in Jesus alone and not by works or rituals. Evidently many people, at the time the Bible was written, thought that they were saved by a circumcision ritual that they couldn't even remember. This would be like buying food to nourish you and putting a picture of the food on your refrigerator to remind you it is there. If you begin to trust in the picture for nourishment instead of eating the food, you will soon die!

God, as we see here, clearly tells us that a ritual given as a reminder, circumcision in this case, will not save anyone, so Christians abandoned circumcision. But amazingly, within about one hundred years another ritual, also performed upon unwitting babies, came to take its place. That ritual would be infant baptism, and it doesn't save anyone any more than circumcision. I'm sure you can think of many people, including many notorious atheists, who were baptized as babies who have no interest in God and some who are anti-Christian. I'm sure you've also noticed that children who are not baptized have about as good a chance of becoming Christians as those who were—provided they are told of Jesus, of course.

So, what is wrong with trusting in Jesus in addition to works or rituals like circumcision or infant baptism? The problem is that to the extent we are trusting in something else is the same extent we are *not* trusting in Jesus. When God tells us, in these verses and in hundreds of others, that when we "believe" in Jesus we are saved, He means that 100 percent of our faith, however great or small it may be, must be in our real Savior, Jesus. Then, and only then, we can actually know that we have eternal life (I John 5:13), simply because we have done exactly as God has told us and we can thus expect exactly what God has promised. The religious leaders of Jesus' day convinced a lot of people to do it man's way. As you seek eternal life, are you doing it man's way or God's way? Works/rituals or "belief"? Religion or Jesus?

ROMANS 4

For if they which are of the law be heirs, faith is made void, and the promise made of none effect. Because the law worketh wrath, for where no law is, there is no transgression. Therefore it is of faith, that

it might be by grace; to the end the promise might be sure to all the seed; not to that only which is of the law, but to that also which is of the faith of Abraham; who is the father of us all (Romans 4:14–16).

In these verses, we are once again told very clearly that if we trust in our good works under the Law (the Ten Commandments), then "faith is made void." These verses tell us that if we trust a little bit in our good works (the Law) and even a lot in Jesus, our "faith" is void. These verses are like Galatians 5:2–6, which tell us that if we trust a little bit in rituals (like circumcision, baptism, etc.) and some in Christ, then Jesus has "become of no effect" for us. When the Bible tells us, as it clearly does, that we are to "believe" in Jesus and in His shed blood as the price to cover our sins, that means 100 percent, not 50 percent, 75 percent, or even 99 percent.

You may say, "Well, my faith is very, very small." That is just fine, as long as all of it is in Jesus and not in something else, or in Jesus plus something else. Your faith may be small but the object of your faith (Jesus) is sufficiently strong and all powerful. Our salvation does not depend on what we do (Praise God!) but upon what He has done. All we need do is place our trust there. You may not know everything there is to know about the airplane but if you trust it enough to get on, the airplane will do the rest. If you don't, you won't get there. Or maybe you want to go with one foot on the wing of the plane and one foot on the hood of the car?

The problem that the Pharisees had with Jesus, and vice versa, was that people trusted in these religious leaders and their rituals to get to heaven. Then along comes Jesus Who tells them that their faith must be in Him alone. You know what happened.

A church, any church, is doing the greatest, highest, and most valuable job in the world when it is pointing people to Jesus alone, and it is doing the greatest harm in the world when it tries to crawl on the throne with Jesus. A doctor, whom you trust, for xample, could prescribe the right medicine and cure you or the rrong medicine and kill you. May each of us trust in Jesus alone, iereby gaining eternal life, and then do what we can to point thers to our great Savior!

ROMANS 4

He staggered not at the promise of God hrough unbelief; but was strong in faith, giving lory to God; And being fully persuaded that, what Ie had promised, He was able also to perform. And herefore it was imputed to him for righteousness Romans 4:20–22).

We have examined one verse after another that clearly tells us that we gain eternal life by trusting and believing solely 1 our Savior, Jesus. This is very hard for us to believe because in iis world, there are very few really good things that come free. ut the Bible tells us that our natural way of thinking, as to alvation, is the wrong way to think (Proverbs 14:12). Further omplicating matters, from the days of the Pharisees until today, iere are those who, for purposes of power and control, will take dvantage of our natural tendency to trust in works, rites, and ituals to earn salvation. Yet the proper way to look at salvation is ke a loving parent who sacrifices for the child and gives the child ood things, with no expectation of repayment. Perhaps this is /hy the Bible tells us that we must become like little children, /ho find it much easier to trust, to gain eternal life (Luke 18:17).

When Jesus died on the cross and shed His blood at Calvary, His precious holy blood paid the price, in full, for our ins—past, present, and future. What He asks in return is that we elieve and trust in Him and His sacrifice. We are saved by faith," however small it may be, as long as all our faith for ternal life is in Him alone. When we transfer our faith from self nd its works and rituals, to Jesus, at that moment we gain eternal fe. It is at that moment that His righteousness is imputed to us and when God looks at us, He sees Jesus' righteousness and gives us eternal life, as a gift (Romans 6:23).

These verses tell us that Abraham gained righteousness through "faith." This is exactly how we gain righteousness. The Bible tells us that our righteousness, however good we may be or think we are, is as "filthy rags" to God (Isaiah 64:6). This is because our so-called righteousness is invariably mixed with sin, and is thus not sufficient. We hear a lot of talk today about people who say they are humbled, but this is the real thing, isn't it? And maybe we're not interested in real humility? But this is why we need a Savior and, praise God, we have one in Jesus! In the words of a song, **"I owed a debt I could not pay; He paid a debt He did not owe!"** Praise God!

ROMANS 44

But for us also, to whom it shall be imputed, if we believe on Him that raised up Jesus our Lord from the dead; Who was delivered for our offenses, and was raised again for our justification (Romans 4:24–25).

The "it" that shall be imputed to each of us who "believe" is righteousness. In other words, considering these verses with the verses immediately around it, God is telling us that if we simply have enough "faith" to believe that Jesus died on the cross, that His blood paid the penalty in full for our sins, and that God then raised Jesus from the dead, then Jesus' righteousness is "imputed" to us. Since Jesus' righteousness is perfect, and my righteousness is far from perfect, I will place my trust in Jesus and forget about my own righteousness. How about you?

This would be like my owning a thirty-year-old car that is always breaking down and which I cannot rely upon to transport myself. Then along comes someone who loves me, and for that reason alone, expecting nothing in return, offers me a brand-new reliable car. But maybe I've become prideful and for that reason, I

rn down his offer. Or maybe, in my own mind, I've convinced
yself that my old broken down car is a better car than what I
n being offered, and I turn down the new car for that reason. If
allow my pride to stand between myself and a car that will
liably transport me about, would you think that I had made a
ise decision? And if I pridefully reject and give back a gift such
this, how do you think the one who loved me enough to offer
e gift would feel?

You won't get it any more plain than these verses tell us.
we "believe," Jesus' righteousness is imputed (given) to us. For
hatever unfathomable reason, God delivered His own son,
sus, to pay for our offenses (sins). When we believe, we are
stified (just as if I'd never sinned). Praise God! So what is our
ecision? We are born trusting in self and so we learn to trust in
ur own devices and systems. The eternal question is this: will we
ansfer that trust to Jesus? Self, rituals, or Jesus?

ROMANS 5

***Therefore being justified by faith, we have
eace with God through our Lord Jesus Christ
Romans 5:1).***

There are several spiritual truths in this short verse. The
phrase "justified by faith" is repeated five times in the New
estament, and the truth it conveys is repeated many times more
an that. It must be important! A dictionary definition of *justify*
"to free from blame." Don't we spend a lot of time trying to
stify ourselves and to free ourselves from blame? We may try
xcuses, we may try psychologists, we may try finger pointing, we
ay try works, we may try rituals, or any number of things. But
e Bible tells us that it is by "faith" that we will become "free
om blame." Is it really that simple? According to God it is!

Furthermore, when we are justified or free from blame,
e Bible then tells us that we have "peace with God." Isn't this
hat everyone is really looking for? Again, we may try all the false

trails like drugs, alcohol, fame, fortune, etc., but "peace with God" is the only thing that will ultimately satisfy. Doesn't it make sense to be "justified" so that we can have "peace with God"?

But how? The last part of the verse ties it all together when it says "through our Lord Jesus Christ." "Faith" must be in "Jesus Christ." When we trust Jesus and Him alone, as having paid the price for our sins with His blood, and stop trusting in the other things, then we have gained "peace with God" and eternal life with Him. Praise God for His great plan that we need only accept by simple faith.

By whom also we have access by faith into this grace wherein we stand, and rejoice in hope of the glory of God (Romans 5:2).

This verse is referring to Jesus, by Whom we have access to God. The Bible tells us that there is only one mediator between God and man, and that is Jesus (I Timothy 2:5). When Jesus died on the cross, and the veil in the temple, which had previously separated God from man, was miraculously torn in two (Matthew 27:51), this showed us that we now can and should come directly to God through our Savior, Jesus. If anyone pretends to be an intermediary between God and man, he is pretending to be Jesus—that won't work.

There are many today who pretend to forgive our sins, but there is only One Who can actually do it—Jesus. When Jesus walked this earth and began to forgive the sins of the people, He felt compelled to prove His authority by healing the sick (Matthew 9:6). If someone other than Jesus is forgiving your sins, can he do likewise? Down through the ages there were many who attempted to come between the sinner and Jesus. Based upon what the Bible says, it would be wise to ignore such imposters and gain access to God by faith in Jesus alone, thereby gaining eternal life, which is the hope of the glory of God. When you

ross that great divide into the next life, if God asks how you
dealt with your sin, do you think it would be better to respond as
man taught you or as God told you in the Bible? When Jesus was
on earth, did He quote the religious leaders of the day or did He
quote Scripture?

ROMANS 5

*But God commendeth his love toward us, in
that, while we were yet sinners, Christ died for us.
Much more then, being now justified by his blood,
we shall be saved from wrath through him (Romans
5:8–9).*

These verses, like many others, tell us in very simple terms
that we can be saved from the wrath of God (which is
directed against our sin because God is holy) and live in heaven
with Him forever, through Jesus and His blood that He shed on
the cross. How can we escape all penalties for all our sins? Isn't
there a price that must be paid for our sins? We have difficulty
believing that someone else, Jesus, would pay the penalty for all
our sins, even though the Bible tells us so. The human way of
thinking, which is the wrong way of thinking (Proverbs 14:12),
causes us to think that we must work or pay some price for our
salvation.

Perhaps we don't understand how serious sin is. It is good
to read the whole Bible to understand that even seemingly little
sin is terribly offensive to a holy God. When we realize this, we
can see that none of our good works or any other efforts could
possibly pay the price for our sins. But the price was paid. The
blood of God Himself, our Savior Jesus Christ, was that price,
and it was paid when it was shed at Calvary. What we need to do,
as the Bible says, is trust in that sacrifice and our Savior, nothing
more and nothing less!

Let's say you needed 10 million dollars for an operation to
save your life. You don't have anywhere near that much money.

Yet a person who loves you gives you the money and it saves your life. Would you then go around pretending that a few good works on your behalf toward him would pay him back for that great gift? No, you would do good things for that person out of gratitude for what he did for you, but you wouldn't pretend that you had in any way earned his great gift. Let us accept God's great gift of eternal life as a gift and then, out of gratitude, do what we can to obey and please Him!

ROMANS 5

For if, when we were enemies, we were reconciled to God by the death of his Son, much more, being reconciled, we shall be saved by his life. And not only so, but we also joy in God through our Lord Jesus Christ, by whom we have now received the atonement (Romans 5:10–11).

We are born enemies of God and remain enemies of God, because of our sin, until we become "reconciled" to God. How? As this verse, and many others, declare—through the death and resurrection of our Savior, Jesus Christ. Please note, once again, that these verses do not tell us that we become saved by being good enough, performing rituals, or any other thing that we can do in our own strength. We are saved through Jesus Christ when we believe in Him and His death on the cross. Then there is "atonement" with God. *Atonement* means to "make amends" with God or to "reconcile" with God. We could never reconcile with God on our own or through our feeble works, and it is just prideful thinking to believe that we could. The good that we may do is ruined by the sin that we may commit, just as a six-egg omelet is ruined by one bad egg. It took a perfect sacrifice to pay the great price for our sins and that was Jesus, the perfect Lamb of God. May we each place our belief and trust solely in the perfect Lamb of God for eternal life, and thereby gain God's great gift, just as the Bible tells us.

But not as the offence, so also is the free gift. For if through the offence of one many be dead, much more the grace of God, and the gift by grace, which is by one man, Jesus Christ, hath abounded unto many (Romans 5:15).

This verse refers to Adam's original sin, through which all of us became sinners. Since Adam, each of us is powerless to resist sin and the devil, until we place our trust in Jesus. Furthermore, each of us is born in sin, as anyone who has spent much time around an undisciplined child can verify. Maybe this doesn't seem fair to you. So does that mean because one man, a long time ago, sinned, each of us is doomed to be sinners as well?

If that's not fair, how about this? God, Who is as far above us as a man is above a worm, sends a part of Himself, Jesus, to die and pay the price for our sins, in our place. Is that fair?

I will freely admit that there are many things about this that I do not know. I do not know where sin came from. I do not know why God could not or did not destroy sin the first time it raised its head. I do not know why Adam fell for sin so easily. The only reason I know that God would send His Son to die for us is that He must love us and love beyond anything we could comprehend. There is certainly nothing I can do for God that He can't do for Himself. And there is one other thing I know for certain about all this, based upon what the Bible says. God's "gift" of forgiveness of sins, and thus eternal life, is a "gift" and it comes totally and only by "grace."

If someone offers you a great gift, for which you could never possibly repay, simply because he loves you, do you turn around and insult him by pretending you could pay for it by some little thing you might give him back? I think each of us would know better than that. Let us therefore simply, with gratitude, accept the great gift of eternal life, through Jesus Christ and His suffering on the cross, that God freely offers each of us! It is really no more complicated than that.

And not as it was by one that sinned, so is the gift, for the judgment was by one to condemnation, but the free gift is of many offences unto justification (Romans 5:16).

This verse tells us that because Adam sinned, each of us became, and still are, powerless to resist sin and the devil, that is, until we trust in Jesus and His shed blood covering our sins. This verse tells us it is our sins that condemn us. This verse also tells us that Jesus' "free gift,"—the forgiveness of sins and eternal life that He offers us if we simply believe and trust in Him and His shed blood to cover our sins—is much greater than Adam's sin and thus, for us, conquers sin and death.

Let's say that you have an old car that you need in order to get to work. You let a friend use the car, he wrecks it, and now he can't pay for it. Now you don't have a car and you could lose your job. That wouldn't really be fair, would it? Then a real friend comes along and buys you a brand-new car, much better than the old one that was wrecked. He gives you the car, only on the condition that you accept it as a gift, given only because he loves and cares for you. I guess that wouldn't really be fair either, would it? But the big question is, what do you do? Do you spend all your time thinking about the unfairness of life and never getting around to accepting the new car that would improve your condition greatly? Or are you too prideful to accept the new car as a gift? Or maybe you decide that you are going to do it your own way and won't take the gift. Instead of humbling yourself and taking the gift, will you work until you can buy your own car? Perhaps you have forgotten that without a car, you don't have a job.

Yes, there is a lot of sin and evil in this world, and it could consume us if we spent all our time dwelling upon it. Why not dwell instead upon the greatest truth in the universe—God loves each of us. And then, through his Son, Jesus Christ, and His death and resurrection, He offers us forgiveness of sins and eternal life. You do it your way if you want—I am more than grateful and happy to do it God's way!

ROMANS 5

For if by one man's offence death reigned by one; much more they which receive abundance of grace and of the gift of righteousness shall reign in life by one, Jesus Christ (Romans 5:17).

Once again, God is telling us that because Adam sinned, each one of us is a sinner and powerless to resist sin, until we trust in Jesus. You may, and we all often do, deceive yourself and others into thinking that your particular sin is not really as bad as someone else's sin, and that therefore you are really quite a good person. But deep down, I think that each of us knows that we have a sin problem that all of our efforts will never solve. I think we also know, as the Bible says, that God is righteous, and without sin, and that we need to be righteous to live in heaven with Him (Ezra 9:15). This verse, as with many others, tells us, praise God, that we sinners can become righteous through Jesus Christ.

The Bible tells us repeatedly (Romans 3:21, 25, 4:3, 6, 10:3; II Corinthians 5:21; Philippians 3:9, etc.) that by simple faith in Jesus Christ, we gain Jesus' righteousness. I believe, on Judgment Day, that it will be a lot better to have Jesus' righteousness covering me than the righteousness of myself, my church, my religion, or any other thing or person. In other words, as the Bible tells us in Isaiah 61:10, when we trust in Jesus, we are covered with Jesus' "robe of righteousness." Thus, when God then looks at us, sinners that we are, He sees Jesus' "robe of righteousness" covering us, which is then our "garment of salvation." That "robe" cost a lot—Jesus' suffering and death on the cross. Can't we regard it highly enough to accept it as offered? Remember, if we try to put one stitch of our own into this perfect garment, we'll ruin the whole garment. Not a good idea when God demands perfection! (Matthew 5:48).

We are reminded in the Bible that while God tells us how to gain eternal life, there will be some, like Abel, who obey God and gain this righteousness necessary for eternal life. Yet, sadly, there will be also others, like Cain, who seek to be religious and righteous in their own way and suffer the consequences (Hebrews 11:3–5). May we each, through our great Savior Jesus Christ, gain our perfect "garment of salvation," while praising and seeking to serve Him through all eternity!

ROMANS 5

Therefore as by the offence of one judgment came upon all men to condemnation; even so by the righteousness of one the free gift came upon all men unto justification of life (Romans 5:18).

Once again, God is driving home His point to us that all of us are sinners, we are therefore under the judgment of a righteous God, and that judgment will result in our condemnation. But we receive justification unto eternal life. How? Through the "righteousness of one" (which means through Jesus Christ and the penalty that He paid for us on the cross), we have received the "free gift" of eternal life.

Today, just as when Jesus walked this earth, there are many who would appeal to our human way of looking at things by telling us that there is something that we must do to earn eternal life. Maybe we have to do good works; maybe we have to engage in their rituals; or maybe this, or maybe that, they say. Stop with me and think about this for a moment. If we earn eternal life with our works or our rituals, it's not a free gift, is it?

If our efforts or our religious leaders give us eternal life, it doesn't really come from Jesus alone, does it?

If God offers us something as wonderful as eternal life as a free gift, as it states here and in many other verses, do you think it is wise for us to pretend that we have earned it by our works, our rituals, or whatever? Just as in Jesus' day, there are a lot of religious leaders who don't mind your thinking that they alone or maybe they **AND** Jesus will get you to heaven. But when we stand before God, and if He asks why He should let us into His heaven, do you think it would be better to have a reason that is from our own imagination, from what some other man has told us, or from what God has told us in the Bible? I think you know the correct answer.

ROMANS 5

For as by one man's disobedience many were made sinners, so by the obedience of one shall many be made righteous (Romans 5:19).

This verse tells us that because Adam sinned, sin entered the world, and each and every person who has ever lived, except Jesus, is a sinner (Romans 3:23). But we may think that our sin really doesn't matter very much because we haven't killed anyone or done the terrible things we read about in the newspapers. However, God tells us that even those "little" sins that we commit every day are just the same in His eyes as murder (James 2:10). It is not that murder is okay—it is that God is so holy that even a seemingly little sin is terribly offensive to Him. I think that in twenty-first-century America we have forgotten that, haven't we? But God hasn't!

Considering that we are all sinners, have you ever thought about how good you would have to be to get to heaven? Actually, God tells us in Matthew 5:48. You must be PERFECT! That is very bad news for each of us, because none of us are righteous and without sin.

Yet, praise God, this verse tells us that we can be righteous through the "obedience of one," meaning Jesus' obedience in going to the cross and paying the penalty for all our sins. But how do we gain this righteousness that is waiting for us as a result of Jesus' obedience? The simple answer is by simple faith in Jesus and His great sacrifice (Acts 16:31). May we each gain this robe of righteousness that awaits us through faith in Jesus!

ROMANS 5

Moreover the law entered, that the offence might abound. But where sin abounded, grace did much more abound. That as sin hath reigned unto death, even so might grace reign through righteousness unto eternal life by Jesus Christ our Lord (Romans 5:20–21).

There are many who think that they will get to heaven by being good enough or at least not sinning very much. Maybe some think it is a combination of faith and works. But these verses tell us that wherever we find the Law (the Ten Commandments), and people trying to follow them, all we are really going to find is a lot of sin. The Law is like a schoolteacher who must first show us we are doing things the wrong way (working for salvation under the Law—impossible) before he can show us the right way (faith in Jesus alone) so that we will no longer need the teacher (Galatians 3:23–26). No one can keep the Ten Commandments, let alone the spirit of the Ten Commandments as found in the Sermon on the Mount (Matthew chapters 5–7). That is not good news, because we must be sinless, perfect, and righteous to get to heaven (Matthew 5:48).

Then what hope is there? I can sum it up in one word—Jesus. These verses and the entire Bible tell us that we gain righteousness, through which we can go to heaven, by believing in Jesus. Jesus did what we cannot do—He paid a sufficient price for all our sins by shedding His blood on the cross. No other payment is good enough!

But shouldn't we try to follow the Law and Jesus' Sermon on the Mount? Of course we should, but we should do so out of gratitude to Jesus for what He did for us, not because we assume that any feeble good works on our part can purchase our place in heaven. Jesus did that. Our salvation is like a beggar receiving a priceless gift from a billionaire. The beggar could never on his own repay the billionaire, and he shouldn't pretend that he could. That would be an insult. But he can do good deeds for his great benefactor out of simple gratitude for the great gift. So should we!

ROMANS 6

Know ye not, that so many of us as were baptized into Jesus Christ were baptized into his death? Therefore we are buried with him by baptism into death that like as Christ was raised up from the dead by the glory of the Father, even so we also should walk in newness of life. For if we have been planted together in the likeness of his death, we shall be also in the likeness of his resurrection. Knowing this, that our old man is crucified with him, that the body of sin might be destroyed, that henceforth we should not serve sin. For he that is dead is freed from sin. Now if we be dead with Christ, we believe that we shall also live with him (Romans 6:3–8).

Those who are baptized will live forever with Jesus in heaven. The question though is whether we are saved because we are baptized or because we believe, with baptism the symbol of our belief and consequent salvation. Is baptism the cause or the symbol of salvation? Do these verses teach us that baptism saves or that baptism is the symbol of Jesus' death and resurrection, a symbol that every believer should seek to undertake? Should we trust in our baptism, in those who baptize us, in Jesus, or in all three? If baptism causes salvation, is the unbeliever who is baptized saved? The Bible always shows believers baptized *after* they have believed and are thus saved, and never before belief.

If we are to interpret the Bible so that all its verses are consistent and not contradictory, we must say three things: (1) all believers, whether or not baptized, are saved (John 3:16; I Corinthians 1:16–18, etc.); (2) all believers should be baptized (Matthew 28:19). If a "believer" tells God he won't do something this important, is he really a believer? and (3) unbelievers, whether baptized or not, are never saved because baptism is our public identification with Jesus' death and resurrection and our declaration of belief (Acts 8:37). Yes, I know, the newer Bibles have simply chopped out this verse to avoid this issue, but also see Mark 16:16. If we accept these principles, there are no contradictions in any of the salvation verses.

The foregoing verses teach us that our baptism is a symbol of Jesus' death and resurrection, by which Jesus paid for our sins and purchased each of us a place in heaven. He offers us this gift, if only we will believe and accept!

ROMANS 6

Likewise reckon ye also yourselves to be dead indeed unto sin, but alive unto God through Jesus Christ our Lord. For sin shall not have dominion over you, for ye are not under the law, but under grace (Romans 6:11, 14).

Before we place our trust in Jesus, we are powerless to resist sin. In fact, the Bible tells us that before we believe, everything we do is sin (Romans 14:23 ["whatsoever is not of faith, is sin"]). But this verse, written to those who are believers, tells each believer that he is dead to sin. In other words, sin no longer has the person who has become a believer in its all-powerful grasp. The believer can resist sin. While believers often fail to exercise their power to resist sin, the point is that each believer has that power available, and should, out of gratitude for what Jesus has done for him, resist sin.

In any event, this verse also tells us that because the believer is dead to sin, and because sin does not have dominion over the believer, the believer is no longer under the Law and is not required to earn his way to heaven. Praise God because this would be impossible. The believer is under grace (GRACE=God's Riches At Christ's Expense) simply because he trusts and believes in Jesus as his Savior. Praise God for His great gift of eternal life through belief in Jesus!

ROMANS 6

For the wages of sin is death, but the gift of God is eternal life through Jesus Christ our Lord (Romans 6:23).

The key word here is "gift." Eternal life is a gift. It is not something that we earn or deserve because there is no amount of good works/religious rituals we could perform that would earn us eternal life—the price is more than we could pay. This verse also tells us that the wages of sin is death, and each of us is a sinner, so how do we avoid our wages of death and gain the "gift" of eternal life?

In this verse, and in many others, we are told that it is "through Jesus Christ." Jesus did many good things while He was on earth, but He came primarily to do one thing—to pay the penalty, in full, for our sins. When Jesus died on the cross, His shed blood paid **IN FULL** the penalty for our sins (I John 1:7). This would be like the man who walks into a car dealership and pays for all of the cars on the lot. That man is now free to go out and make a "gift" of each of those cars to whomsoever he chooses. In this case, Jesus paid for all the sins of the entire world, in full, and there is nothing more that needs to be done, *except* for one thing. As with any gift, it needs to be accepted.

Each of us needs to place our trust in Jesus for having paid the price in full, and thereby gain His great gift of eternal life.

There is therefore now no condemnation to them which are in Christ Jesus who walk not after the flesh, but after the spirit (Romans 8:1).

This verse tells us that we are not under condemnation **IF** we are in "Christ Jesus." When we have escaped condemnation, we have gained eternal life with God in heaven forever. The result of being "in Christ Jesus" allows the Christian to walk after the spirit and not after the flesh. We are "in Christ Jesus," the moment that we place all our trust in Jesus for eternal life (John 3:16).

You may say, "I don't have enough faith." Each of us is given a certain measure of faith. But the issue is not how large our faith might be (none of us is perfect, including in the faith category), but rather where we might place the faith that we have. Do we place our faith in our own good works? Or in religious rituals that we have performed? Or in Jesus? Or maybe in all three? The Bible tells us, repeatedly, that when all of our faith, however small it might be, rests in Jesus and in His blood sacrifice for all our sins, then, praise God, we have gained eternal life! And once we have become a believer, we now have the power to walk after the Spirit and not after the flesh. Let us always strive to do so out of gratitude for what our great Savior has done for us!

For the law of the Spirit of life in Christ Jesus hath made me free from the law of sin and death. For what the law could not do, in that it was weak through the flesh, God sending his own Son in the

likeness of sinful flesh, and for sin, condemned sin in the flesh. That the righteousness of the law might be fulfilled in us, who walk not after the flesh, but after the Spirit (Romans 8:2–4).

In His Sermon on the Mount (Matthew chapters 5–7), Jesus tells us that we violate the Law even when we think evil or hateful thoughts. The Law sets a standard that none of us could possibly live up to. Why not? Because we are sinful. It is impossible for us to keep the Law. Yet, we must be righteous, and without sin, and perfect (Matthew 5:48) to be with God in heaven. What hope is there for any of us?

The hope, as these verses tell us, is in Jesus Christ. Jesus paid the penalty for all our sins—past, present, and future—with His blood on the cross. Whatever your sins may have been, they are paid for in full. With His blood, Jesus purchased for each of us a place in heaven. When we believe and trust in Jesus alone, and accept His great gift, we have then gained eternal life in heaven. Praise God!

ROMANS 8

But ye are not in the flesh, but in the Spirit, if so be that the Spirit of God dwell in you. Now if any man have not the Spirit of Christ, he is none of his. And if Christ be in you, the body is dead because of sin; but the Spirit is life because of righteousness (Romans 8:9–10).

The Holy Spirit comes to indwell each believer the moment that a person comes to believe and trust solely in Jesus for eternal life (Acts 11:15–17). No matter how good or religious we may seem to be, and despite how many religious rituals we may have done, each of us is dead in sin until we believe in Jesus and the Holy Spirit comes to indwell us. The Law, and all its requirements, causes death because we cannot possibly live up to it. With Jesus, though, comes life—eternal life!

Each week, as we search for truth, let me again suggest that you follow along in your own Bibles. There are several reasons for this. If you are a believer, the Holy Spirit indwells you, and the Holy Spirit will guide you to truth (John 16:13). You will often gain insight into these verses beyond that mentioned here. If you are not a believer, I suggest reading ahead each week to find the next verse that tells you how to gain eternal life. If you do this with a prayerful and open heart, asking God to teach you the meaning of each such verse, you are seeking God. When you do this, the Bible promises that you will find Him (Jeremiah 29:13). If you think you don't have the faith to believe, the Bible also promises that faith comes by searching the Bible (Romans 10:17). God commends you for always checking up on anyone who teaches you anything from the Bible (Acts 17:11). If God commended Christians for getting out their Bibles and checking up on what the great apostle Paul was teaching them, should you do any less, regardless of who is teaching you?

May each of us use the greatest book given to mankind, the Bible, to find the greatest gift given to mankind, Jesus Christ and His shed blood, and thereby gain eternal life.

ROMANS 8

For we are saved by hope, but hope that is seen is not hope, for what a man seeth, why doth he yet hope for? (Romans 8:24).

The hope of every Christian believer is our Lord and Savior Jesus Christ. As the verses we have already studied teach us, we are saved the instant we believe in Jesus and trust Him enough to make Him our exclusive hope for eternal life. Some may say that it is foolish to put our trust and hope in something or someone we cannot see, but we do this all the time. We take our cash to the bank and then we don't see it anymore. Yet we trust hat it is there if we ever need it. Why? Because of the institution, he bank, that backs that trust.

We either believe that there is a God or we don't. We know there is a God because of all of God's creation that we see around us. It is simply preposterous to believe that the earth and everything on it created itself. And the Bible contains so many prophecies that eventually came true (including the one about little Israel someday being the center of world attention) that it is impossible for this to be a man-made book. See www.About BibleProphecy.com for details. If we then believe that the Bible came from God, we know that we can trust its promises with more certainty than any promise given to us by any bank, no matter how strong that bank may be. When God promises that if we will simply believe and trust in Jesus that we thereby gain eternal life, as simple as that may sound, we know that we can stake our eternal lives upon it. We can do this not because of anything we may do or merit, but rather because of what Jesus has done and what God has promised.

ROMANS 8

Who is he that condemneth? It is Christ that died, yea rather, that is risen again, who is even at the right hand of God, who also maketh intercession for us (Romans 8:34).

This is not a direct salvation verse, but it is very important. Do you see in this verse Who is at the right hand of God and Who always makes intercession for us? It is Jesus! You might think of Jesus as the best defense attorney anyone could ever hire. But there is one precondition. As with any legal relationship, you must first retain him as your attorney before God. The Bible tells us we do this by believing and trusting in Jesus alone. And as with any attorney, you can elect not to retain Him. If you are not believing or trusting in Jesus for your eternal life, you have not retained Him. God makes it very plain in the Bible that Jesus does not operate with co-counsel. You may not retain your pastor, priest, church, or yourself instead of Jesus or even as co-counsel with Jesus. Jesus is a solo practitioner. With Jesus, you either trust in Him entirely, or not at all. I want Jesus to be my attorney before God and I don't think He needs any help. How about you?

ROMANS 9

What shall we say then? That the Gentiles, which followed not after righteousness, have attained to righteousness, even the righteousness which is of faith. But Israel, which followed after the law of righteousness, hath not attained to the law of righteousness. Wherefore? Because they sought it not by faith, but as it were by the works of the law. For they stumbled at that stumblingstone. As it is written, behold, I lay in Sion a stumblingstone and rock of offence and whosoever believeth on him shall not be ashamed (Romans 9:30–33).

The Bible tells us that the Jewish people are God's chosen people, through Abraham. Yet they stumbled at the stumblingstone, which is Jesus, and gaining eternal life by faith in Jesus.

We are born trusting in ourselves and when it comes to eternal life, we accordingly think that we must have to earn it through our good works and practices. However, the Bible tells us the way that seems right to our natural minds leads to death (Proverbs 14:12). These verses tell us that if we try to gain righteousness—which we need to get to heaven—through our works, we will fail. If the Jewish people, who had established an entire system of works, the likes of which we could never possibly keep, cannot get to heaven by works, neither can we. To get to heaven by good works we must be perfect (Matthew 5:48).

the Law (the Ten Commandments) shows us how sinful we are; is not our road to heaven.

But, praise God, there is another way; it is as simple as believing in Jesus as our Savior and as the perfect Lamb of God who was sacrificed for our sins. When we set aside all our pride and works and trust in Jesus instead of ourselves, we gain Jesus' perfect robe of righteousness—this then covers our sins and it is what God sees when He looks at us.

So, let's do it God's way! Instead of Jesus being our stumblingstone, let Him be our stepping stone to heaven!

ROMANS 10

For they being ignorant of God's righteousness, and going about to establish their own righteousness, have not submitted themselves unto the righteousness of God. For Christ is the end of the law for righteousness to everyone that believeth (Romans 10:3–4).

We need to become righteous to get to heaven. We are told here that there are people who are "ignorant" of God's righteousness, seek to establish their own righteousness, and therefore do not submit to the righteousness of God. But it is God who has the keys to heaven. Don't you think it is better to find God's righteousness, by which He will let us into heaven, than seek to do it our own way and fail? Doing it our own way is like never having been to Los Angeles but pridefully thinking we can drive there by instinct instead of following a road map. The Bible is our road map to heaven, given to us by God.

So what is God's righteousness? When we try to keep the Law and lead sinless lives, we know from experience that we will fail. But these verses tell us that Jesus is "the end of the law" for all who believe. In other words, the moment we trust in Jesus, we have Jesus' perfect righteousness imputed to us. This is the righteousness of God, and this is the pathway to heaven. Praise

God for providing the way, through Jesus, that we could not make on our own!

> *For Moses describeth the righteousness which is of the law, that the man which doeth those things shall live by them. But the righteousness which is of faith speaketh on this wise, say not in thine heart, who shall ascend into heaven? That is to bring Christ down from above. Or, who shall descend into the deep? That is to bring up Christ again from the dead. But what saith it? The word is nigh thee, even in thy mouth, and in thy heart that is the word of faith, which we preach (Romans 10:5–8).*

These verses tell us of two different kinds of righteousness. This is very important because we need to be righteous to get to heaven and to live with God. The first kind of righteousness is from Moses, which is the Law—the Ten Commandments, and the rules and regulations that come from the Ten Commandments. We can get to heaven this way, by our good works, but only if we keep the entire Law. That is not good news because everyone is sinner and no one has kept the entire Law, except Jesus (Romans 3:23).

But, praise God, there is a second way. That is the righteousness, which comes by "faith," and that is the kind of righteousness that God tells us will bring us to heaven. This "faith," as we have learned in other verses, must be in Jesus so that we trust solely in Him and in His perfect sacrifice on the cross to cover our sins.

This was a simple issue then and it is a simple issue today. Will we trust in ourselves, our good works, and our man-made ceremonies to get us to heaven, or will we trust in Jesus to bring us to heaven? We see here the answer that God gives.

ROMANS 10

That if thou shalt confess with thy mouth the Lord Jesus, and shalt believe in thine heart that God hath raised him from the dead, thou shalt be saved. For with the heart man believeth unto righteousness, and with the mouth confession is made unto salvation. For the scripture saith, Whosoever believeth on him shall not be ashamed (Romans 10: 9–11).

In the Bible, we are repeatedly told by God that "faith" and "belief" will save us. These verses expand on that a little. These verses tell us that we must believe that God raised Jesus from the dead—He died on the cross to shed His blood to pay the penalty for our sins, and God raised Him from the dead, as evidence that Jesus was man but also God. If we believe this, as simple as it may seem, we have gained eternal life. We must also be ready to confess that Jesus is our Savior. Peter denied Jesus, and we know that Peter was saved, but Peter did go on to confess Jesus and preach Jesus on many different occasions. The Bible tells us that after we have placed our trust in Jesus for eternal life, we will not be ashamed of Him.

Maybe you think that you are too shy to ever tell anyone about Jesus. The Bible tells us here that after we believe, God will make us not to be ashamed of Jesus. In other words, as with the rest of our lives, we must believe and let God do the rest! God will then cause us to do things that we cannot possibly do on our own, not to gain our salvation, but as a result (fruit) of it.

ROMANS 10

For whosoever shall call upon the name of the Lord shall be saved (Romans 10:13).

I remember once showing a person that the Bible tells us that if we simply believe and trust in Jesus for eternal life, then we have gained eternal life. We need to simply call upon Him, trusting in His promise. There are no other requirements. The person responded, "I can't believe it; it's too simple." I think that a lot of people think this when confronted with the truth of what God tells us in the Bible, like in this verse. This is because, on this earth, few things come free or without a great deal of effort or skill. Yet, the greatest gift of all, and it *is* a gift (Romans 6:23), comes without any work or effort on our part. This is because the price for our sins was so great that we could never pay it, and Jesus paid it by shedding His blood on the cross. Now He freely offers us this great gift—eternal life. It's like someone paid dearly to open an account for us at a store that we can draw upon if we only ask. Let us be mindful that the way that seems right to our natural minds, earning eternal life with our works and ceremonies, is the wrong way, but believing in Jesus is the right way (Proverbs 14:12; John 3:16).

There is something in this world that we can count upon and that is each of the various promises of God. As we have seen, God has promised repeatedly in His Bible that if we believe and trust in Jesus alone, however great or little our trust might be, and however good or bad a person we may be, we have then gained eternal life. Have you examined the Bible enough to convince yourself of this truth regardless of what your natural mind or other men may tell you? Then, call upon the name of the Lord and be saved!

So then faith cometh by hearing, and hearing by the word of God (Romans 10:17).

B y now it should be quite apparent that the Bible is filled with verses that tell us that we gain eternal life by believing and trusting solely in Jesus and the blood He shed on the cross to pay the penalty in full for our sins. Maybe this sounds so incredible to you that it is hard to believe. Maybe you know of others who seem to have great faith and you just have a very little faith. Remember that no person on this earth has perfect faith. Each of us is given a certain measure of faith by God, but we choose where we will place that faith. Many people place that faith in themselves and in their good works to get to heaven. Other people place that faith in institutions, churches, or church leaders to get to heaven. These, in and of themselves, may be good things, but none of them will get you to heaven. In fact, to the extent that you are trusting in something or someone other than Jesus is the same extent you are not trusting in Jesus, and that is bad. In the verses that tell us we gain eternal life by believing in Jesus, I really don't see any exceptions. The question is not how great your faith might be but whether **ALL** of your faith is in Jesus and in His shed blood to cover your sins.

Is this a hard thing for you to do? It probably is because this is a spiritual battle. This verse tells us that we can build our faith by the "word of God" or, in other words, by reading the Bible. May I make a suggestion? Make it a point to read your Bible on a daily basis in this fashion. Go to a book that contains a lot of salvation verses, like maybe Romans or John. Read until you have found a verse that tells you how to gain eternal life and circle that verse. Then consider that verse, pray over it, and ask God to show you the meaning of that verse. As this verse tells us, I don't think it will be long before you will want to place your entire trust in Jesus and thereby gain eternal life!

ROMANS 11

Even so then at this present time also there is a remnant according to the election of grace. And if by grace, then is it no more of works, otherwise grace is no more grace. But if it be of works, then is it no more grace, otherwise work is no more work (Romans 11:5–6).

In these verses, God is telling us the importance for relying upon grace and not upon our good works for our salvation. By "grace," God means for us to rely only upon our belief in Jesus and the shedding of His blood as a payment for our sins, for our eternal life. We are pointedly told that if we trust in anything besides Jesus, then it is no longer grace and we don't have it.

Why? No one, of course, knows all of the purposes and reasoning of Almighty God, so therefore it is simply better to just do what He says. But let me attempt an explanation in this fashion.

Let's say you labored long and hard for enough money to buy a really nice gift for a relative or a dear friend. Then you gave that gift and the person you gave it to took out a few pennies, gave them to you, and said, "Now I've earned the gift." I think that could be taken as arrogance or insulting. The price that had to be paid for our sins was Jesus' blood, suffering, and death. No work or ceremony that you or I will ever do will come close to matching that great effort and gift of Christ. Let's forget about trying to pay for eternal life and accept as the gift that God offers (Ephesians 2:8–9). Then, let's try to do good works out of GRATITUDE for this great gift, but never for a moment believing that those good works will EARN our eternal life—it was earned and bought and paid for nearly two thousand years ago on a cross at Calvary. That payment was perfect and it was all sufficient. It was then and there "finished" (John 19:30). Let us believe and accept it with a heart full of gratitude!

ROMANS 11

Well, because of unbelief they were broken off, and thou standest by faith. Be not highminded, but fear (Romans 11:20).

God tells us in these verses that some people were "broken off." In other words, they would not be able to live with

God in heaven forever, because of their "unbelief." These people did not believe that Jesus came to earth to shed His blood on the cross as the penalty for our sins or that He rose again from the dead as God. There is much evidence that the Bible is true—from the hundreds of prophecies that were fulfilled to the letter, to the many accounts of Jesus rising from the dead, to the good that we see coming from Christianity all around the world. And, perhaps most of all, it is simply preposterous to think that this world and everything in it created itself out of nothing. People come to unbelief down many different roads, each of which is carefully constructed by the devil, most of which originate somewhere in pride. But each of those roads leads to one destination and it is not good.

But let's look upon the bright side. This verse tells us that we stand by "faith," meaning we will be with God forever in heaven when we believe in Jesus as our Savior. As this verse instructs us, this great truth, founded upon the great sacrifice by our Savior, should never cause us to be "highminded" or prideful, because it was all of Jesus and none of self that brought this great gift of God to us.

ROMANS 14

And he that doubteth is damned if he eat, because he eateth not of faith, for whatsoever is not of faith is sin (Romans 14:23).

In the preceding chapters, God, through Paul, tells us of all the things that we should or should not do (the Law) but He then summarizes with this verse that tells us, again, how we might gain acceptance by God, and thus eternal life. There are many good things that we should do and many bad things we should avoid, but if we have not first believed in Jesus, even the seemingly good things are sin—if it is not of faith it is sin. How can this be?

As we are learning, week by week, God has given us one way to gain eternal life. Our sin is so offensive in God's eyes that only the blood of Jesus, shed on the cross, could pay the great penalty for our sins; that blood is the only payment that is sufficient. None of our works, goodness, or ceremonies is good enough, and we should never think that they are. When we accept God's great gift—Jesus' blood covering our sins—and when God looks at us, He then does not see our sins but sees Jesus' blood and righteousness. Then, and only then, we can go on to do good works and ceremonies and avoid bad things out of gratitude for what Jesus has done for us, but never for a moment thinking that any of this is sufficient to gain the eternal life that Jesus Himself bought and paid for.

If we do the good works and ceremonies and avoid the bad things in order to earn our eternal life, we are basically saying that Jesus is not sufficient and this is most certainly sin, even though, seemingly, some good may come from it. Isn't it better to do it God's way?

ROMANS 15

Wherefore receive ye one another, as Christ also received us to the glory of God (Romans 15:7).

In this verse, Paul, inspired by the Holy Spirit, writes that Jesus "received us." How did Jesus receive Paul and those to whom he was writing? The same way that Jesus receives you and me—the moment that we believe and trust in Him alone as the perfect sacrifice for our sins and as our Savior. It was no more complicated than that for the great apostle Paul, and it is no more complicated than that for you and me. Yes, man, in his human way of thinking, is always trying to add to this simple truth and make it more complicated. But we will never improve upon John 3:16 and we must never try, if we hope to see God in heaven.

We should also be good and kind to our neighbors, just as Jesus sacrificed for us. This is often hard to do and we often fail, but this is the goal, and we must keep striving for this goal. We should not do this to earn our salvation but do it out of gratitude for what Jesus did for us. Let us first believe and then obey!

For Christ sent me not to baptize, but to preach the gospel; not with wisdom of words, lest the cross of Christ should be made of none effect. For the preaching of the cross is to them that perish foolishness; but unto us which are saved it is the power of God (I Corinthians 1:17–18).

The great apostle Paul is telling us here that he came not to baptize but to "preach the gospel" and "the cross." Jesus suffered and died on the cross to pay the penalty for our sins and if we simply believe in Jesus, and His sacrifice for us, we have gained eternal life. As these verses tell us, we become "saved" through the "power of God," which is his preaching of the gospel and of the cross so that we might believe.

The other simple message here is that this great evangelist, Paul, who was perhaps the greatest of all evangelists, tells us plainly that he came to preach so that we might believe. He further tells us that Jesus did not send him to baptize. If you were saved by being baptized, don't you think that Paul would have come to baptize instead of preach? Let us accept the gospel (believe in Jesus) and thereby gain the great gift of eternal life that Jesus bought for each of us, by paying for our sins on the cross.

For after that in the wisdom of God the world by wisdom knew not God, it pleased God by the foolishness of preaching to save them that believe (I Corinthians 1:21).

D oes it come any more clear than this? God tells us directly here that He does "save them that believe." Believe what? The surrounding verses tell us that when we believe that Jesus died on the cross to pay the penalty for our sins, and that He rose again from the dead because He was God, we have then gained eternal life.

God tells us here that those who are wise in the eyes of the world reject God (because God does not fit into their wisdom) and are thereby foolish. Anyone who rejects God may be respected by the world for a few years but will then spend eternity suffering. I don't think that is very smart. In fact, in this chapter of the Bible, God tells us how He often calls and uses people who are seemingly weak or foolish to accomplish His mighty purposes. He does this, He tells us, so that man will glory in God and not in man's own ability or strength. How about you? Are you working your way to heaven on your own or in a way that seems right or appealing to you? Or are you following the road that God has laid out in verse after verse of the Bible, thereby trusting in Jesus and not your wisdom or devices?

I CORINTHIANS 1

For the Jews require a sign, and the Greeks seek after wisdom. But we preach Christ crucified, unto the Jews a stumblingblock, and unto the Greeks foolishness; But unto them which are called, both Jews and Greeks, Christ the power of God, and the wisdom of God (I Corinthians 1:22–24).

T hese verses tell us that Jesus is the "power of God" and the "wisdom of God" to those who are "called," meaning those who are saved. The preaching of "Christ crucified" is sufficient for each of us to be saved. The preaching of "Christ crucified" means teaching about how Jesus died on the cross to shed His blood as a penalty for our sins and that if we simply believe in Jesus and His sacrifice, we are saved.

Sometimes you might hear someone say, "If God is real and if He is all powerful, then certainly He can do miracles," and certainly He can! And such a person might say, "If only God would show me a miracle, then I would believe." Others, like the Greeks in this verse, might say, "If we could, with some clever words or argument, demonstrate the truth of what the Bible says, then we would believe." However, God tells us that today He is giving us, and all He plans on giving us, is the preaching of "Christ crucified." If that is not good enough for you, then you will have to reject Jesus and suffer the consequences.

So why won't God show us a miracle(s) and why won't He give us arguments that would destroy the arguments of the skeptics? I don't know because certainly He could. It may have to do with the fact that if people were not persuaded by the miracles of God Himself and the wisdom of God Himself when He walked on this earth in the form of Jesus, then it probably wouldn't work today either. The problem, you see, is not in the head; it is in the heart. We can look around us and see the earth and everything on it and know that there is a God Who created it all. Or we can rebel against God and foolishly start thinking that this earth created itself and everything on it, so as to hide from the God that, deep down, we know is there (I Timothy 6:1–2; Jeremiah 2:27). Will you allow the preaching of "Christ crucified" to touch you or not? Will you believe and place all your trust in Jesus or not?

I CORINTHIANS 1

But of him are ye in Christ Jesus, who of God is made unto us wisdom, and righteousness, and sanctification, and redemption (I Corinthians 1:30).

Once again, we see a verse that tells us that we have "redemption," in other words, eternal life "in Christ Jesus."

Some may say that if salvation is as simple as trusting solely in Jesus, then we could go out and break the commandments and live as we please. While this is technically true, the Bible indicates that if we are saved and choose to live in sin, our lifespan could well be shortened. Furthermore, once we are saved, portions of the Bible that never made any sense to us now begin to make sense (I Corinthians 2:14). Once we realize the great sacrifice that Jesus made for us, and the great gift of eternal life that we have gained through Jesus, our attitude will become that we want to please Him and not disobey Him. This is called sanctification. Things that once looked burdensome and looked like legalism to us, now become what we desire to do. It is like a good friend who might sacrifice to give you a great gift. If this occurred, would you want to harm that friend or obey him and be kind to him? Would you rebel at hearing what that friend liked or disliked, or would you want to know? I think you know the answer to that. And so it is with salvation. Let us always be thankful to Jesus and seek to please Him for this great gift for which we could never repay.

I CORINTHIANS 2

And I, brethren, when I came to you, came not with excellency of speech or of wisdom, declaring unto you the testimony of God. For I determined not to know any thing among you, save Jesus Christ, and him crucified. And I was with you in weakness, and in fear, and in much trembling. And my speech and my preaching was not with enticing words of man's wisdom, but in demonstration of the Spirit and of power. That your faith should not stand in the wisdom of men, but in the power of God (I Corinthians 2:1–5).

The great apostle Paul is telling us that the one thing that means everything is "Jesus Christ and him crucified." God, hrough Paul, is telling us that neither clever speeches nor great wisdom, nor anything else for that matter, is of any lasting ignificance compared to Jesus. Why? Because as we know from he many other verses we have studied, we gain eternal life hrough believing in Jesus and the blood that He shed at His rucifixion as having paid in full the penalty for our sins, thereby ;iving us His righteousness, so we can live in heaven with God orever. It is a simple message and it does not depend upon the :leverness of man; in fact, our pride of intellect may well keep us rom accepting this message.

Aren't we, as believers or nonbelievers alike, all too often nfluenced by appealing speeches, clever arguments, or intellectual prilliance? According to God, it is Jesus Who is and should be paramount in each of our lives. The Bible is a book unlike any other because it is a book written by God. We gain a relationship with God and eternal life by simple childlike faith and trust in esus, and Him alone. Then, as we study the Bible to learn more about Jesus and how to follow Him better, we find wisdom that owers over the intellect and wisdom of man. As Christians, as with the great apostle Paul, may we always remember that everything, including our very salvation, depends not upon self or any other thing but upon loving and trusting solely in our Savior, Jesus Christ.

I CORINTHIANS 2

But the natural man receiveth not the things of the Spirit of God; for they are foolishness unto him; neither can he know them, because they are spiritually discerned (I Corinthians 2:14).

A man I know once told me a story of how he had presented the gospel to a very intelligent man, a college professor. The simple gospel is that we gain eternal life by believing and trusting n Jesus alone. After much discussion, the professor told my friend that he would not believe the Bible until he understood it.

My friend then told the professor, "Then you will die and spend eternity in hell, because you will never understand it until you believe it." That unfortunate truth is exactly what this verse is telling us.

Much of the Bible does not make any sense to us until we believe in Jesus. We do, however, know enough so that we can either accept Jesus in childlike faith, or reject Him, and thereby determine our own fate. But once we believe in Jesus, the Holy Spirit comes to live within us, as the verses preceding the above verse tell us, and the things that are in the Bible begin to make more and more sense to us.

May each of us, in simple childlike faith, trust in Jesus as our Savior and then, more and more, begin to understand, accept, and follow the teachings of the Bible by the wisdom that the Holy Spirit gives us and out of gratitude to Jesus for what He has done for us.

I CORINTHIANS 3

Who then is Paul, and who is Apollos, but ministers by whom ye believed, even as the Lord gave to every man? (I Corinthians 3:5).

In this verse, the great apostle Paul tells us what the goal of every pastor, priest, or Christian on this earth should be—to tell the gospel story of salvation through faith in Jesus so that others might also "believe" and be saved. Please note that the great apostle Paul, who many agree is the greatest preacher of all time, did not pretend to have any supernatural devices at his exclusive disposal, like rites or rituals, by which he could save people. In this verse, as throughout all his writings, he regards his primary function on this earth to tell people about Jesus so they might "believe" and be saved. If a preacher with the credentials of Paul tells us that we should not trust in preachers (like Paul or his friend, Apollos, for example) for salvation, do you think it is wise to trust in today's preachers and/or the institutions they

epresent for salvation? Or might it be better to do it God's way
nd simply "believe" and thereby gain eternal life?

I CORINTHIANS 3

*For other foundation can no man lay than that
s laid, which is Jesus Christ (I Corinthians 3:11).*

God, through the great apostle Paul, is talking here about our
"foundation," referring to the Christian foundation, which
s our basis for eternal life. I think we all know that the
oundation is the most important part of the house. If the
oundation is bad, eventually the house will collapse. Or if the
oundation is partly good cement and partly bad dirt, the house
vill still collapse, will it not? Please note that the great apostle
²aul is telling us that our foundation must be "Jesus Christ"
lone. I don't see anything else mentioned in the foundation other
han Jesus Christ, do you? Does Paul say that our foundation
hould be Jesus Christ plus baptism? Does Paul say that our
oundation should be Jesus Christ plus works? Does Paul say that
ur foundation should be Jesus Christ plus rites or rituals? Here is
vhat God says through the great apostle Paul, but the key
question is, what do you say?

Not being a chemist, I don't know why it is that only
ement, and not dirt mixed with cement and water, will make a
;ood foundation. And not being God, I don't know why it is only
pelief in Jesus Christ that will save us. But I do know that God
10lds the keys to heaven, and this is what He tells us. Shouldn't
his be our foundation regardless of what our human minds,
raditions, or others may tell us?

I CORINTHIANS 5

*Purge out therefore the old leaven, that ye
nay be a new lump, as ye are unleavened. For even*

Christ our passover is sacrificed for us (I Corinthians 5:7).

The reference to *unleavened* here is an analogy to being unsaved but that when a person becomes "new" he is saved. In II Corinthians 5:17 we read: ". . . if any man be in Christ, he is a NEW creature." When we are "in Christ" or trust in Christ, we are saved. This verse tells us that Jesus is our Passover.

You may have noticed in reading the Bible that there is a great deal of symmetry in the Bible. Much of what occurs in the Old Testament is a picture of the New Testament. The Passover is described in Exodus 12:1–33. When the time came for God to deliver His people, the Israelites, from Egypt, God hit Pharaoh with one plague after another, but the stubborn Pharaoh would still not let the Israelites go. The final plague occurred when the death angel, after adequate warning to Pharaoh, passed through Egypt killing the first-born in every household. However, each Israelite was told that if he would take the blood of a lamb and put it on the doorposts of his house, then everyone inside would be safe. Thus, a child in that house was saved if there was just enough faith to obey God and put the blood on the doorposts. Our salvation is likewise just that simple. If we, by simple faith, believe that Jesus died on the cross for us and shed His blood as the penalty for our sins, and we accept that blood as a complete and total covering for all our sins—past, present, and future—in that moment of belief we are saved forever. There are many things we learn in the Bible that God has done that neither I nor anyone else can explain, but I do know that the Bible says that gaining eternal life is just that simple, and praise God for it!

I CORINTHIANS 6

And such were some of you; but ye are washed, but ye are sanctified, but ye are justified in the name of the Lord Jesus, and by the Spirit of our

God
(I Corinthians 6:11).

The verses leading up to this verse describe many forms of sin. The Bible tells us not to sin and we should not sin, but each of us knows that we do sin. We are powerless to resist the devil until we are saved. This verse gives us many important truths of our salvation. It begins with being "washed" or washed in the blood of Jesus. We are washed in the blood of Jesus when we believe that Jesus died on the cross and shed His blood for our sins, and we thus accept that blood as the penalty or covering of all our sins. In other words, that blood, when we believe enough to accept it, pays the price for all our sins, a price that we could never pay on our own. The verse also tells us that we are "justified" in the name of Jesus. The word "justified" means "just as if I'd never sinned." Again, when we trust in Jesus, all our sins are covered under His blood. His Holy Spirit comes to live within us at the moment of belief (Ephesians 1:13). After we are saved, for the first time in our lives, we can resist sin (Romans 6:14). A Christian is sanctified by studying the Bible and thus gaining faith (Romans 10:17). The new believer will resist sin more and more out of gratitude for what Jesus has done. May we always be grateful to Jesus for His great sacrifice, which allows us to gain eternal life with Him in heaven forever!

I CORINTHIANS 15

Moreover, brethren, I declare unto you the gospel which I preached unto you, which also ye have received, and wherein ye stand; by which also ye are saved, if ye keep in memory what I preached unto you, unless ye have believed in vain. For I delivered unto you first of all that which I also received, how that Christ died for our sins according to the scriptures; and that he was buried, and that he

rose again the third day according to the scriptures (I Corinthians 15:1–4).

These verses tell us that we are saved by the preaching of the "gospel." What is the gospel? In summary, as these verses tell us, it is that Jesus died on the cross, that His shed blood would pay the full penalty for all our sins, and that He was buried and rose again on the third day to prove that He was God. This really says it all, doesn't it?

All of us, deep down, know that a price must be paid for our sins. But incredibly, God has gone ahead and paid that price on our behalf with the blood of His Son, Jesus Christ.

John Wesley said, "If you show me a worm who can understand a man, I will show you a man who can understand God." God is that far above man, and even much farther above. Can you conceive of a man dying for a worm? This is why it is so difficult for us to believe the Son of God, Jesus Christ, would die for us. Yet it is true because the Bible tells us so. So, will you believe and accept this great gift, or will you try to do it your own way?

I CORINTHIANS 15

And that he was buried, and that he rose again the third day according to the scriptures; And that he was seen of Cephas, then of the twelve. After that, he was seen of above five hundred brethren at once; of whom the greater part remain unto this present, but some are fallen asleep. After that, he was seen of James; then of all the apostles. And last of all he was seen of me also, as of one born out of due time (I Corinthians 15:4–8).

These verses, if we examine them and their implications, give an important proof that Jesus did indeed rise from the dead, which proves that He was the Son of God and that the Bible is true. This means that we can place all our trust in God's promise that if we simply believe in Jesus, we have gained eternal life, and we thus never again need to worry about where we will spend eternity.

Eleven of the twelve apostles died a martyr's death for preaching about Jesus and that we gain eternal life by believing in Him. These verses tell us that each of the apostles, as well as five hundred other people, saw Jesus after He had risen from the dead, and thus knew the truth of the matter. Does it make any sense to you that these eleven men, who knew whether or not Jesus had risen from the dead, would die a martyr's death for preaching this, if it was all a big lie? What would their motive be for doing so? Atheists, skeptics, and secularists say that there is no proof that Jesus rose from the dead. We have a book, the Bible, written by the men who saw these events, telling us that Jesus rose from the dead. There are eleven people, and many more, who gave their lives to testify to the truth of what they saw —that Jesus rose from the dead. Much of history that many of us would never question is written on the basis of a handful of witnesses. What about five hundred? Or what about eleven who gave their lives to verify the truth of this great message? But the great question is this: which way will you stake your life?

I CORINTHIANS 15

For as in Adam all die, even so in Christ shall all be made alive (I Corinthians 15:22).

When Adam, the first man, sinned, sin came upon the human race. Each person after Adam has sinned and all of us are thus sinners (Romans 3:23). Sometimes we get the idea that our sins are not very great compared to someone else's sin and that God will maybe accept us for this reason. However, God tells us that even some sin we may find to be insignificant is just the same, in God's eyes, as seemingly terrible sins like murder (James 2:10). This is not because great sins are okay, but rather because God is so holy that even a seemingly little sin offends Him greatly. Therefore each of us, because of our sins, stands on the edge of eternity in hell.

However, the great news is that in Jesus Christ we can all be made "alive" or, in other words, alive with Jesus in eternity in heaven forever. How? By simply believing and trusting in Jesus, with His death and suffering on the cross, as the complete, total, and final sacrifice for our sins (Romans 3:24–26; I John 2:2, 4:9–10). Yes, as the Romans and the I John verses tell us, we know we are sinners, **BUT** if we believe and trust in Jesus, when God looks at us, He will not see our sins but rather the blood of Jesus covering our sins. And the perfect payment that Jesus made is **FINAL**—just like when you make the final mortgage payment on your house. You then don't need to keep paying. Praise God for His great and all-sufficient gift!

I CORINTHIANS 15

The sting of death is sin; and the strength of sin is the law. But thanks be to God, which giveth us the victory through our Lord Jesus Christ (I Corinthians 15:56–57).

These verses tell us that the Law brings sin and death, which means eternal separation from God in hell. The Law is man working his way to heaven through trying to obey the Ten Commandments, good works, religious rites, and rituals. In other words, the Law, which was established by God and is perfect, shows us that we cannot get to heaven this way. The Law is like having the only perfect diamond in the world and then comparing every other imperfect diamond to that perfect standard—they would all fail. God gave us the Law so that we could compare ourselves to the Law and see for our own selves that we cannot meet its standards and thus cannot work our way to heaven or become religious enough to make our way to heaven. There has to be another way, if we are to get to heaven.

Yes, praise God, there is another way! There is a way that gives us "victory" and it is "through our Lord Jesus Christ," just as this verse tells us. There are many other verses in the Bible that tell us that the Law condemns us, but Jesus fulfilled the Law for us, much like a parent or friend who helps us when we cannot help ourselves (Romans 8:1–3, 10:3–5; Galatians 2:15–17, 3:23–25, 5:3–5). When we set aside everything else that we are trusting in, and believe and trust in Jesus alone for our salvation, then, praise God, we have that great gift of eternal life that we could never purchase or earn on our own!

II CORINTHIANS 1

But we had the sentence of death in ourselves, that we should not trust in ourselves, but in God which raiseth the dead. Who delivered us from so great a death, and doth deliver: in whom we trust that he will yet deliver us (II Corinthians 1:9–10).

These verses tell us that each and every one of us is under a death sentence—physically and spiritually. We should not trust in ourselves, not in our works, not in our efforts, and not in our man-made systems. So, what should we do? Just as this verse tells us, we should do the only thing we can do and that is to trust in God and more specifically his Son, Jesus Christ, Who paid the death penalty for us when He died on the cross at Calvary.

Yes, each of us will die physically unless the Lord returns while we are still alive. But when we trust in Jesus, Who paid the price to deliver us from spiritual death, at that moment of trust, He saves us and gives us spiritual life that continues even when we physically die. We will live with Him in heaven forever. This is how God, in His great love, paid the price for our sins and "delivered" us from spiritual death and hell forever. Where we will spend eternity is a lot more important than how many years we spend on this earth, isn't it?

Our situation is like that of a condemned man who is offered a pardon by the governor. He can either trust the governor and accept the pardon, or he can refuse the pardon and die. Or he could foolishly refuse the pardon because he is a proud man and may hope to escape the death penalty in some other fashion. Don't you think it best that we accept God's pardon His way, by trusting in His Son, our Savior, Jesus Christ?

For the Son of God, Jesus Christ, who was preached among you by us, even by me and Silvanus and Timotheus, was not yea and nay, but in him was yea. For all the promises of God in him are yea, and in him Amen, unto the glory of God by us. Now he which stablisheth us with you in Christ, and hath anointed us is God; Who hath also sealed us, and given the earnest of the Spirit in our hearts (II Corinthians 1:19–22).

Here, the great apostle Paul tells us that he is preaching Jesus Christ. In fact, this is all that Paul preached. If there were another way to be saved, other than faith in Jesus Christ, and trust in Him as the great sacrifice for all our sins, wouldn't Paul have been preaching this supposed other way? We are told today that there are ways to heaven other than or in addition to Jesus, but Paul evidently did not believe that and neither should we.

We are also told here that Jesus fulfilled the promises of God. These would be the promises God gave in the Old Testament (Isaiah 53) that He would send a Savior and a Redeemer who would save us from our sin. That Savior was, of course, Jesus, Who was the perfect sacrificial Lamb of God. Until Jesus came, a perfect lamb had to be sacrificed repeatedly for the sins of the people (Leviticus chapters 3 and 4) who were, at that time, looking forward to their Savior, Jesus, coming. After Jesus, the perfect Lamb of God, came and was sacrificed on the cross, the debt owing for our sins was paid in full, once and for all. Sacrificing a lamb before Jesus came was like making a payment on a mortgage. When Jesus came and was sacrificed, it was like paying off that mortgage in full so that no more payment need ever be made.

God has one condition and one only. We must believe and trust Jesus as the perfect and all-sufficient sacrifice for our sins. When we transfer our trust from self or anything else we may be trusting in, to Jesus, we have then gained eternal life. At that time, the Holy Spirit comes to live in our hearts and guides us into further truth through His Word, the Bible (John 16:13). Praise God!

II CORINTHIANS 3

And not as Moses, which put a veil over his face, that the children of Israel could not stedfastly look to the end of that which is abolished. But their minds were blinded for until this day remaineth the same veil untaken away in the reading of the old testament; which veil is done away in Christ. But even unto this day, when Moses is read, the veil is upon their heart. Nevertheless when it shall turn to the Lord, the veil shall be taken away. Now the Lord is that Spirit and where the Spirit of the Lord is, there is liberty (II Corinthians 3:13–17).

These verses tell us that the people who lived before Christ—who only had the Old Testament to guide them—were given indications of the coming Savior (as in Isaiah 53), but it was not totally clear. It was like they were looking through a veil. But today we have the New Testament and we are told clearly about Jesus, our Savior, and the "veil" is taken away. The Old Testament, with the Ten Commandments (the Law), showed the people then, as well as now, that we are sinners and sin separates us from God. It is also evident, if we are honest with ourselves, that none of us can keep the Ten Commandments, and thus be good enough to get to heaven. And if this were not evident from the Old Testament, then we should read Matthew chapters 5–7, the Sermon on the Mount, and refresh our memories as to just how high God's standards really are. If the Law and our own "goodness" were all there is, then each of us is hopelessly lost.

But, praise God, there is another way—our Savior, Jesus Christ. Jesus, with His shed blood at Calvary, paid the price in full for our sins, giving us the great gift of eternal life. We just need to believe and trust in Him and His great sacrifice ("turn to the Lord" like the verses tell us). This is "liberty" indeed! Does this mean that we can or should use this great liberty to disobey the Ten Commandments? If someone has given you a great gift, do you want to hurt that person?

Jesus paid the price for our sins and earned for each of us the gift of eternal life that we could never earn for ourselves. We should use this great "liberty" that He has given us, and the power to resist sin, to do just that—resist sin and help others find our great Savior.

II CORINTHIANS 4

But if our gospel be hid, it is hid to them that are lost. In whom the god of this world hath blinded the minds of them which believe not, lest the light of the glorious gospel of Christ, who is the image of God, should shine unto them. For we preach not ourselves, but Christ Jesus the Lord; and ourselves your servants for Jesus sake (II Corinthians 4:3-5).

The great apostle Paul, perhaps the greatest evangelist ever, and the man whom God inspired to write much of the New Testament, devoted his entire life and ministry to one thing— preaching the gospel. What is the gospel? It is summarized in John 3:16, often called the "Bible in a verse"—when we believe solely in Jesus Christ, we are saved! Yet, a lot of what we hear today is Jesus plus, plus, plus, isn't it? Paul tells us that the gospel is "light" but that much of the gospel is "hid" from them who are "blinded" to the truth of the gospel (by the devil and his helpers) and thus do not "believe." When we "believe" (as these verses reference), we see the "light" and are saved.

Paul tells us clearly in these verses that he does not preach "ourselves," but rather "Christ Jesus the Lord." There is a division today, as there always has been, between those who are preaching themselves and pretending that they can save you with their devices, and those who are preaching Jesus Christ and Him alone as all sufficient (II Corinthians 3:5). Whom are you following? Who is your Savior?

II CORINTHIANS 5

And that he died for all, that they which live should not henceforth live unto themselves, but unto him which died for them, and rose again. Therefore, if any man be in Christ, he is a new creature: old things are passed away; behold, all things are become new. And all things are of God, who hath reconciled us to himself by Jesus Christ, and hath given to us the ministry of reconciliation; To wit, that God was in Christ, reconciling the world unto himself, not imputing their trespasses unto them; and hath committed unto us the word of reconciliation (II Corinthians 5:15, 17–19).

These verses tell us that we are "reconciled" to God "by Jesus Christ." Sin keeps us from God. But these verses tell us that we can be "reconciled" to God, which means that we can live with Him in heaven forever, and that comes "by Jesus Christ." Our trespasses (or sin) will not be "imputed" to us because of Jesus. And how can it be that our many sins will not be imputed to us by God? How can we be "reconciled to God"? How can

God overlook sin? The answer is that God can't overlook sin because He is holy. A price must be paid for our sins. Jesus paid that price on our behalf when He suffered and died on the cross at Calvary. When we simply believe and trust in Jesus (John 3:16), our sins are no longer imputed to us, but the righteousness of Jesus is imputed to us. When God looks at us, He sees Jesus' blood covering our sins (I John 1:7), and He sees the righteousness of Jesus (Romans 3:22) that we gain by simply trusting in Him.

Does this seem too good to be true, even though God tells us it is true? Does this mean that we can then go out and sin all we want because our sins are no longer "imputed" to us? I'll let you answer that question. When we realize what Jesus has done for us, and when we trust Him and thus gain eternal life, we should no longer live for ourselves in our sins, but rather we should live for our Savior Who died for us and do what we can to please Him. Our good works have nothing to do with our salvation because our feeble good works could never cancel our sins; God tells us this in Ephesians 2:8–9. But our good works have everything to do with our expressing gratitude to our great Savior for what He has done for us!

II CORINTHIANS 5

For he hath made him to be sin for us, who knew no sin; that we might be made the righteousness of God in him (II Corinthians 5:21).

When we gain the "righteousness of God," we have gained eternal life with God in heaven forever. How do we gain this righteousness? Is it by trying as hard as we can to do good works, avoid sin, and obey the Ten Commandments? We should do these things out of gratitude for what Jesus has done for us. But do you really think that we can gain the "righteousness of God" in this way? Just think of the many times that each of us sin in a day or in a week. Let's say that you or I sin three times a day. This is over a thousand sins in a year. Then, let's multiply our age by these one thousand sins per year. Can you really stand before God with this much sin and claim the "righteousness of God"? You may say that you do many good things for each sin. But if you make an omelet with five good eggs and one bad egg, what is the result? No, we will never get to heaven by being good enough or by trying to live a sin-free life. There must be another way.

This verse tells us about that other way. When Jesus died on the cross at Calvary, God placed the entire sin of the entire world—past, present, and future—upon Him. Jesus, with His shed blood, paid the price for all that sin (Hebrews 9:19–28). The blood of God (Jesus), and **ONLY** this blood, was equal to the price for all our sins. The price for your salvation and my salvation has already been paid. It is as if a bank were holding a check with your name on it. But you would have to show up and claim it. We must claim God's great gift of eternal life by believing and trusting in Jesus and His perfect sacrifice for our sins, and nothing else. It is as simple as that. When we transfer our trust from ourselves, and our own perceived goodness, to Jesus, we have gained eternal life. Praise God!

II CORINTHIANS 7

For Godly sorrow worketh repentance to salvation not to be repented of; but the sorrow of the world worketh death (II Corinthians 7:10).

This verse implies that repentance brings salvation. Does this mean then that repentance is a work that we must do in addition to believing in Jesus to be saved? No, it does not. Salvation comes by belief in Jesus alone (Ephesians 2:8–9). This verse complements all those other verses we have been studying. It is an elementary rule of Bible interpretation that when one interpretation will conflict with other verses in the Bible, and when a different interpretation will harmonize all verses, one always uses the interpretation that harmonizes.

This verse (read in conjunction with our previously studied verses) means there is one great sin of which we must repent before we can be saved—our previous failure to trust solely in Jesus for eternal life. When we repent of that sin and turn our hearts and minds toward Jesus, we are then saved.

If this verse meant that we must repent of *all* our sins, as opposed to the great sin of not trusting in Jesus, then we would be lost. Why? For one thing, you can't even remember all your sins. In fact, you can't even remember all the sins you committed last week, let alone in a lifetime. Also, we may define sin a little differently than God (Matthew chapters 5–7). When we consider that God is so holy that even a seemingly innocent sin, like a little white lie, is as great as murder in God's eyes (James 2:10), we see that we could never hate sin as much as God and be as sorry for our sins as God demands.

Does this mean then that we should not be sorry for our many sins or that it is okay to ignore them? Of course not. Once we have accepted the great gift of eternal life, we will naturally be sorry for our sins. This is because we will then know that it was our sins that put Jesus on the cross, and still, in His great goodness, He willingly died for us.

II CORINTHIANS 8

For ye know the grace of our Lord Jesus Christ, that, though he was rich, yet for your sakes he became poor, that ye through his poverty might be rich (II Corinthians 8:9

Here, Paul is writing to "brethren" (II Corinthians 8:1), meaning fellow Christians, reiterating that these Christians "know" the "grace" of Jesus. Yes, a Christian gains eternal life ot through any work, ritual, or his own merit but rather entirely Jesus' expense, as a pure and total gift from Jesus. Please do ot let any self-appointed intermediary convince you that you are aining eternal life through anything other than believing and usting in Jesus alone!

This verse also explains that Jesus was rich. Of course He as. He was God (part of the triune God), and God has all eaven and earth under His control and at His disposal. He alone olds the keys to heaven. But as unbelievable as it may seem, od became "poor," meaning that He, Jesus, became a man, lived poverty, took the abuse of us sinners, and eventually allowed imself to be crucified because of my sin, your sin, and the sins f the entire world. Would you not agree that this is one great od? Why did He do this? So, as this verse says, we too then ight be "rich," meaning that we might have eternal life with sus in heaven forever. Tell me; is that not Good News? Have ou accepted this great gift?

II CORINTHIANS 13

For though he was crucified through veakness, yet he liveth by the power of God. For we lso are weak in him, but we shall live with him by he power of God toward you. Examine yourselves, vhether ye be in the faith; prove your own selves. Know ye not your own selves, how that Jesus Christ s in you, except ye be reprobates? (II Corinthians 3:4–5).

These verses tell us that we shall "live with" Jesus—an eternal life in heaven with Jesus. How? By "faith." Do you see a attern here? Each time the Bible tells us directly, or indirectly, ow we might gain eternal life, it is always by "belief" or "faith" Him alone. When we believe that Jesus died on the cross to ay the penalty in full for our sins and that His shed blood ompletely covers our sins, we are then trusting only in Him to give us His great gift of eternal life. In other words, it is all Jesus, and none of self. Isn't it much better to be able to place our trust in Jesus rather than self, works, rituals, or any other thing, all of which can and will fail?

We can know that we will have eternal life because, as these verses tell us, the same God Whose power caused Jesus to rise from the dead, will use that power to give us eternal life in heaven with Jesus. I would rather be trusting in a God and a Savior Who have demonstrated their power, than in persons or systems whose power has not been demonstrated, wouldn't you?

Grace be to you and peace from God the Father, and from our Lord Jesus Christ. Who gave himself for our sins, that he might deliver us from this present evil world, according to the will of God and our Father (Galatians 1:3–4).

These verses tell us that Jesus gave Himself for our sins that we might be delivered from this present evil world, meaning that we might gain eternal life in heaven with Jesus. Being in heaven for eternity is to be our goal, not the presumed pleasures of this world.

Many think that believing and trusting in Jesus and His sacrifice for our sins is too easy or too good to be true, as the only means of going to heaven. Thus, they add things to trusting in Jesus as the means, and the only means, of gaining eternal life. However, God, in the Bible, does not add to believing or trusting in Jesus to gain eternal life (John 3:16), so we should not either. But how can it be that simple?

Let's say that you need a complicated operation to save your life. You need one million dollars to pay for the operation, and you cannot have the operation unless it is paid for in advance. You may be a hard-working person and you may have some savings, but if you don't have the one million dollars, you

n't have the means to save yourself. You may have relatives or
iends who are good people and want to save you but if they do
ot have the one million dollars, they do not have the means to
ve you. Then, along comes a billionaire, Mr. X, and for some
ason he takes pity upon you and pays the one million dollars on
ur behalf; you are saved. Did it cost him something? Yes. Do
e know why he chose to save you? No. Can you explain it? No.
ut you can accept it. While this is not a perfect analogy, gaining
ernal life is just about that simple, according to the Bible. God,
His great love, and Jesus, to His great detriment, chose to save
. I believe we should accept it exactly on their terms and then,
 best we can, try to do the good that will please them instead of
e bad that will disappoint them.

GALATIANS 1

*I marvel that ye are so soon removed from him
at called you into the grace of Christ unto another
ospel. Which is not another; but there be some that
ouble you, and would pervert the gospel of Christ.
ut though we, or an angel from heaven, preach any
ther gospel unto you than that which we have
reached unto you, let him be accursed. As we said
efore, so say I now again, if any man preach any
ther gospel unto you than that ye have received, let
im be accursed (Galatians 1:6–9).*

The "gospel of Christ" is that portion of the Bible that tells
us how we might be saved. The word "grace," coming from
od, means that we are saved totally as a gift of God, totally
rough "faith" in Jesus our Savior, with no works of any kind on
ur part (Ephesians 2:8–9). God evidently knew that people
ould come along who would preach "another gospel" and
pervert" the gospel of Christ. This gospel that we are warned
gainst is evidently a gospel that teaches that we are saved by
eans other than faith in Jesus or in addition to faith in Jesus.

How should we respond to persons, institutions, or even "angels from heaven" who preach a different gospel? I will simply answer by quoting the words of God: "let him be accursed"!

Knowing that a man is not justified by the works of the law, but by the faith of Jesus Christ, even we have believed in Jesus Christ, that we might be justified by the faith of Christ, and not by the works of the law; for by the works of the law shall no flesh be justified (Galatians 2:16).

The background to this verse is that some believers were being pressured to be circumcised (a religious ritual usually performed upon infants, much like infant baptism). These believers were being told that this religious ritual was a part of salvation (Galatians 2:3–4, 7–9, 12–13). We see God's response above. The word "justified" in the Bible means standing before God as if we had never sinned. We are clearly taught in this verse that we are not "justified" by works (being good enough) or religious rituals (like circumcision, etc.), but we are justified by "faith" in Jesus. Is that too simple for you? It is evidently not too simple for God. Do you want to add something to faith in Jesus to obtain eternal life? God is warning against it. If we were to take the road of adding works, rituals, or whatever to faith in Jesus to gain eternal life, we are then saying that Jesus alone is not sufficient. Do we want to stand before God someday claiming that Jesus alone was not sufficient for us? Or would it perhaps be better to stand before God claiming faith in Jesus alone, nothing more and nothing less? I suggest letting this verse be our answer.

I am crucified with Christ, nevertheless I live, yet not I, but Christ liveth in me and the life which I now live in the flesh I live by the faith of the Son of God, who loved me, and gave himself for me. I do not frustrate the grace of God, for if righteousness come by the law, then Christ is dead in vain (Galatians 2:20–21).

In these verses, the great apostle Paul is telling us that Jesus lives in him, which means that he has gained eternal life. He further tells us that he is living by "faith" in Jesus. Many other verses have repeatedly told us that we gain eternal life by faith in Jesus alone (Ephesians 2:8–9 etc.). Apparently, this was good enough and not too simple for Paul.

Paul was perhaps the greatest preacher, greatest evangelist, and greatest man of God who ever lived. Did this great Christian gain eternal life by all his great and mighty works for God? He did not. In fact, he tells us that he would not even try to do so and thereby "frustrate" God's "grace" of salvation by faith alone. Is that clear enough?

And if the great apostle Paul could not gain eternal life through his great and mighty works for God, then neither can you or I. So, let's discontinue our useless and futile striving and climbing to heaven; rather, let's enter through that God-guaranteed way, the one and only bridge from this life to the next, Jesus! Then, solely out of gratitude to Jesus for what He did for us, let us try to do the good things that we know that God wants us to do in return for His great love and sacrifice.

GALATIANS 3

This only would I learn of you, received ye the Spirit by the works of the law, or by the hearing of faith? Are ye so foolish, having begun in the Spirit, are ye now made perfect by the flesh? (Galatians 3:2–3).

In these verses, God continues to tell us that we receive the Holy Spirit, Who comes to each of us at the time we gain eternal life (Ephesians 1:13), by faith (in Jesus) and not by the Law (meaning our own good works—the good things the Bible tells us to do, Ephesians 2:8–9). Sometimes we are tempted to think, though, that while we might be saved by faith or trust in Jesus and His blood that was shed as the all-sufficient sacrifice for our sins, we must then do enough good works or rituals to stay saved. But this would be "saved by faith and unsaved by works." The Bible does not teach this. In fact, the idea that we are saved by faith, but not yet perfect, and then made perfect by works, or rituals is, in these verses, labeled "foolish." We do have to be "perfect" to get to heaven (Matthew 5:48). But when we believe in Jesus, His shed blood covers our sins and God then sees the righteousness of Jesus and not our sins (I John 1:7). We are made "perfect" in God's eyes through Jesus, at the moment of belief.

Let me use this analogy. We had a stain in our carpet that nothing would take out, including two professional cleanings by two professional carpet cleaners. We were told nothing would take out the stain. Then, one day, we bought an amazing product at the Dollar Store. I had been told that it would probably remove the stain in our carpet. I tried it and, to my amazement, it did. I had tried various good things that would not take out that stain, but this one product did the job. It is somewhat like that with our sins. There are many good things we can do, and that God wants us to do like good works, trying to obey the Ten Commandments, religious rituals, and so forth, but these things, as good as they may be, will not remove our sins. But there is one thing that will—the blood of Jesus. When we trust solely in that blood, then, praise God, all our sins—**PAST, PRESENT, AND FUTURE**—are gone. How do I know this? The God of heaven Himself, in His Bible, tells me so. Why would I try anything else? The stain of my sin is too deep for any thing or any one other than Jesus to take it away.

He therefore that ministereth to you the Spirit, and worketh miracles among you, doeth he it by the works of the law, or by the hearing of faith? Even as Abraham believed God, and it was accounted to him for righteousness. Know ye therefore that they which are of faith, the same are the children of Abraham (Galatians 3:6–7).

Once again, we are told that we gain "righteousness" not by "works of the law" (good works that we may do like avoiding sin, or doing religious rituals), but rather by "faith." You know the story of Abraham from the Bible. Abraham did many mighty works for God, including moving to a strange land (Israel) when God told him to do so, fighting evil, and founding the Jewish nation. Abraham also not only practiced but established the ritual of circumcision, a religious ritual similar to infant baptism (Genesis 17). Maybe you could call Abraham the King of Good Works. But how did Abraham gain the "righteousness" that each of us needs to live in heaven forever with God? Was it by his good works, of which there were many? Was it by religious rituals that he in fact established? No, it was because he "believed" and it was by "faith." If Abraham did not get to heaven by good works, neither will we. We are explicitly told at the conclusion of these verses that we also, by "faith," become "children of Abraham," meaning children of God. Faith in what? As we have learned in many other verses, it is by faith in Jesus and that His shed blood is all-sufficient to pay the penalty for our sins that we gain eternal life. Abraham looked forward to his Savior, Jesus, and we look backward to the same Savior, Jesus. We may never have the great faith of an Abraham, but do you have enough faith to believe that Jesus' sacrifice covers your sins, and nothing more and nothing less?

> **And the scripture, foreseeing that God would justify the heathen through faith, preached before the gospel unto Abraham, saying, In thee shall all nations be blessed (Galatians 3:8).**

There are at least two important truths in this great verse. First, God is telling us that through Abraham (or the Jewish people) "shall all nations be blessed." The Jewish people, for the most part, have sadly rejected their Savior, Jesus, and God especially wants to see them saved because they are still His chosen people. In this verse, as well as many others, God tells us as individuals and as a nation, that we must be kind to the Jewish people and then we shall be "blessed." I believe that one reason that God does not simply destroy America for all its wickedness and perversion is that America is still the great refuge for and champion of the Jewish people and nation. History is littered with examples of what happens to nations that have harmed the Jewish people. If that ever happens here, then America's real problems have just begun.

Second, even more important than God's blessing on this earth, as important as that is, is being blessed for all eternity by being in heaven with God. This verse tells us that we can be justified, which means that we can be viewed by God "just as if I'd never sinned." How? God tells us "through faith." Yes, when we take whatever faith we have, whether it is great or small, and remove that faith from ourselves, our good works, our religion, our rituals and place it solely upon Jesus and His shed blood, at that very moment we are "justified" and have gained eternal life. Praise God for this critical directive for successful living in this life and the next

So then they which be of faith are blessed with faithful Abraham (Galatians 3:9).

God blessed Abraham because of his faith. God blessed Abraham in many ways on this earth but, most importantly, God blessed Abraham with eternal life in heaven, all because of his faith. How do we gain eternal life in heaven as Abraham did? In the same way—faith! (Galatians 3:13–15).

But faith in what? Faith in Jesus.

Each of us has faith or trusts in something to save us when we die. It might be self (good works), religion (a church or an earthly spiritual authority), or rituals. But rituals (like circumcision, baptism, etc.) are signs and not a means of salvation, and trusting in works (the Law) voids faith (Romans 4:9–14). Why not do it God's way, not man's way, and trust in the real thing—Jesus and Him alone? When all these verses tell us that Jesus alone is sufficient, who are we to try coming to heaven another way?

For as many as are of the works of the law are under the curse; for it is written, cursed is every one that continueth not in all things which are written in the book of the law to do them. But that no man is justified by the law in the sight of God, it is evident; for, the just shall live by faith (Galatians 3:10–11).

If you were to go out and stop people randomly on the street and ask them how they might get to heaven, I think that eight out of ten would tell you that they hope to get to heaven because they are not a bad person, because they have done more good than bad, they are better than someone else, or some other works-related reason. Yet, sadly, this is directly contrary to what the Bible teaches.

Sometimes we will hear someone say they are living by the Sermon on the Mount. This would be untrue, because no one can live by the Sermon on the Mount (Matthew chapters 5, 6, and 7). In the Sermon on the Mount, Jesus tells us of all the sins we must avoid and all the good things we should do, all of which originate in the Ten Commandments. Jesus tells us that unless our righteousness exceeds that of the Pharisees, we cannot enter into heaven (Matthew 5:20). The Pharisees, as you may recall, were so strict about obeying every last element of the Law, that they would hire people to come into their homes on the Sabbath and light their stoves so that they would not violate the Sabbath. You will never exceed the righteousness of the Pharisees. As if this is not bad enough, Jesus then tells us in Matthew 5:48, not only must we keep all these laws, but rather that we must be "perfect" as God is perfect. So, what hope is there for any of us?

Our hope is that God has provided another way—Jesus. As we see in these verses (and in the Sermon on the Mount and in many other places), we will never be justified in God's eyes by obeying the Law (the Ten Commandments). The Law merely shows us what terrible sinners each and every one of us is, if we're honest enough to admit it. But when Jesus died on the cross and shed His blood, His blood paid the full penalty for all our sins and paid a price that we could never pay ourselves. It is by "faith" in Jesus and His blood sacrifice that we overcome the Law, sin, and death and gain eternal life with Jesus in heaven forever. Praise God!

GALATIANS 3

Christ hath redeemed us from the curse of the law, being made a curse for us; for it is written, cursed is everyone that hangeth on a tree. That the blessing of Abraham might come on the Gentiles through Jesus Christ; that we might receive the promise of the Spirit through faith (Galatians 3:13–14).

These verses tell us that we receive the "blessing of Abraham," which means eternal life in heaven with God, "through Jesus Christ." These verses also tell us that we receive the Holy Spirit (which we receive upon the event of being saved, Ephesians 1:13) "through faith." In other words, we are saved through faith in Jesus Christ. Once again, I don't see any other pre-conditions like works, being good enough, or rituals.

How can this be? Can a person actually be saved, no matter how good or bad he might be in his own eyes or in the eyes of others, simply by believing and trusting in Jesus and His blood sacrifice for his sins on the cross? You might ask, "Doesn't someone have to pay for my sins?" Yes and yes. Let's say, for example, that you had a large mortgage on your house, it was due, and you couldn't pay it. You wanted to keep the house but the bank had to be paid. You couldn't pay the bank. What could you do? The only answer would be to find someone loving and kind enough to pay the debt on your behalf. And that, reader friend, is exactly what Jesus did for us on the cross at Calvary. Let us not be so foolish as to ignore His great gift or try to do anything other than accept it in simple trusting faith!

GALATIANS 3

Now to Abraham and his seed were the promises made. He saith not, and to seeds, as of many; but as of one, and to thy seed, which is Christ. And this I say, that the covenant, that was confirmed before of God in Christ, the law, which was four hundred and thirty years after, cannot disannul, that it should make the promise of none effect. For if the inheritance be of the law, it is no more of promise; but God gave it to Abraham by promise (Galatians 3:16–18).

These verses remind us that people in the Old Testament looked forward to a promised Savior, Jesus, and today we look backward to that same promised Savior, Jesus, Who willingly suffered on the cross and shed His blood to pay the penalty for all our sins, past, present, and future. By trusting in this Savior, people in the Old Testament, and we today, are equally saved (Hebrews 11, 12:2).

There is another interesting point in these verses. These verses tell us that once we are saved, the moment that we place our trust in Jesus alone for eternal life, we cannot become "unsaved" later on. We are not saved by faith and unsaved by the Law. The "law" means the Ten Commandments, religious rituals, and other works. These verses tell us that the "law" cannot "disannul" the "promise" from God (our salvation). How can this be? When we trust in Jesus, His blood covers every one of our sins. Yes, out of gratitude for what Jesus has done for us, we should try to keep the Law, attend church, and do the other things that God wants us to do. But, praise God, our salvation is dependent on Jesus and what He has done (PERFECTION) and not ourselves and what we do (IMPERFECTION). Praise God!

GALATIANS 3

For if the inheritance be of the law, it is no more of promise, but God gave it to Abraham by promise (Galatians 3:18).

Our "inheritance" from God, as children of God, is eternal life in heaven with God. But how do we gain this "inheritance"? How do we become God's children? By faith in Jesus alone, Who paid the price for our sins for us (see the preceding eight verses). Why would God do this? I don't think anyone really knows how or why this can be, but it is what God decided, and it is what He promises. It seems hard to believe, doesn't it, that by putting one's faith in Jesus and the blood He

.hed on the cross as the penalty for our sins, that all of our sins (past, present, and future) are thereby forgiven and covered under Jesus' blood so that we might gain eternal life? Doesn't it seem, to our human way of thinking, that if we place our trust in Jesus and then later commit some terrible "big" sin, or a bunch of "little" sins, that God might not save us at all? Yet, God addresses that very question in the above verse.

God tells us here that His promise (eternal life through faith in Jesus, referring back to prior eight verses) is valid regardless of whether or how we may break a Law or Commandment (disobedience to God). He tells us that if our eternal life depended upon our being good enough or following the Law, then that would nullify God's promise of salvation by faith in Jesus. God won't do that, as He tells us here. If someone of great character who loves you promises you a gift if you will accept it, and you accept the gift, it does not then depend on how good you are or if you deserve the gift, does it? Yes, we should try and obey the Ten Commandments and the Law out of gratitude to God and Jesus for what they have done for us. But, praise God, our salvation does not depend upon it, because if it did, we would all be in very serious trouble. May we spend each of our days thanking Jesus for His great love and sacrifice!

GALATIANS 3

Wherefore the law was our schoolmaster to bring us unto Christ, that we might be justified by faith (Galatians 3:24).

Once we are justified in God's eyes (meaning when God looks at us, He only sees Jesus' perfect blood), we have then gained eternal life in heaven with God. But many want to work their way to heaven with good works and rituals. If this is your plan, what good work or ritual is worth as much to God as one drop of Jesus' blood? Do you really think that all the good works or rituals in the world will cover your sins to the extent that Jesus' blood will cover your sins? Both Cain and Abel brought God a sacrifice, but Cain's sacrifice was not the one God wanted and God rejected it (Genesis 4:1–7). Let us not make the same mistake.

If we are saved by trusting solely in Jesus and His blood, where does the Law and rituals come in? We should do all these good things only out of gratitude to Jesus for what He has done for us, and never for a moment think that these things can earn us what only Jesus and His shed blood can gain for us. As this verse tells us, the Law (God telling us through the Bible about things we should and should not do) is merely our "schoolmaster" or teacher to show us that we are terrible, habitual sinners and we do not deserve to be in heaven with God. Once our teacher, the Law, has taught us this lesson, let us then look for the real pathway to heaven. May each of us find and follow that pathway—Jesus. It is the only road to heaven! (John 14:6). All the other pathways to heaven, even though they may seem right, lead to death (Proverbs 14:12).

GALATIANS 3

For ye are all the children of God by faith in Christ Jesus. For as many of you as have been baptized into Christ have put on Christ (Galatians 3:26–27).

These verses, like all the others we have studied, teach us that we become "children of God" by "faith in Christ Jesus." Everyone who puts his faith or trust in Jesus is a saved child of God. These verses also teach us that everyone who is baptized is also saved. In order for both verses to be true, one who is saved must have believed before he is baptized. Otherwise, one verse or the other is false. This also coincides with what we see in the Bible because, in the Bible, everyone who is baptized first believed in Jesus, with the baptism being the believer's declaration to the world that he or she is a Christian. None of the disciples

r anyone else in the Bible ever baptized anyone who had not
rst believed. Baptism without belief is like a pen without ink; it
impotent. And don't we see a lot of examples of that today?
Vhy then do a lot of churches today baptize nonbelievers and
retend this saves them? Because it is a great way to build church
nembership and devotion, but it is not the teaching of Jesus or
ne Bible. If we allow people to decide for themselves whether
ney want to be a Christian, some may say no, but that's the way
esus did it.

Every believer should be baptized. If not, we are
ccepting God's great gift of salvation through faith in Jesus and
His suffering on the cross, which paid the penalty for our sins,
ut then telling the world that we are ashamed to identify with
Him through baptism. These verses teach us that everyone who
relieves (verse 26) is saved and everyone who is baptized (verse
7) is saved (provided they are baptized after believing as the
Bible teaches), but what about the category of people who
relieve but are not baptized? If both verses are true, and they are,
hey are a saved but sorry Christian. Let's rather do both, as God
lesires!

GALATIANS 4

*Even so we, when we were children, were in
bondage under the elements of the world. But when
he fullness of the time was come, God sent forth his
on, made of a woman, made under the law. To
redeem them that were under the law, that we might
receive the adoption of sons. And because ye are
sons, God hath sent forth the Spirit of his Son into
your hearts, crying, Abba, Father. Wherefore thou
art no more a servant but a son, and if a son, then an
heir of God through Christ (Galatians 4: 3–7).*

God tells us in these verses that we were slaves to sin and
servants to sin until God sent His Son, Jesus, to redeem us.

How and why? Since God loves us, He wants us to be with Him in heaven forever. But since God is also just, like the just judge, He cannot ignore our sins and crimes; there must be a price paid for these sins. God is so holy that the good things we do could not possibly outweigh the sins we commit, whether we think that is fair or not. There is only one sacrifice that would pay the sufficient penalty for our sins. So, what is that sacrifice?

Do you remember how the Israelites would sacrifice a perfect lamb periodically as a sacrifice for their sins? But this was not sufficient and they had to keep sacrificing such a lamb. When Jesus, the perfect Lamb of God, came to earth as man and as God, He allowed Himself to be sacrificed on the cross, and His blood then paid the full penalty for all of our sins. Jesus redeemed each and every one of us just as these verses say. But as with any gift, it must be accepted or we do not have it. When we place all our faith in Jesus for eternal life (and that means we cannot place part of our faith in Jesus and part in works, ceremonies, etc.) then, praise God, we have gained eternal life, but at Jesus' expense. May we each believe in Jesus and spend the rest of our lives trying to obey God in thankfulness for His great gift!

GALATIANS 4

But now, after that ye have known God, or rather are known of God, how turn ye again to the weak and beggarly elements, whereunto ye desire again to be in bondage? Ye observe days, and months, and times, and years. I am afraid of you, lest I have bestowed upon you labour in vain. Brethren, I beseech you, be as I am; for I am as ye are; ye have not injured me at all. Ye know how through infirmity of the flesh I preached the gospel unto you at the first (Galatians 4:9–13).

God is telling us in these verses that the great apostle Paul preached the "gospel." The gospel is the center of the Bible and it is the message of the Bible that tells us that we are saved by faith alone in Jesus and the blood that Jesus shed as the perfect and all-sufficient sacrifice for the sins of each and every one of us.

Yet, the people to whom Paul preached this salvation-giving and life-changing "gospel" were apparently turning away, in whole or in part, from the sufficiency of the "gospel" and toward observing "days, months, times, and years." This undoubtedly referred to the ceremonies that the religious leaders of the day were conducting, such as the observance of the sabbath, the Passover celebration, and various other temple ceremonies. These ceremonies are good things, when they serve as a reminder of Jesus and what He would do for us. May we never forget that when the devil seeks to turn our attention away from Jesus, he is smart enough to use good things as well as bad things to do so. For instance, here the devil was using ceremonies that believers should observe as a reminder of Jesus, to take the place of Jesus as the only means of salvation. This should never occur. Do you see any similarities to some religious ceremonies of today? The devil often uses the same tricks that he has for the past six thousand years to trick people out of their salvation. And the devil is smart enough to use seemingly good people and seemingly good practices to do so. May we always be alert (I Peter 5:7), and may our trust for salvation be in Jesus alone.

GALATIANS 5

Stand fast therefore in the liberty wherewith Christ hath made us free, and be not entangled again with the yoke of bondage. Behold, I Paul say unto you, that if ye be circumcised, Christ shall profit you nothing. For I testify again to every man that is circumcised, that he is a debtor to do the whole law. Christ is become of no effect unto you, whosoever of

you are justified by the law; ye are fallen from grace. For we through the Spirit wait for the hope of righteousness by faith (Galatians 5:1–5).

Circumcision was the Old Testament's equivalent of infant baptism today. Jews of the Old Testament, who were looking forward to their Savior, Jesus, were commanded to circumcise their babies as a "token of the covenant" between God and man (Genesis 17:11). Today, every believer is commanded by God to be baptized, after he has believed, as a sign that he is a Christian. The Jews of the Old Testament became saved by believing and trusting in their coming Savior, Jesus, just as we become saved by looking backward to that same Savior, Jesus.

However, over time, the Jews began to cut Jesus out of the picture, in whole or in part, preaching that circumcision was a means of salvation instead of a reminder of salvation. In this manner, the Jews began to trust in their religious leaders, the Pharisees, instead of Jesus, for their salvation. Needless to say, this was okay with most of the religious leaders of the day. In fact, it was so okay with them that these religious leaders hated Jesus when He came and, yes, crucified Him. Now, let me ask you: What happens today, and more importantly, what is your reaction, when you are told that it is Jesus alone, not religious rituals, nor the religious leaders who perform them, that provide your salvation? And if the religious leaders of Jesus' day could come back from the dead, what do you think they would now say?

GALATIANS 5

For in Jesus Christ neither circumcision availeth any thing, nor uncircumcision; but faith which worketh by love (Galatians 5:6).

God is clearly telling us that salvation does not come by any religious ritual but rather by "faith" in Jesus Christ.

There seems to be a tendency on the part of man either to push Jesus aside or try to crawl upon the throne with Him. The religious leaders of Jesus' day pretended that circumcision saved people. You may recall that Jesus roundly condemned the religious leaders of that day for not recognizing and teaching that Jesus alone was the only way to heaven. Why didn't God, in the Bible, explicitly tell us that infant baptism (or any other baptism, which is a sign and not a cause of belief and salvation) doesn't save anyone, just like He explicitly tells us here that circumcision does not save anyone? The simple answer is that infant baptism didn't even exist until about one hundred years after the Bible was written. It would seem difficult to contend that a practice that neither Jesus nor any of the disciples practiced or mentioned is in fact the way to gain eternal life, especially considering how often Jesus tells us that eternal life is gained through faith in Him alone. God also certainly knew that if it were not circumcision or infant baptism, man would have concocted some other religious ritual whereby man and his institutions would do the saving, instead of or in purported partnership with Jesus.

The religious leaders of Jesus' day ended up hating Jesus because Jesus told the people the truth about how to gain eternal life. This truth conflicted with the grip that these leaders had over their people. If religious leaders of Jesus' day could come back from their place of eternal destiny, I wonder if they would tell us that it was worth it to keep their followers in their rituals and traditions in place of their Savior. Some churches do a lot of good by teaching the Bible message, that trust in Jesus alone brings you eternal life, and some don't. May each of us be certain that when we leave this earth, our trust is in Jesus alone.

JAMES R. ANDERSON

As we have therefore opportunity, let us do good unto all men, especially unto them who are of the household of faith (Galatians 6:10).

In this verse, God is using the term "household of faith" to describe the true church. The true church is made up of all who are believers in Jesus Christ. The true church, I believe, cuts across all denominations and is comprised of individuals who have learned and accepted the great gospel truth of the Bible—that salvation comes by faith in Jesus alone (John 3:16). Many churches do a lot of good by preaching this simple message and others do a lot of harm by either not preaching this message or preaching some alteration of it. Each of us should try to find the best church that we can, which would be the church that comes closest to the Bible on important matters. Regardless of where we attend church, let each of us be certain that we are trusting in Jesus alone for eternal life. Let each of us be certain that we have taken such faith as we have, however great or small it may be, and have placed all of it upon Jesus and His shed blood, and nothing or no one else, for the salvation of our souls.

Then, out of gratitude, to our great Savior, Who suffered on the cross to shed His blood to pay the price for our sins (a price we could not pay ourselves in a million years of good works), let us go out, as best we can, and "do good unto all men." The Christian, of course, should do good works, but let us never get the idea that our feeble good works can pay even the smallest part of the purchase price of our salvation. That required a far greater price—the precious blood of our loving Savior.

For neither they themselves who are circumcised keep the law; but desire to have you circumcised, that they may glory in your flesh. But

od forbid that I should glory, save in the cross of
ur Lord Jesus Christ, by whom the world is
rucified unto me, and I unto the world. For in Christ
esus neither circumcision availeth anything, nor
ncircumcision, but a new creature (Galatians 6:13–
5).

hen Jesus walked this earth, the religious ritual that the religious leaders claimed would save their followers was rcumcision, a religious procedure that these leaders performed pon infant babies. But the great apostle Paul tells us that "in hrist Jesus" neither circumcision nor uncircumcision (in other ords, religious rituals) means anything. When we are "in Christ sus" we are saved, and the only way to get there, as we have arned in verse after verse, is to place our trust in Jesus and the lood that He shed on the cross as the full, complete, and all-ufficient penalty for each of our sins. This is why Paul is telling s that he will not glory in religious rituals but will glory in Jesus nd the cross. So should we.

Paul also tells us that the reason the religious leaders were ushing the line that circumcision would save people was so that ney themselves might be glorified. It stands to reason, doesn't it, nat if a religious leader can get you thinking that he has saved ou, that you will then start glorifying that religious leader instead f or along with the real Savior, Jesus?

There is an important message here that is just as relevant oday as the day it was written. There is only one Savior. May ach of us be aware of Who it is and place our trust in Him lone.

EPHESIANS 1

To the praise of the glory of his grace, wherein
e hath made us accepted in the beloved. In whom
e have redemption through his blood, the

forgiveness of sins, according to the riches of his grace (Ephesians 1:6–7).

As these verses tell us, we are "accepted," or saved, through God's grace. Remember the mnemonic for GRACE?— God's Riches At Christ's Expense. Can salvation be stated any better than this?

The verses go on to teach us that we are redeemed (or saved) through Jesus' blood, which is the price that **JESUS** paid for the forgiveness of **OUR** sins.

Why is it that our sins are forgiven by the shedding of Jesus' blood (and our subsequent trust in Jesus and that blood as our salvation) rather than through effort on our part? The answer is simple: none of us has the means for the price required to wipe out our sins and thus gain salvation (eternal life in heaven with God). Let's stop and think for a moment. What if you needed an expensive car to adequately perform your job, let's say a car that cost $30,000. But let's say that all the money you could raise was $1,000. What could you do? Unless you could find someone to give you the other $29,000, or credit for $29,000, you couldn't have the car. It is a little like that with salvation. Our sin is so offensive to God (if you don't believe that, just spend some time in the Old Testament) that all the good works we might be able to do will not wipe out (or pay for) our sin in God's eyes. Our good works, despite what we may think, are just not that valuable. But the Bible tells us that just a drop of Jesus' blood, shed on the cross at Calvary, is of sufficient value to God that it will wipe out and cover every sin of every person who has ever or will ever live. That makes some sense when we look at it this way. All of our good works are nothing that God can't create for Himself in an instant, if He so desires, just as He created this world and everything in it in an instant. But the blood of the One, Jesus, Who is also God, is very, very valuable. In God's eyes, it is so valuable that it will cover our sins when nothing else will. Thus, wouldn't it be a good idea to lay aside all of our useless striving and place our trust in that blood, and in the Savior from Whom it me, for our salvation? Especially since God says so? Why try anything else?

That we should be to the praise of his glory, who first trusted in Christ. In whom ye also trusted, after that ye heard the word of truth, the gospel of your salvation, in whom also after that ye believed, ye were sealed with that holy Spirit of promise. Which is the earnest of our inheritance until the redemption of the purchased possession, unto the praise of his glory (Ephesians 1:12–14).

When we have "trusted in Christ" (or "believed"), God's Holy Spirit then comes to live within us. God tells us in the Bible that until we believe and trust in Jesus, many things in the Bible will not make a lot of sense to us. However, once we place our trust in Jesus to save us, the Holy Spirit comes to live within us, as these verses tell us, and the Holy Spirit then helps us to understand the Bible (John 16:13; I Corinthians 2:9–14). Furthermore, the Holy Spirit living within the Christian, after he believes, is the "earnest" or binding proof from God of our "inheritance," which means eternal life with God in heaven.

Therefore, may each of us place our trust in Jesus and gain eternal life in heaven, and let us trust the Holy Spirit Who will help us better understand the Bible. Praise God for His great gifts!

And what is the exceeding greatness of his power to us-ward who believe, according to the working of his mighty power, Which he wrought in Christ, when he raised him from the dead, and set him at his own right hand in the heavenly places,

Far above all principality, and power, and might, and dominion, and every name that is named, not only in this world, but also in that which is to come; And hath put all things under his feet, and gave him to be the head over all things to the church, Which is his body, the fulness of him that filleth all in all (Ephesians 1:19–23).

Who is the head of the church? According to these verses, Jesus. Who comprises God's church? According to these verses, every believer. I guess this could cut across all denominations, couldn't it? But as broad as this can be, it is limited to those "who believe." Yes, once again, we are taught that we gain eternal life by believing in Jesus. The church, which means all those who will live with Jesus eternally in heaven, is comprised of those "who believe."

What must we believe? As these verses teach us, we must believe that Jesus died on the cross, to pay the penalty for the sins of each of us, and after three days in the grave, He rose from the dead and now He is in heaven with God. Why should we believe this? Because God, through the Bible, tells us so. Don't you think it is more likely that there is a God Who created this earth and all the intricate things on it than that this earth and everything on it created itself? Doesn't it seem unlikely to you that eleven of the twelve apostles would die a martyr's death spreading the gospel if they knew that Jesus did not walk out of the grave? If there really is a God and a Jesus Who died for us and rose from the dead, and They, Who should know, tell us that gaining eternal life is as simple as believing and trusting in Jesus, shouldn't we do so? I believe that I shall trust Jesus instead of self or man and his devices and works to gain eternal life. How about you?

EPHESIANS 2

But God, who is rich in mercy, for his great love wherewith he loved us, even when we were dead in sins, hath quickened us together with Christ, (by grace ye are saved). And hath raised us up together, and made us sit together in heavenly places in Christ Jesus (Ephesians 2:4–6).

This verse tells us that each of us, no matter how good we think we are or how many good deeds we have done, is "dead in sins." But God quickens us, or makes us alive, "with Christ" by His grace. Like the just judge who must punish a criminal that he may personally like, God must punish our sins. Yet, as the verses tell us, He loves each of us. So, what can He do?

God sent his own Son, Jesus, to die on the cross to pay the penalty for the sins of each and every one of us. If we will put aside our pride and simply accept and trust in Jesus and His sacrifice, we have thereby gained eternal life. Why? Because God says so. A penalty must be paid and Jesus paid it for us.

Sometimes we will hear someone say that they like us or that they love us. How do we know for sure? I think the best test is whether the one professing love will actually sacrifice for the one he says he loves. Since God is God, He could have dealt with our sins by destroying this earth and every one of us on it. Yet, He chose to send His Son, Jesus, to die for us. While we certainly may not understand each and everything that God does, or why, wouldn't you say that this is incontestable evidence that God loves us? Shouldn't we accept His great gift of eternal life and place our trust solely in Jesus for eternal life?

EPHESIANS 2

For by grace are ye saved through faith; and that not of yourselves, it is the gift of God; not of works, lest any man should boast (Ephesians 2:8–9).

It does not get any clearer than this, does it? I've heard it said that the difference between heaven and hell is two letters—it is the difference between *do* and *done*. We do not have to do anything to gain eternal life; Jesus did it all (done) by suffering on the cross at Calvary to pay for our sins. We gain eternal life by trusting in what is done—Jesus and His sacrifice on the cross. The great irony is if we try to earn this gift, we are saying that Jesus' sacrifice is not sufficient, and we thereby lose eternal life by trying to substitute our feeble works for Jesus' all-sufficient sacrifice.

Should the Christian do good works and the things that God tells us to do in the Bible? Of course. But like the beggar who has received a great gift from the king, let us never start thinking or pretending that our good works have **EARNED** any part of God's great gift of eternal life. Let our good works, small as they may be in comparison to what Jesus has done for us, be simply a small thank you to Jesus for what He has done for us.

EPHESIANS 2

That at that time ye were without Christ, being aliens from the commonwealth of Israel, and strangers from the covenants of promise, having no hope, and without God in the world. But now in Christ Jesus ye who sometimes were far off are made nigh by the blood of Christ. For he is our peace, who hath made both one, and hath broken down the middle wall of partition between us; having abolished in his flesh the enmity, even the law of commandments contained in ordinances; for to make in himself of twain one new man, so making peace; and that he might reconcile both unto God in one body by the cross, having slain the enmity thereby (Ephesians 2:12–16).

This is a message to us Gentiles (those of us who are not Jews) by the great apostle Paul.

Before Jesus came to earth, it appeared that only the Jews could be saved. And their religious leaders taught them that they were saved by doing certain ceremonies, rituals, or ordinances (like circumcision) that only these Jewish religious leaders performed. These ordinances thus created hatred between Gentiles and Jews. Like the "know it all" who knows better than the instruction book, twisting or adding to the Bible brought trouble two thousand years ago, just as it does today in our lives. But it still happens.

Then along comes Jesus and His disciples. Jesus clearly taught that people weren't saved by keeping commandments and ceremonies; they were saved by believing in Jesus and trusting Him alone. The religious leaders hated Him for this. He was destroying their grip on the people.

There is still hatred between different religious groups and other groups of people but, as these verses teach us, if we will simply trust in Jesus, this breaks down the barriers and we have peace with fellow man. Our pride, our denominations, and our rituals become much less important. Even more importantly, the blood that Jesus shed on the cross satisfied God as the penalty for breaking His commandments, which all of us do. Yes, by trusting in Jesus and His shed blood as the perfect covering for our sins, we not only gain peace with fellow Christians, but also peace with God, thereby gaining eternal life in heaven. Isn't Jesus' way better than man's way?

EPHESIANS 2

For through Him we both have access by one Spirit unto the Father. Now therefore ye are no more strangers and foreigners, but fellow citizens with the saints, and of the household of God. And are built upon the foundation of the apostles and prophets, Jesus Christ himself being the chief corner stone. In whom all the building fitly framed together groweth unto an holy temple in the Lord (Ephesians 2:18–21).

These verses, again, tell us that through Jesus we become members of the "household of God," meaning that we go to heaven when we die. It is Jesus, and not any of His self-proclaimed partners, Who is the sole Savior and the "chief corner stone" of His church. The true church is comprised of all Christians, across all denominations, who believe and trust solely in Jesus as their "corner stone" for eternal life. It is through Jesus that we have "access" to God. Who or what is your cornerstone? Is it self, works, religion, a person, possessions, your reputation, your job, politics . . . or is it Jesus? If your cornerstone is anyone or anything other than Jesus, or even along with Jesus, even if it is someone or something good, you probably know that things aren't fitting together quite right. Think of what the building will become if the cornerstone is a little off. If your cornerstone is throwing your building off, transfer your trust to Jesus alone, and everything will fit together as it should. God guarantees it!

EPHESIANS 3

How that by revelation he made known unto me the mystery; (as I wrote afore in few words, whereby, when ye read, ye may understand my knowledge in the mystery of Christ). Which in other ages was not made known unto the sons of men, as it is now revealed unto his holy apostles and prophets by the Spirit. That the Gentiles should be fellow heirs, and of the same body and partakers of his promise in Christ by the gospel (Ephesians 3:3–6).

You may have heard people say how the Bible is one big mystery, not understandable, etc. It is true that there are many things about God and the Bible that remain a mystery, but it is also true that there are many things about God and the Bible that are no mystery at all, and are a mystery only to those who do not like what the Bible tells us. In fact, the greatest mystery in the

Old Testament—how people other than Jews might be saved—is clearly revealed with the coming of Jesus, just as the great apostle Paul tells us in these verses.

Before Jesus came to earth, it may have appeared to Gentiles (non-Jews) that they could not be saved and that God was thus unfair. Yet, we now know that Jews and Gentiles alike are saved in the same way—"in Christ" just as God's gospel promises to each and every one of us. Each of us comes to be "in Christ" by trusting Jesus and His blood sacrifice on the cross as the full, complete, and sufficient payment for each of our sins. Let's remember; when it comes to salvation, Jesus does not need or claim any partners (Acts 20:28; Romans 3:24–26, 5:9; Ephesians 1:7; Colossians 1:14; Hebrews 9:12–14, 13:12; I Peter 1:18–19; I John 1:7). Either we trust only in Jesus or we say that Jesus alone is not sufficient. Jesus plus something else doesn't work. Let us each be "in Christ" entirely and heir to eternal life in heaven!

EPHESIANS 3

In whom we have boldness and access with confidence by the faith of him (Ephesians 3:12).

This verse tells us that we have access to Jesus. This means that we have access to Him while we are alive on this earth and then eternally in heaven. How? Once again, the key word is "faith." When we place all of our faith, however small it may be, in Jesus, then we have access to Him. This verse also tells us that we may come "boldly" to Jesus. Hebrews 4:15–16 also tells us that by trusting in Jesus, we may "boldly" come to Him. Why? The Bible tells us that when we trust in Jesus and His death on the cross, our sins are covered with Jesus' blood and God does not see them anymore (Romans 3:24–26). The New Testament is filled with references to those who preached boldly and came directly to Jesus boldly. However, until we have transferred our trust to Jesus from self, people, rituals, religion, or any other thing, our sin is not covered and we hesitate to approach Jesus. Many religious leaders, like the Pharisees in Jesus' day, pretended to be a mediator between God and man, but the Bible tells us that there is only one mediator between God and man and that is Jesus (I Timothy 2:5).

Thus, let us come directly to Jesus, let us place our trust in Him alone, seek forgiveness from Him alone, and let Jesus be our mediator with God so that we may boldly have access to our great Savior, now and forever!

EPHESIANS 4

Till we all come in the unity of the faith, and of the knowledge of the Son of God, unto a perfect man, unto the measure of the stature of the fulness of Christ. That we henceforth be no more children, tossed to and fro, and carried about with every wind of doctrine, by the sleight of men, and cunning craftiness, whereby they lie in wait to deceive; but speaking the truth in love, may grow up into him in all things, which is the head, even Christ. . . . And that ye put on the new man, which after God is created in righteousness and true holiness. . . . And be ye kind one to another, tenderhearted, forgiving one another, even as God for Christ's sake hath forgiven you (Ephesians 4:13–15, 24, 32).

There are many important truths in the fourth chapter of Ephesians and I have selected five verses that I believe deal most closely with the subject of salvation. The "unity" that is spoken of here by God is the unity among Christians, or those people who are saved. We see that it comes by "faith," meaning faith in Jesus and in Jesus' sacrificial death on the cross as being the complete sacrifice for all our sins. When we place our trust in Jesus alone, we become the mentioned "new man" and thus

aved (II Corinthians 5:17; Galatians 6:15). God tells us that
when we have this "faith," we also become "perfect" in God's
eyes, and thus can live with Him in heaven forever. How and
why? Because of Jesus and His great sacrifice for us. Yes, indeed,
a price had to be paid for our sins and none of our good works
and religious expressions could ever repay it, so Jesus paid the
price on the cross. He can offer us the forgiveness that we must
have to gain eternal life, if only we will accept His offered gift by
faith. At Christmastime, we will probably be offered gifts. But any
gift will be ours **ONLY** if we accept it, will it not? Jesus offers us
the greatest gift of all, and I pray that each of us may accept it,
unconditionally, with a heart full of gratitude and a desire to
henceforth please God.

Do you also see the warning? The Bible tells us there are
many cunning and crafty men who will seek to deceive us with
their doctrines. Who will these men be? I assume that some of
them will be religious men, because we see the word *doctrine*. I
also assume that the devil is smart enough not to use the town
grouch, the town idiot, or the man wearing horns when he seeks
to deceive you or me with false doctrine. How then are we to gain
the right kind of saving "faith"? As God tells us, by studying the
Bible (Romans 10:17). With your eternal soul in the balance, it is
best to accept nothing that any man, myself of course included,
tells you regarding salvation, unless you can verify it in the Bible.
If you were buying a house, would you take someone's word for
it or would you check it out yourself? Your soul is more
important than your house. By investigating, you will come to be
the sort of searching Christian that God commends and rewards
(Acts 17:11; Jeremiah 29:13).

EPHESIANS 5

*And walk in love, as Christ also hath loved us,
and hath given himself for us an offering and a
sacrifice to God for a sweet-smelling savour
(Ephesians 5:2).*

We have found and studied many verses that clearly tell us that we gain eternal life by believing and trusting in Jesus alone. We each know that we are sinners (Romans 3:23). Let us say, hypothetically, that we were so holy that we committed only one little sin during our entire life. Even then, God is so holy and that sin is so offensive to Him that it would be the same as if we had broken every one of the commandments (James 2:10). We may think that we are pretty good by comparing ourselves to someone seemingly worse, but God doesn't look at us that way. And none of us can do anything for God that He can't do for Himself, whether it be good works, religious rituals, or whatever. Our sin is like a cancer growing within us that we cannot cut out ourselves. Then along comes a kindly doctor (Jesus) Who cuts out our cancer and asks for nothing in return, except that we accept His gift of the operation. Since God holds the keys to heaven, isn't it better to accept God's remedy for our sins rather than the phony quack cures that man offers?

You may say, "How can salvation be a free gift?" The Bible tells us that we should avoid sin and do good things. Doesn't this imply that we have to earn our salvation in some way? I suggest reading the rest of chapter 5 and the following chapter, Ephesians 6. The above verse tells us that **BECAUSE** Jesus sacrificed Himself on the cross to pay the penalty for our sins, and **BECAUSE** He showed His love for us this way, and **BECAUSE** He offers us eternal life as a free gift as a **RESULT** of that sacrifice, there are many things we should do out of love as a thank you to Him for His gift. These two chapters tell us many of the things we should do out of gratitude to Jesus. But we must never think that the good things we may do will earn our salvation because only Jesus could pay that price. Our faith and trust must be entirely in Jesus and not in self.

> ***Yea doubtless, and I count all things but loss for the excellency of the knowledge of Christ Jesus my Lord; for whom I have suffered the loss of all things, and do count them but dung, that I may win Christ, and be found in him, not having mine own righteousness, which is of the law, but that which is through the faith of Christ, the righteousness which is of God by faith. That I may know him, and the power of his resurrection, and the fellowship of his sufferings, being made conformable unto his death. If by any means I might attain unto the resurrection of the dead (Philippians 3:8–11).***

In the first part of chapter three (Philippians 3:1–7), the great apostle Paul points out that if anyone could boast about religious experiences, religious good works, and the religious rituals that they have performed then he, Paul, is the man who could boast. Yet, Paul himself says that all these religious things mean absolutely nothing (the word he uses is "dung") compared to faith in Jesus Christ. Paul himself tells us that the "righteousness" that comes from the Law (meaning religious rituals and good works) means nothing and that it is "faith" in Jesus Christ that means everything where our salvation is concerned. It is faith in Christ that gives us the "righteousness which is of God" without which we will never see heaven. If all the religious works and rituals that the great apostle Paul performed did not save him, will yours save you? Is it wise to put all or part of your trust in these things when all of it, according to Paul, must be in Christ?

The Bible tells us repeatedly that it is faith in Jesus alone (and His sacrifice on the cross for all our sins) that saves us. Let's not pretend that Jesus alone is not sufficient. Let us say, hypothetically, that there is a ten thousand-pound barbell somewhere and that God told you that if you or any other person on earth could lift that barbell with his own natural strength and hold it in the air for one minute, then you would gain eternal life. The problem though is that neither you nor anyone you know can perform that task. Yet, Jesus could do it because He has all the strength of the God Who created the universe. Getting back to reality, do you see that your sin is like that barbell? Neither you nor any of your earthly friends or spiritual advisors could lift that barbell of sin off your back. Jesus can and offers to do so. The question is, will we stop putting our faith and trust in all those things that we know are bound to fail, and place our trust in the One Who will never fail us?

COLOSSIANS 1

Giving thanks unto the Father, which hath made us meet to be partakers of the inheritance of the saints in light. Who hath delivered us from the power of darkness, and hath translated us into the kingdom of his dear Son. In whom we have redemption through his blood, even the forgiveness of sins (Colossians 1:12–14).

This verse tells us that we have "redemption" through the blood of God's Son, Jesus, and then the consequent forgiveness of sins. When our sins (past, present, and future) are forgiven, we can live in heaven with God forever when we die (our "inheritance" mentioned here is heaven). According to the dictionary, the word *redemption* means to "buy back." God created man and we were God's sinless children. But then Adam sinned, and this separated each of us that followed Adam from God. But God's own Son, Jesus, paid the price for our sins when He suffered and died and shed His blood on the cross (Jesus' perfect blood being the only payment that would satisfy the price for sin). God Himself bought us back; He redeemed us.

This would be a little like you owing your banker a huge amount of money on your house, an amount so huge that you

ould never hope to repay it. But your banker has pity on you and
e himself pays off your mortgage so that now you can live in
our house forever. Your banker would have "bought back" his
wn mortgage and freed you from its payments. I guess you
ould refuse to accept your banker's payment (out of pride, poor
dvice, or whatever) and continue to struggle under the payments
hat you could never meet. God redeemed us with Jesus' blood,
ut we have to have enough faith and trust in Jesus to accept that
lood as the full payment for our sins, nothing else. Will you
ccept Jesus' blood as full payment for your sins, so that you can
ive with God in heaven forever? Or will you, like Cain (Genesis
:1–16), insist upon paying your sin debt in your own way—a way
hat will never be good enough? Why not set aside pride,
radition, poor advice, worldly friendships, or any other thing that
eeps you from your Savior and, in humble faith and trust, accept
His great gift?

COLOSSIANS 1

*And, having made peace through the blood of
his cross, by him to reconcile all things unto himself,
by him, I say, whether they be things in earth, or
things in heaven. And you, that were sometime
alienated and enemies in your mind by wicked
works, yet now hath he reconciled. In the body of his
flesh through death, to present you holy and
unblameable and unreproveable in his sight. If ye
continue in the faith grounded and settled, and be
not moved away from the hope of the gospel, which
ye have heard, and which was preached to every
creature which is under heaven; whereof I Paul am
made a minister (Colossians 1:20–23).*

These verses, once again, tell us that if we place our "faith" in
Jesus, and keep it there, we have "peace" with God. When
we gain peace with God, we have gained eternal life in heaven

with Him. What do we have to do to earn this "peace" with God? Nothing—Jesus has already earned it "through the blood of His cross" by suffering, dying, and shedding His blood as the full and sufficient penalty for our sins.

Yet, that blood, as valuable as it may be, because it can take away all the sin of every person of in the world, will do us absolutely no good unless we place our "faith" in Jesus and in that blood. This is like having the finest automobile in your garage that you know for certain will take you to Minneapolis. You don't need to do anything to gain that automobile because it is already yours and it is already sitting there, ready to take you to Minneapolis. If you irrationally do not have any faith that the vehicle will take you to Minneapolis, you will not get in the vehicle, and it will not take you to Minneapolis. Your faith must place you in that fine automobile before it can take you to your destination. In the more important matter of eternal life, your eternal life has already been purchased by Jesus with His blood, but you have to have enough faith to place your trust in Jesus alone for eternal life. In the matter of your car, you couldn't very well get to Minneapolis by half riding in your car with the other half of you in some other car because you didn't fully trust your own car, could you? Neither can you get to heaven by half trusting in Jesus and half in something else. Why not throw all your striving, which has accomplished nothing, overboard and place all your trust in the blood that will heal you and give you "peace"?

COLOSSIANS 1

Whom we preach, warning every man, and teaching every man in all wisdom; that we may present every man perfect in Christ Jesus (Colossians 1:28).

Have you ever wondered how good you must be to get to heaven? The Bible gives the answer to that question. After

us gave much of His Sermon on the Mount, in which He told
how easy it is to sin and how difficult it is to do the good that
od requires of us, He then told us how good we must be to get
heaven. He told us that we have to be "**PERFECT**" (Matthew
48). "But," you say, "no one can be perfect." That's right; so
w can anyone get to heaven? As you do your daily tasks,
rhaps you've noticed that if you cannot obtain your goal in one
y, then perhaps some other way will work. Since Jesus Himself
d us that if we want to get to heaven by being good enough,
 will have to be perfect, and since no one can be perfect, I
ess that's not the road to heaven. Let's see if there is another
y.

And yes, praise God, there is! This verse tells us that we
n be "perfect," but it comes about "in Christ Jesus." If we try
 keep the commandments and do other good works, we can
ver attain the perfection we need to get to heaven, because we
ll sin (Romans 3:23). But when we are "in Christ Jesus," we are
erfect" and thus ready for heaven. As this verse indicates and
 Romans 4 plainly tells us, by putting our trust solely in Jesus
d in His shed blood, our sins are covered. When God then
oks at us, He no longer sees our imperfect selves but rather the
ghteousness of Jesus and we are perfect in God's eyes, all
cause our great Savior paid the price for us. Why would anyone
t want to place his trust in a Savior such as this? May each of us
 so and then spend a lifetime trying to do good, **NOT** to earn
lvation, **BUT** out of gratitude for that great gift!

COLOSSIANS 2

As ye have therefore received Christ Jesus the
ord, so walk ye in him. Rooted and built up in him,
nd stablished in the faith, as ye have been taught,
bounding therein with thanksgiving. Beware lest
ny man spoil you through philosophy and vain
eceit, after the tradition of men, after the rudiments
f the world, and not after Christ. For in him

dwelleth all the fulness of the Godhead bodily. And ye are complete in him, which is the head of all principality and power (Colossians 2:6–10).

We see in these verses, as we have in many other verses, that "faith" in "Christ" must be the foundation for each of us. In fact, these verses tell us that when we have Christ, or in other words, when our "faith" for eternal life is in Christ, then we are "complete." There is really nothing to add to something that is complete is there? Jesus died on the cross so that His shed blood would pay the full penalty for the sin of each of us, and when our faith is in Jesus and in that shed blood to cover our sins, we have gained eternal life and become "complete." Yes, praise God, it is that simple according to the Bible!

However, simply because we gain eternal life the moment we place our faith in Jesus, does not mean that the Christian does not have a lot of growing to do. In fact, these verses also tell us that as we are "taught" we become "rooted and built up" in Jesus. As any farmer knows, a young plant has life but it takes a lot of care, protection, and nourishment to yield fruit. For the Christian, all of those inputs come from the Bible. God specifically tells us that the faith, which we place in Jesus gives us eternal life, will grow as we study and read the Bible (Romans 10:17).

However, there is also a warning here. The warning is that people could be led away from the simple Bible truth of salvation (faith in Jesus alone). We are told that it is the "tradition of men" that could lead us away from this great Bible truth. What would be a "tradition of men"? It would be any practice or means of salvation that one does not find explicitly in the Bible that is invented by man (even and most likely religious men) and taught and practiced for so long that it becomes a "tradition." In Paul's day, such traditions included salvation by circumcision and salvation by works (instead of or along with faith in Jesus). Today such traditions include salvation by infant baptism (which replaced salvation by circumcision as a means of religious figures purporting to save people) and the old reliable, salvation by works. You can perhaps think of other "traditions" that are not found in the Bible but with which religious leaders seek to elevate themselves and diminish Jesus as the sole means of salvation. The great apostle Paul tells us "beware"!

COLOSSIANS 2

In whom also ye are circumcised with the circumcision made without hands, in putting off the body of the sins of the flesh by the circumcision of Christ. Buried with him in baptism, wherein also ye are risen with him through the faith of the operation of God, who hath raised him from the dead. And you, being dead in your sins and the uncircumcision of your flesh, hath he quickened together with him, having forgiven you all trespasses (Colossians 2:11–13).

These verses tell us that we are "risen" with Jesus through "faith," meaning we gain eternal life with Jesus through faith. This means, as the Bible tells us (John 3:16; Acts 16:31, etc.), trusting in Jesus alone as our sole means of salvation. It means trusting in the blood He shed on the cross as the full payment for each of our many sins.

In Paul's day, the religious leaders pretended that they (instead of or along with Jesus) could save people by performing the ritual of circumcision. Today, religious leaders pretend that they can save people by performing the religious ritual of infant baptism. The religious ritual of infant baptism is not mentioned anywhere in the Bible. This should tell us that it doesn't save anyone; if it did, God would have told us. The reason that it is not mentioned in the Bible is that it did not exist till one or two hundred years after the Bible was complete. The religious ritual of circumcision fell away because it is so roundly and directly condemned in the Bible (Galatians 5:1–6), but it did not take religious leaders long to invent a substitute. It is too tempting for a church or its leaders to pretend that they are a part of the salvation process instead of simply the messenger.

It is not the physical circumcision that saves but rather the "circumcision of Christ" (symbolic and spiritual circumcision). In other words, it is not the ritual itself that saves, but rather what the ritual symbolizes. So too with the ritual of baptism. In fact, it is no coincidence that the ritual of baptism is mentioned in these same verses with the ritual of circumcision. Since most of the people that Paul was speaking to had been circumcised and were still "dead in your sins," it is obvious that that ritual had not saved them. Any ritual, whether circumcision, baptism, or whatever is a symbol of Jesus and placing our faith in Jesus. Trusting in the symbolic ritual instead of or along with Jesus would be like trusting in your wedding ring to raise the children, bring home the paycheck, or do any of a thousand things that a loving spouse in a marriage will do. The wedding ring (or the ritual) may remind us of the real thing, but it is not a very good substitute. Let's get real and place our trust solely in Jesus.

COLOSSIANS 2

Blotting out the handwriting of ordinances that was against us, which was contrary to us, and took it out of the way, nailing it to the cross; and having spoiled principalities and powers he made a shew of them openly, triumphing over them in it. Let no man therefore judge you in meat, or in drink, or in respect of an holy day, or of the new moon, or of the sabbath days, which are a shadow of things to come; but the body is of Christ (Colossians 2:14–17).

These verses, and those preceding it, tell us about as clearly as God can that the "ordinances"—all our rituals or sacraments —were NAILED TO THE CROSS by none other than Jesus Himself. The "body" (the body of believers who will be with esus in heaven) is "of Christ." We become a member of God's eternal "body" simply by believing and trusting in Christ and the blood that He shed on the cross as the penalty for all of our sins, rebellion, and imperfections. Jesus paid in full the price of our salvation and all we need do to gain that salvation is trust in Jesus. But like the man who has a gift waiting for him at the store, if he doesn't believe it, he will never go to the store to receive it. Eternal life is one "gift" (Romans 6:23) I don't want to miss!

In the Old Testament, ordinances included ritual events like performing the Passover and today they include ritual events like baptism and communion. Some even call these events sacraments. Like the Passover, baptism and communion are symbols that remind us of Jesus, but they are merely symbols and "a shadow of things to come" as these verses tell us. When Jesus came and died on the cross, these ordinances were nailed to the cross with Him. All believers should be baptized and take communion because God tells us in the Bible that He wants us to do these things. Since we should be grateful to our Savior for what He has done for us, why would we not want to do these things? But to trust in something that is merely a symbol and has been "blotted out" and "nailed to the cross" instead of trusting solely in the real thing, Jesus, would be like trusting in a picture of food instead of real food to provide us nourishment. The devil would like us to trust in anything (even good things) instead of or along with Jesus for salvation. Let's do it God's way instead! Whatever man may say, it is always best to do what God says!

COLOSSIANS 2

Wherefore if ye be dead with Christ from the rudiments of the world, why, as though living in the world, are ye subject to ordinances, (touch not; taste not; handle not; which all are to perish with the using;) after the commandments and doctrines of men? (Colossians 2:20–22).

In this entire chapter of Colossians, God has been teaching and showing us that it is "faith in Christ" (Colossians 2:5) that saves us and not rituals or ordinances (like circumcision or baptism or communion, etc.). The ordinances are merely reminders, imperfect symbols, or "shadows" (Colossians 2:17) of Jesus and how He saved us by dying on the cross to pay the penalty for our sins. A "shadow" is not going to save us. Even in Paul's day (and I'm sure long before that), there were those who taught that these symbols, which are always performed by the religious leaders of the day, will save you. We should practice these symbols but only as symbols and nothing more. God tells us that when we have trusted Christ alone for salvation, we are "dead" to the world, its devices, and its "commandments of men." In other words, it is Jesus, and Him alone, Who saves us, and nothing or no one else. Yes, we should try and follow the Ten Commandments out of gratitude for what Jesus has done for us. Yes, we should participate in the ordinances like baptism and communion as a reminder and a symbol, or "shadow," of Jesus and what He did for us. But the moment we start trusting in these things, then we have chosen not to place our entire trust in Jesus, and that is a fatal mistake.

Imagine a large, flat, solidly anchored rock in the middle of quicksand. If we stand with both feet on that rock, we will be saved. If we get into the quicksand, we will be lost. Would you want to stand with both of your feet on that rock (Jesus) or with one foot on the rock and one foot on the quicksand?

I THESSALONIANS 1

For this cause also thank we God without ceasing, because, when ye received the word of God which ye heard of us, ye received it not as the word of men, but as it is in truth, the word of God, which effectually worketh also in you that believe (I Thessalonians 2:13).

We have learned in many other verses that by simply trusting in Jesus alone, we gain eternal life in heaven. This means we believe that Jesus was man and also God, as the Bible tells us. We also believe that when He died on the cross, His suffering and blood paid the entire penalty for all our sins. When we simply trust in Jesus, His blood covers all our sins so that we might be seen by God as perfect and live in heaven with Him forever (Colossians 1:14; I John 1:7).

There are many reasons that a person should know that the Bible is true. The Bible is the only book that explains how this earth and everything on it came into being, unless of course one believes that this earth and everything on it created itself. Unlike every other religion in the world, including secularism, the Bible is the only book that contains any degree of **ACCURATE** prophecy (there are several hundred prophecies in the Bible) almost all of which have come true with only a handful yet to be fulfilled. Since today's so-called fortune-tellers can't even predict what will happen next year with any accuracy, let alone hundreds of years out, if this were a matter of logic, we would all agree that the Bible must come from God. The reason that many will not accept these simple facts as proof in the truth of the Bible is not merely because there is something wrong with their logic, but because this is a spiritual battle and the devil blinds the minds of unbelievers. Only after one becomes a believer, does the Bible begin to make any sense (I Corinthians 2:14).

Once a person stops trusting in all the other ways to get to heaven and begins believing and trusting in Jesus, then the Bible (Word of God) begins to work in us and make sense, and more and more of that small amount of faith that caused us to believe in Jesus becomes greater and greater (Romans 10:17). The first step is to toss away all those other things that one might believe in to gain eternal life in heaven and begin trusting in the real thing—Jesus!

> *But I would not have you to be ignorant, brethren, concerning them which are asleep, that ye sorrow not, even as others which have not hope. For if we believe that Jesus died and rose again, even so them also which sleep in Jesus will God bring with him. For this we say unto you by the word of the Lord, that we which are alive and remain unto the coming of the Lord shall not prevent them which are asleep. For the Lord himself shall descend from heaven with a shout, with the voice of the archangel, and with the trump of God; and the dead in Christ shall rise first. Then we which are alive and remain shall be caught up together with them in the clouds, to meet the Lord in the air, and so shall we ever be with the lord (I Thessalonians 4:13–17).*

These verses tell us quite plainly that if and when we believe that "Jesus died and rose again," we are saved and we will be with Him in heaven when we die or when Jesus returns, whichever comes sooner. We seem to find that word *believe* when the Bible references heaven, don't we?

The verses before these, like much of the Bible, tell us things that we should and should not do as Christians. This would be the Ten Commandments and other commands that God gives us in the Bible. But doing good things and obeying the commandments will never save us. Only believing in Jesus, as these verses and many others tell us, will save us. Why then does God tell us in many places in the Bible various things that we should or should not do? Because, after we believe, for the first time, we have the power to resist the devil and sin (Romans 6:14). We should then do so not because we believe that our feeble good works can save us, but rather out of gratitude to Jesus for having suffered and died so that we might be saved. Perhaps your spouse or a loved one hints at things that they might want as a birthday or Christmas present. If that person loves you, these are not prerequisites to love, but rather a means of showing you how to make them happy. Considering what our great Savior has done for us, why would we not try to follow God's commandments and please Him for all He has done for us?

I THESSALONIANS 5

But let us, who are of the day, be sober, putting on the breastplate of faith and love; and for an helmet, the hope of salvation. For God hath not appointed us to wrath, but to obtain salvation by our Lord Jesus Christ, who died for us, that, whether we wake or sleep, we should live together with him (I Thessalonians 5:8–10).

We see here that Jesus "died for us" so that "we should live together with Him." We further see that we obtain our salvation "by our Lord Jesus Christ." We know that Jesus did not have to die for us because He was God. He did not have to come to earth at all, and He did not have to die on the cross once He came to earth. So why did He die for us? It is because we are sinners and none of us, with all our good works or rituals, or anything else, can pay the price that God requires to wipe out our sins so that we can live with a holy God in heaven. What price is required to pay for our sins? According to the Bible, only the blood of a perfect individual, that being Jesus, would pay that price. I can't tell you why, but that's the way it is.

Sometimes we hear people say that it is unfair that God would send anyone to hell to suffer for eternity. Yet, sin, while we may wink at it today, is very offensive to a holy God. And what more could He do than send His own Son to suffer and die in our place and pay the penalty that justice requires for our sins? In "everyone is a victim" America today, it is fashionable and even benevolent to overlook wrongdoing and sin. But God is perfectly just and cannot do so. God could not bring us to heaven to live with Him forever without the price being paid for our sins and Jesus paid that price. Praise God!

How do we gain that great gift for which Jesus paid? By virtue of that one key word in the above verses, "faith." Nothing more and nothing less. When we believe and trust in Jesus alone and the blood that He shed on the cross to cover our sins as a final and complete sacrifice for all our sins, at that moment, we have gained eternal life in heaven. Praise God for His great gift!

I THESSALONIANS 2

But we are bound to give thanks always to God for you, brethren beloved of the Lord, because God hath from the beginning chosen you to salvation through sanctification of the Spirit and belief of the truth (II Thessalonians 2:13).

In the second chapter of II Thessalonians, God is warning us, once again, that there is a devil, and he is very real. He opposes everything that God does and his primary goal is to trick people away from the truth of the Bible. I should not have to waste space identifying his many tricks and myriad of helpers today. God tells us that as we approach the end of time, the devil will become more active and people will fall for this strong delusion the devil creates. Wouldn't you say that this just about describes where we are at today? When we look around today and see that sodomy is exalted, baby killing is revered as a matter of choice, pornographers of Hollywood are worshipped, and America keeps lurching farther away from the God Who has given us everything, would you not say that many people are suffering from a strong delusion? Things that would not have been tolerated a hundred years ago, because they are so clearly contrary to what God tells us, are now prerequisites to social acceptance. But just as people, societies, and cultures change—staggering from morality to immorality and then back again—

God does not (Malachi 3:6). We may be very pleased with our enlightened attitudes of today, but God still calls it sin. What is one to do in the midst of a society that is wholesale turning its back upon its God? This verse tells us in all simplicity that in the midst of a society rushing after the devil's delusions, we must always give thanks to God for our salvation and the salvation of others. As we have learned again and again, this salvation comes from "belief of the truth." Jesus is the way, the truth, and the life. And through Him, we come to God and salvation (John 14:6). Yes, although the world as we know it may be crumbling around us, we gain eternal life in heaven simply by believing and trusting in our Savior, Jesus Christ. May the devil and his helpers not delude us otherwise!

I TIMOTHY 1

This is a faithful saying and worthy of all acceptation, that Christ Jesus came into the world to save sinners; of whom I am chief. Howbeit for this cause I obtained mercy, that in me first Jesus Christ might show forth all longsuffering, for a pattern to them which should hereafter believe on him to life everlasting (I Timothy 1:15–16).

The great apostle Paul regarded himself as the "chief" of all sinners. Before Paul was saved, trusting in Jesus, upon the event of his miraculous encounter with Jesus on the Damascus road, he had done many terrible things. He participated in the killing of Christians. Paul was also a religious leader who led many people astray by teaching that people got to heaven by obeying the commandments and rituals that the religious leaders formed and taught. Yet, as this verse tells us, He saves all who "believe" in Jesus. This means, believing that Jesus was real, that He came to earth, and that He died on the cross so that His shed blood would pay the full penalty for our sins. All we need do, and all we can do, is to simply believe because Jesus has done all the rest.

The devil has a bag full of tricks and one of his greatest is to cause us to believe that salvation cannot be as simple as simply "believing" in Jesus. The devil appeals to our instincts, which tell us that there is no such thing as a free lunch. But in the matter of salvation, we must take our instruction from the Bible and not from our instincts (Proverbs 14:12). Charles Spurgeon said to the effect, "If we try to put one stitch in the perfect garment of our salvation, which Jesus made for us, we are lost." Why? Because by pretending that our works or our man-made rituals accomplish, or help accomplish, something that Jesus was not sufficient to accomplish, to that extent, our trust is in self or something other than Jesus. Yes, like the great apostle Paul, simply "believe" in Jesus, His finished work, and leave it at that!

I TIMOTHY 2

Who will have all men to be saved, and to come unto the knowledge of the truth. For there is one God, and one mediator between God and men, the man Christ Jesus. Who gave himself a ransom for all, to be testified in due time (I Timothy 2:4–6).

Jesus gave Himself as a "ransom for all." This means that He paid the price for our sins, He paid all of it, and this is the "truth" that saves, when we simply accept and believe it.

These verses also tell us that there is "one mediator" between God and man and that is Jesus. But that does not prevent a lot of men and religious institutions from trying to wiggle between the sinner and the Savior, does it? I shall again recount the story of an old Scottish woman who lay dying. Her neighbors were concerned with her spiritual well-being but they did not know her denominational preference. They sent for the local priest and when he arrived, he announced that he was there to give her absolution. She did not understand the meaning of

ie word and asked the priest to explain. He said that he was
iere to forgive her sins. She asked to see his hands. Puzzled, he
omplied with the request. The godly old lady announced, "You
r are an imposter. The One who forgives my sins has nail prints
1 His hands." There are many today who pretend to do all the
iings that only Jesus can do, from baptizing your babies into
eaven to forgiving your sins. But on that last day, when I pass
rom this life to the next, I am going to be depending
iNTIRELY upon a real Savior. How about you?

I TIMOTHY 4

*For therefore we both labour and suffer
reproach, because we trust in the living God, who is
he Saviour of all men, specially of those that believe
I Timothy 4:10).*

In this verse God tells us, as He does in all the other verses
we've studied, that eternal life is for those who "believe." It is
or those who "trust in the living God"—the God Who can be
he Savior "of all men" and is the Savior of "those that believe."
Iow can one believe? How can one gain faith if one does not
iave faith now? The answer to that question, as well as many
ither important questions, is in the Bible. The Bible tells us we
;ain faith by reading, studying, and searching the Bible (Romans
0:17).

In this chapter, for example, we're told many things that
ve should avoid. As we avoid the spiritual things that are wrong,
;e can then concentrate upon the spiritual things that are right.
n other words, we cut out the clutter and we begin to part the
og.

Once again, my reader friend, I would like to encourage
ou to read ahead from the verse we are studying every week. Try
o find the next verse that tells us how to gain eternal life and
hen prayerfully ask God to teach you its meaning. I try very hard
o find all the salvation verses and I try to interpret them

properly, but I don't discount for one minute that I could make mistakes. When anyone, regardless of their position is teaching you from the Bible, you should check those teachings against the Bible. The Bereans double checked the great apostle Paul and were commended, not condemned, for doing so (Acts 17:11). If God commended people in those days for double checking the great apostle Paul against what the Bible taught, do you think that God wants us to blindly accept whatever we are taught about the Bible today? In Jesus' day, as we saw in Jesus' last days on earth, the percentage of people and religious authorities who came to the truth was very small. Those who did, did so through learning and accepting the unfiltered words of Jesus. I would say it is very important to search the Bible to learn the pure, unfiltered words of Jesus and these God-inspired Bible writers—wouldn't you?

I TIMOTHY 6

Fight the good fight of faith, lay hold on eternal life, whereunto thou art also called, and hast professed a good profession before many witnesses (I Timothy 6:12).

Here again, we see that we gain hold of eternal life by "faith." Please notice the word *fight* in this verse. Much of the Bible is about love. It is God's love for us that caused Him to send a part of Himself, Jesus, to earth to suffer and die on the cross so that the blood that Jesus shed would pay the penalty for our sins—the penalty that we could never pay with our feeble good works and efforts. God did not have to do this but He did it for one reason—love. We are taught in the Bible that we should love God and love our neighbors, not to earn eternal life, which we could never do, but out of gratitude for the great gift that our Savior has given us.

However, this verse tells us, unfortunately, that life is not one big lovefest. Sometimes we must fight. Why? Because there is a devil roaming around blinding the eyes of people to the great

ospel message of salvation by faith in Jesus alone. And the devil
as a lot of helpers on this earth. It would seem that when you
ccept the great Bible message of salvation by faith in Jesus alone
nd tell others about this great truth that everyone would be
appy about this, right? Wrong! When Jesus came to earth to give
His life so that we might live, He was hated beyond measure and
he religious leaders and authorities of His day sent Him to the
ross. Today, if you take this great truth and share it, you will be
pposed by the same type of political and religious authorities
hat opposed Jesus. As we see, you can spread any false religion
ou want in America today, and no one will get too concerned,
ut mention the word *Jesus* and watch the demons fly out of hell
t you. There are many things we can do on this earth to show
ur gratitude to our Savior for all He has done for us; fighting the
good fight of faith" is simply one more. May we use every
pportunity to share with our friends and neighbors the great
ospel message that brings eternal life to all who hear and accept
, regardless of who may not like it!

II TIMOTHY 1

*Paul, an apostle of Jesus Christ by the will of
God, according to the promise of life which is in
Christ Jesus (II Timothy 1:1).*

We see that we have "life," meaning eternal life "in Christ
Jesus." And please also note that this eternal life in heaven
s not a "maybe" or a "wish for" or "if I'm good enough" but
ather is a "promise" from God. And a promise from God is not
s good as gold; it is *better* than gold!

Let's say that you stand before God when you die, as you
ertainly shall, and God asks you, "Why should I let you into My
eaven?" What would you say? I think a good answer might be,
Because of your promise." Then, if God should say, "What
romise?" perhaps it might be good to quote this verse or any of
he hundreds of other verses in the Bible that tell us that eternal

life in heaven comes through believing and trusting solely in Jesus Christ. A Christian could say, "Because I am trusting and believing in Jesus, nothing more."

There would be other ways that one could answer. One could state, "Because I have done all these great things." I don't think that will work (Matthew 7:22–23). Or maybe one could say, "Because I have trusted in Jesus and then, just to be safe, in case that wasn't enough, I did this other thing." Wrong again! Do you really think, in light of this verse, and the hundreds of others that tell us that Jesus alone is sufficient, that God will want to hear that we were trusting partly in Jesus and partly in something else, no matter how good that other thing might be?

Let us all be "in Christ Jesus" and thus safe from the storms around us, in this life and the next.

II TIMOTHY 1

Who hath saved us, and called us with an holy calling, not according to our works, but according to his own purpose and grace, which was given us in Christ Jesus before the world began. But is now made manifest by the appearing of our Saviour Jesus Christ, who hath abolished death, and hath brought life and immortality to light through the gospel (II Timothy 1:9–10).

The "gospel" is the part of the Bible that tells us about Jesus and how we can be saved by believing and trusting in Him and the blood He shed on the cross that paid the full penalty for our sins. These verses tell us that when Jesus came to earth and died on the cross He "abolished death" and He brought "life and immortality," meaning eternal life in heaven. The "gospel" is the "light" by which we discover the road to eternal life. These verses tell us that we gain eternal life by "grace." In other words, eternal life in heaven is a free gift that was bought and paid for by Jesus and His suffering on the cross. And please note that eternal life in

eaven has not come "according to our works." This means that
o matter how seemingly good or how seemingly bad we may be,
iis does not affect whether we receive God's gift of eternal life.
'his gift of eternal life is so valuable and precious that only the
lood of Jesus could pay the required price and this is the price
iat God required to pay for and wipe out our sins. Any thought
iat any of our good works could pay any part of that price is
othing but sheer vanity. So Jesus gives that gift to whomsoever
Ie pleases, regardless of what we may think. And, as Jesus tells
s clearly in this verse, and in many others, we will get that gift if,
nd only if, we believe and trust solely in Jesus as the one and
nly pathway to eternal life (John 14:6).

II TIMOTHY 2

Therefore I endure all things for the elect's
akes, that they may also obtain the salvation which
s in Christ Jesus with eternal glory (II Timothy
:10).

This verse tells us that salvation "is in Christ Jesus." As the
great apostle Paul tells us in this verse, he had to endure
iany sufferings to bring the message of salvation "in Christ
:sus." But does this mean that our entire salvation is "in Christ
:sus" and that there is nothing more we need to do or can do
ther than to run to our Lord and Savior, Jesus, and gain that
reat gift of eternal life? Yes, this is exactly the meaning of this
erse.

Earlier I mentioned that the difference between gaining
alvation and missing salvation is two letters—the difference
etween *do* and *done*. If we accept the world's way of thinking that
iere are things that we must "do" to gain eternal life, and that
ur efforts are sufficient to "do" these things, then we have
iissed eternal life (Proverbs 14:12). However, we if we
cknowledge that our own feeble efforts, however seemingly
ood they may be, are totally insufficient and that Jesus has

"done" it all when He paid the full price for all of our sins on the cross, then, by simply believing in Jesus and His great sacrifice as the full and sufficient payment for all our sins we have gained the great gift of eternal life in heaven. Too good to be true? It is good and it is true—we know this because the Bible repeatedly tells us so!

II   TIMOTHY   2

Nevertheless the foundation of God standeth sure, having this seal, The Lord knoweth them that are his. And, Let every one that nameth the name of Christ depart from iniquity (II Timothy 2:19).

This verse indicates that all who "nameth the name of Christ" (or believe in Christ) are "his" (or are saved). Very simple and very true. This is why children often grasp this great truth better or easier than adults. Life often makes adults too cynical (Matthew 18:3). But sometimes the question arises, if we are saved simply by believing and trusting in Jesus Christ, doesn't this mean that we could go out and sin at will and still be saved? Theoretically, yes.

This verse, though, tells us why this should not happen. Let's say that someone who loves you very much, maybe a wife, parent, or child for example, knew that you had need of something that was very expensive. Let's say this person, who loves you, at great sacrifice to himself or herself, finally saved up enough to buy you the gift and did so. Would you then turn around and do the very things that would hurt that person or would you try and express kindness and love in return?

Jesus, who is part God, did not have to come to this earth and He certainly did not have to die on a cross to pay for the sins of all of us, including those who tortured and killed Him. But He did, and that demonstrates the greatest love in the universe. A person who does not believe and is not saved is powerless to resist sin and the devil (Acts 26:18). The only reason that this world is not a lot worse is that the devil likes to have some of his helpers pretend that they are very good and even religious people so that they can trick believers or would-be believers (II Corinthians 11:13–15). (This is another great reason to know what the Bible says on things, so we're not inadvertently taking our cues from the devil's tricksters.) However, the Christian can resist sin, (Romans 6:14) and, as this verse tells us, should use every effort to resist "iniquity" (sin) out of gratitude for what our great Savior has done for us.

II TIMOTHY 3

And that from a child thou hast known the holy scriptures, which are able to make thee wise unto salvation through faith which is in Christ Jesus (II Timothy 3:15).

Once again, we are taught, very clearly, that we gain salvation through "faith" and that this "faith" must be in Jesus. We also learn that it is through the "holy scriptures"— the Bible— that we gain this saving faith. In the next verse after the one above, we are told that the entire Bible comes from God.

This entire third chapter of II Timothy, written about two thousand years ago, tells us that as we approach the end of time, men will become more deceitful, more self-centered, and further away from God. It reads like quite an accurate description of today. This chapter describes such men as "ever learning and never able to come to the knowledge of the truth." Men such as this like to expound upon how this part of the Bible is not true or that part is inaccurate, etc. But let's stop and think for a moment. If there is a God, and He was God enough to create everything, don't you think He could use men to create and preserve a book, the Bible, that is entirely true? Or maybe you prefer to believe, as the evolutionists tell us, that this world and everything on it created itself. Don't you think that's a little farfetched?

There is a God, He created this earth and everything on it, and He gave us a Bible that is true in its entirety. This Bible tells us that we gain eternal life by "faith" in Jesus, and nothing else. Thus, we can be absolutely certain that when we die and leave this earth believing in Jesus, we shall awake in heaven for eternity (I John 5:13). We can with certainty know and believe this because God told us so in His Bible.

II TIMOTHY 4

I charge thee therefore before God, and the Lord Jesus Christ, who shall judge the quick and the dead at his appearing and his kingdom; preach the word; be instant in season, out of season; reprove, rebuke, exhort with all longsuffering and doctrine. For the time will come when they will not endure sound doctrine; but after their own lusts shall they heap to themselves teachers, having itching ears; and thy shall turn away their ears from the truth, and shall be turned unto fables. But watch thou in all things, endure afflictions, do the work of an evangelist, make full proof of thy ministry (II Timothy 4:1–5).

These verses do not tell us how we might be saved, but they most certainly do tell us the importance of being saved. They also give us an important warning about one of the tricks the devil will use to keep people from being saved.

The importance of being saved is that when this world ends, everyone will be judged by God, and His Son, Jesus, Who can be our Savior if we will allow it. Everyone who has believed and trusted in Jesus as Savior, at this judgment, will go to heaven and everyone who has not believed and trusted in Jesus as Savior will go to hell for all eternity (Revelation 21: 3–8). This is wonderful news for all who have been trusting and believing in esus as Savior and terrible news for all who have rejected Jesus as Savior, or decided to do it their own way.

All who have trusted Jesus as Savior can show their gratitude to Jesus by telling others about this great gift of eternal life through Jesus. This is exactly what Paul is instructing his friend Timothy to do in these verses.

But Paul warns that the time will come, which may be today, when many who purport to be Christian teachers or preachers will instead turn away from the truth, meaning the truth of the Bible, and will start teaching and preaching "fables." They will do this because, we are told, people will want to hear fairy tales, rather than the truth of the Bible, because of their own sins and lusts. In other words, to be comfortable in their sin is more important to people than learning the truth from the Bible about how to be saved and how to live. And in a case of getting what one deserves, along will come teachers who are a lot more interested in pleasing their audience than in pleasing God. This deadly combination will seal the fate of these teachers and their followers for all eternity, and it will not be good. When it comes to something as important as eternal life, each of us must be certain that we are getting our teaching straight from the Bible, and not merely from whomever might have the microphone at the moment. Only God can tell us with certainty the road to heaven and He reveals that road in the Bible (II Timothy 3:15), and that roadway is through Jesus Christ alone (John 14:6).

TITUS 2

For the grace of God that bringeth salvation hath appeared to all men (Titus 2:11).

We see here that we gain salvation or eternal life in heaven by the "grace" of God. In other words, eternal life is a gift from God (Ephesians 2:8–9; Romans 6:23) that cannot be earned by us by works that we may do, rituals that we may perform, or by any of our other efforts. Yes, a price had to be paid for our sins, and Jesus paid that price with His blood that He shed on the cross at Calvary. Now He offers that gift to all who will believe and trust in Him. It is just that simple.

Some may say that this is too simple and they feel like they must do something to earn eternal life. In fact, the Bible tells us that many will feel this way and it is dead wrong (Proverbs 14:12). In fact, the Bible tells us that the vast majority of people will choose the wrong road. Don't let the multitudes taking the wrong road divert you from the right road (Matthew 7:13–14).

German molecular biologist and professor of genetics, Benno Muller-Hill, tells the true story of a physics class that he attended as a student. The teacher arranged for all students, including Prof. Muller-Hill, to view a planet and its moons through a telescope. Several students, one after the other, came to the telescope and in response to the questions of the teacher responded that, yes, they could see the planet and its moons. But then, part way through the exercise, one student complained that he couldn't see anything. After some back and forth, the teacher responded angrily, calling that student an idiot and telling him to adjust the lenses. The student did so and responded that he still could not see anything. The teacher, by then beside himself, looked through the telescope and a strange expression came over his face. The teacher only then realized that the lens cap was still on the telescope. Every prior person who "saw" the planet and its moons was merely following the herd—over the cliff.

Dear friends and those you regard as authorities may all be telling you one thing about how to get to heaven but remember, it is the narrow and least-traveled road that leads to heaven. Don't you think it is best to travel the road of GRACE rather than the roads that many others might be urging today? Isn't the Bible the only roadmap to heaven that we can really trust?

TITUS 2

Looking for that blessed hope, and the glorious appearing of the great God and our Saviour

Jesus Christ. Who gave himself for us, that he might redeem us from all iniquity, and purify unto himself a peculiar people, zealous of good works (Titus 2:13–14).

We are reminded to always be watching for the second coming of our Savior, Jesus Christ. When Jesus comes again, as we are told in I Thessalonians 4:15–17, all who are living will meet Him in the air, the dead will rise, and all Christians will live with Jesus in heaven forever. At this time, the fruits of Jesus' suffering and death on the cross will be realized. As these verses tell us, Jesus gave Himself (or died on the cross) to "redeem" us from our iniquity (sin). The dictionary definition of *redeem* is to "buy back."

Let's say that you borrowed money from a pawn shop and gave the pawn shop your work tools to hold until you paid the loan back. But you don't have enough money so you can't pay the loan. And until you pay the loan, you can't go back to work. You are caught in a vicious cycle. But along comes a friend and pays the loan and you get your tools back, and now you can go to work. It is somewhat like that with our sins. When we first sinned, the devil took us into his possession and we could not get loose no matter how many good works, rituals, or anything else we did. But when Jesus shed His blood on the cross at Calvary, He paid the price in full for the sin of everyone who has ever lived. The only condition is that we have to believe and trust in Jesus and in His sacrifice to thus escape the devil's clutches and gain eternal life in heaven. The man whose tools were held in the pawn shop would never get his tools if he didn't believe that his friend could pay the bill so he could now go in and collect the tools. So too with us. If we do not believe that Jesus has paid the price, or that it could be this simple, we will never gain the eternal life in heaven that He has paid for. Wouldn't that be tragic?

> ***Not by works of righteousness which we have done, but according to his mercy he saved us, by the washing of regeneration, and renewing of the Holy Ghost; which he shed on us abundantly through Jesus Christ our Saviour (Titus 3:5–6).***

Since "washing" is taken by some (but not all) to mean baptism, these verses raise the question of whether we are saved because we are baptized or whether we are baptized because we are saved. Is baptism the cause or, rather, the symbol of our salvation? A Christian may wear a cross on a pin or necklace, or may have a painting of a cross in his home. But no one is trusting in that necklace or painting for salvation; these are symbols or reminders of the only One, Jesus, Who is the cause of our salvation. So, as always, we must let the Bible speak for itself and look closely at these verses.

The word *regeneration* probably has about the same meaning as *born again*, both of which mean salvation. When one is saved, one is both born again and regenerated. Some churches stress one phrase over the other. I hope we might agree that whether one is "born again" or is "regenerated" (and a Christian is both), that person is saved. But what about the "washing" phrase? Does "washing" mean baptism, so that if one is washed or baptized, that person is then thus regenerated or saved by the washing? Let's look at what the verse declares. The phrase is "washing of regeneration" and not "regeneration of washing." As the phrase is written, *regeneration* and not *washing* is the action word. The phrase tells us that we are washed by the regeneration, not regenerated by the washing as would be the case if the two words were reversed in order.

In these verses, as in hundreds of others, it is Jesus, not man, Who does the saving. It is all Jesus and none of man. Let us place all of our trust in the only One Who will save us!

TITUS 3

That being justified by his grace, we should be made heirs according to the hope of eternal life (Titus 3:7).

Once again, we are taught that we are justified (meaning "just as if I'd never sinned") by God's grace ("God's Riches At Christ's Expense—GRACE). Each of us instinctively knows that we must be "good" to get to heaven. But we all sin and I think each of us knows that no matter how much good we may do, we can never erase our sins. But this short verse tells us that Jesus, by shedding His blood on the cross, provided our justification. This would be like the child who uses his crayons on the wall and then tries to wash it off. It doesn't work. But then along comes Mom. Mom knows the right cleaning product and makes the wall look good as new. There is only one cleaning product that will wash away our sins, and that is Jesus' blood (Romans 3:25; Ephesians 1:7; Colossians 1:14; Revelation 1:5). Why should we try all the alternatives that will not wash away the stain of our sins? The Bible clearly tells us that when we put our trust in the blood of Jesus, this is the cure we need and it is the only one that will work. Let us stop our futile, useless efforts with the wrong products and place our trust in the right One!

HEBREWS 1

God, who at sundry times and in divers manners spake in time past unto the fathers by the prophets. Hath in these last days spoken unto us by his Son, whom he hath appointed heir of all things, by whom also he made the worlds. Who being the brightness of his glory, and the express image of his person, and upholding all things by the word of his power, when he had by himself purged our sins, sat

down on the right hand of the Majesty on high (Hebrews 1:1–3).

When we become without sin, we can live in heaven forever with God. But since all of us sin (Romans 3:23), how can we become without sin? These verses tell us that the Son of God, Jesus, "Himself purged our sins." How could Jesus do this? If we do something wrong, like injure the property of another, we can make it right by paying for that property or replacing that property. But what is acceptable to God to pay the price for our sins? Actually, God gives us the answer to this question. The price is actually quite steep, as we might expect, and it is a price that neither you nor I could ever pay; the price is the blood of God's Son, Jesus. All we need do is accept and believe that that blood paid the full price for our sins (Romans 3:24–26). This would be like receiving as a gift a check for $10,000. If we don't have enough faith in the giver or the check to cash it, we never receive the gift. But when we do, we receive the riches that were offered.

Someone might say, "If that is true, why doesn't God speak audibly like He has in the past and tell me so?" Actually, these verses give the answer to that as well. These verses tell us that in Old Testament times, God *did* speak audibly through the prophets. But today, God speaks to us through Jesus and the entire Bible (II Peter 1:19–20, and the verses above).

Can one ever be certain that he or she has eternal life? Yes (I John 5:13). We can be certain because God Himself repeatedly tells us in the Bible that we have (not *maybe* have or have if we're good enough) eternal life in heaven at the moment of belief (not later), if we simply believe and trust solely in His Son, Jesus (John 3:16).

If the owner of a motel tells you that you are free to choose any room in the motel and stay there free of charge, that settles it, does it not? And when the owner of heaven, God, tells us that Jesus purges our sins and that we can go to heaven simply

y trusting in Jesus and His sacrifice (John 3:16), that settles it,
oes it not?

> ***Wherefore in all things it behoved him to be
> made like unto his brethren, that he might be a
> merciful and faithful high priest in things pertaining
> to God, to make reconciliation for the sins of the
> people (Hebrews 2:17).***

The verses leading up to this verse make clear that it is Jesus
Whose suffering and shed blood on the cross paid the price
or our sins, and that He is our Savior. Hebrews chapters 8
through 10 makes plain that when we put our trust and faith in
esus, we become children of God and gain eternal life in heaven.
When we place our trust in Jesus, we are also placing our trust in
His shed blood as the complete covering for our sins. The verse
we are studying today makes plain that we are reconciled with
God (or made friendly again with God) through Jesus. In fact, we
are told that Jesus is our "high priest" and brings us to God.

You may recall that in the Old Testament the people had
to continually sacrifice a perfect lamb and that the "high priest"
of that day had to bring the sacrifice into the tabernacle to God
to continually reconcile the people to God. That lamb was merely
a symbol of the truly perfect Lamb sacrifice, Jesus, Whose blood
would wipe away all our sins forever. The people in the Old
Testament were looking forward to the coming Messiah, Jesus,
and placing their trust in Him, and we look backward to Jesus
and place our trust in Him (Hebrews 9:11–10:10). From Jesus'
day until this day, there are many who pretend to be the "high
priest" who can stand between man and God, forgive sins, and
guarantee eternal life. However man may wish otherwise, there is
only one mediator between God and man and His name is Jesus
(I Timothy 2:5). This is the Jesus Who today is our "high priest"
(Hebrews 9:11), and it is Jesus Who made the sacrifice that

perfects every Christian sinner (Hebrews 10:10–14). Jesus alone, and nothing else and no one else, is our great pathway to heaven (John 14:6). May each of us take this narrow way to eternal life, whatever others may think, say, or do!

HEBREWS 3

But Christ as a son over his own house; whose house are we, if we hold fast the confidence and the rejoicing of the hope firm unto the end (Hebrews 3:6).

Jesus' "house" is in heaven and we will be members of that house if we continue in our "confidence" and "hope," which is belief and trust in Jesus as our Savior (John 3:16). And note that this verse tells us that we have eternal life at the moment of belief, not "maybe have" eternal life. There are many other verses that tell us the same thing.

These verses above mean that not everyone who verbally professes Jesus actually believes in Jesus as the only road to eternal life, and this becomes clear as they advance in life. We place our belief in Jesus for eternal life by forsaking all the other things in which we had previously been trusting for eternal life in heaven (like self, works, rituals, etc.) and placing that trust solely in Jesus. But once we place all our belief, confidence, and hope for eternal life in Jesus, then we begin to understand the Bible (which never made sense before, I Corinthians 2:14–15), and then there is nothing else we desire to have as the object of our belief, confidence, and hope (I Corinthians 1:18). Once we have heard and believed, we are His forever (John 10:27–29). Praise God!

HEBREWS 3

For we are made partakers of Christ, if we hold the beginning of our confidence steadfast unto the end; while it is said, today if ye will hear his voice, harden not your hearts, as in the provocation.

*or some, when they had heard, did provoke;
owbeit not all that came out of Egypt by Moses. But
ith whom was he grieved forty years? Was it not
ith them that had sinned, whose carcases fell in the
ilderness? And to whom sware he that they should
ot enter into his rest, but to them that believed not?
o we see that they could not enter in because of
nbelief. Let us therefore fear, lest, a promise being
ft us of entering into his rest, any of you should
em to come short of it. For unto us was the gospel
reached, as well as unto them; but the word
reached did not profit them, not being mixed with
ith in them that heard it. For we which have
elieved do enter into rest, as he said, as I have
worn in my wrath, if they shall enter into my rest;
lthough the works were finished from the
oundation of the world (Hebrews 3:14–4:3).*

We are looking at many verses today because they relate to each other. The message here is that we are saved to eternal life in heaven by "faith" and lost by "unbelief." There is a great symmetry in the Bible, with many events in the Old Testament being a picture of the New Testament, with its message of salvation through belief in Jesus and His shed blood as the complete and sufficient payment for our sins. These verses compare our choice to believe in Jesus and live with Him in heaven forever (with unbelief condemning us to hell) with the Israelites who God led out of Egypt to the Promised Land. Despite the many miracles they had witnessed (today we have the Bible to tell us of these events), they refused to believe and they never did reach their Promised Land. Yet, the few who did believe (Joshua and Caleb) would enter into their "promised land" (Numbers 13 and 14).

There are many important lessons here. First, we learn that there are great rewards for believing what God tells us and there are great penalties for disbelieving what God tells us. Second, the crowd is often wrong and the right way is usually the narrow way (Matthew 7:13–15). Third, it is important to study and know the entire Bible, as many events in the Old Testament point the way to Jesus. By seeking God through reading, searching, and studying the Bible, we will come to place our trust in Jesus and gain eternal life in heaven (Jeremiah 29:13; Psalm 9:10; Romans 10:17). If you were given a map leading to a great treasure, wouldn't you read and study the map? You have such a map in your own home—it is the Bible!

HEBREWS 4

And in this place again, if they shall enter into my rest. Seeing therefore it remaineth that some must enter therein, and they to whom it was first preached entered not in because of unbelief (Hebrews 4:5–6).

These verses speak about entering into God's rest or, in other words, heaven. It also tells us that there are those who did not enter in because of "unbelief." This verse does not tell us that people do not go to heaven because they are not good enough, because they do not belong to the right church, because they have not performed the right rituals, or any other of the man-made ways to heaven. This verse does clearly tell us that the one obstacle to heaven is "unbelief." This unbelief, as many other verses have taught us, is the unbelief of refusing to believe that Jesus suffered and died on the cross to pay the penalty for our sins, and that by simply believing and trusting in Him and His sacrifice, we gain eternal life in heaven (John 3:16).

Can unbelief be such a powerful thing that it can keep us out of heaven? Can belief be so powerful that it can gain us admittance to heaven? Let's think of our everyday lives. Unbelief, which is often fear of the unknown or of a different way of doing things, can keep us from buying the house we should have ught because we did not believe we could make the payments. can keep us from taking the job we should have taken because did not believe we could do the job. It can keep us from tting on the airplane that could take us to our destination. belief can keep us from many good things. Conversely, belief attain for us many good things. But it is the object of our lief that is most important. Each of us trusts in something, but it the right thing? If we believe we can make payments on a use that is far beyond our means, this would be a harmful rage. Therefore, belief is important, but the foundation of our lief would be even more important. What could be a better undation than Jesus? Is there anything besides Jesus that you lieve in to gain eternal life in heaven? If so, is the object of ur belief better or more certain than Jesus? Is your authority r doing so better than the Bible?

HEBREWS 4

Let us labour therefore to enter into that rest, st any man fall after the same example of unbelief. or the word of God is quick, and powerful, and arper than any two-edged sword, piercing even to e dividing asunder of soul and spirit, and of the ints and marrow, and is a discerner of the oughts and intents of the heart. Neither is there ny creature that is not manifest in his sight; but all ings are naked and opened unto the eyes of him ith whom we have to do. Seeing then that we have great high priest, that is passed into the heavens, esus the Son of God, let us hold fast our profession. or we have not an high priest which cannot be uched with the feeling of our infirmities; but was all points tempted like as we are, yet without sin. et us therefore come boldly unto the throne of

grace, that we may obtain mercy, and find grace to help in time of need (Hebrews 4:11–16).

The verses begin by telling us that we will "fall" or fail to enter heaven by "unbelief." The "word of God," or the Bible, is sharp, powerful, and piercing; it is the Bible alone that reveals who and what we are. Today, we are told by everyone from politicians to psychologists that we are really fine people and all that is wrong with us is that our self-esteem is not high enough. Conversely, the Bible truthfully tells us that each of is desperately wicked in our sin, which separates us from a holy God (Jeremiah 17:9–10). Then, lest we start thinking that we are a little better than the guy next door, who is really a bad sinner, we are told in James 2:10 that God is so holy that even that seemingly innocent little sin we just committed is just as bad as the big sin our neighbor commits (James 2:10). So, what hope is there for you or me? There is absolutely none if you or I are going to try to be good enough to get to heaven. But, praise God, there is another way.

Jesus is our "high priest" and that we may "boldly" come directly to Him for mercy and grace. Jesus alone paid the price for our sins on the cross and it is Jesus alone Who saves you and me. Down through the ages, from Jesus' day until today, there are many who have tried to get between man and God, pretending that they can save or forgive sins; they are all imposters. It is Jesus alone Who forgives sins and it is Jesus alone Who saves. Until we accept this, we are crippled with the "unbelief" that will keep us from heaven.

HEBREWS 5

And being made perfect, he became the author of eternal salvation unto all them that obey him (Hebrews 5:9).

I once heard a pastor tell the story of a person who asked him how good he would have to be to get to heaven. The pastor responded, "That's an easy question. The answer is in the Bible." Upon being asked where he could find that answer in the Bible, the pastor responded, "Matthew 5:48. Jesus tells you that you have to be **PERFECT.**" I sure hope there is another way because I know I'm far from perfect. And, praise God, there is!

In Old Testament times, the Israelites were saved from death in Egypt by putting the blood of a "perfect" lamb on their doorposts (Exodus 12) and then sacrificing the perfect lamb to blot out their sins (Leviticus 5). The perfect lamb was the symbol of the coming truly perfect Lamb, Jesus. The animal and its death didn't save anyone but those who believed in it as a symbol of the Messiah were saved. People before Jesus were saved by looking ahead to the coming Messiah and trusting Him, just as we are saved by looking back to the Messiah, Jesus, and trusting Him. For some reason, God needed a "perfect" sacrifice to cover our sins, and that sacrifice was Jesus. Even a "perfect" lamb wasn't really perfect. But Jesus was. By trusting in Jesus and His sacrifice, we gain the greatest gift, eternal life in heaven.

Thus, this verse tells us that Jesus was perfect. Do you see how this fits in with Matthew 5:48, which tells us that we have to be perfect to get to heaven? Perfection was needed and the perfect Jesus took our place. If we are trying to do it on our own or if we are trusting in some imperfect human, institution, etc., we will never make it. It is Jesus alone Who is perfect, and when we obey His command to put our belief and trust in Him alone (John 3:16, 14:6) we gain eternal life in heaven!

HEBREWS 6

Therefore, leaving the principles of the doctrine of Christ, let us go on unto perfection; not laying again the foundation of repentance from dead works, and of faith toward God (Hebrews 6:1).

In the preceding verses, God, in Hebrews, has discussed the "doctrine of Christ." This doctrine is that we gain eternal life in heaven by believing and trusting solely in Jesus and His blood sacrifice on the cross as the perfect covering for all our sins. It is this simple belief in Jesus that gives us eternal life, and it is by that simple act of belief and trust that we are born again into eternal life with God in heaven forever when we die. This is the "foundation" and now that God has communicated this foundation in the preceding verses, He tells us that He will now leave these principles and foundation and show us some things we should do as Christians.

Specifically, once we are saved we can now resist sin as we never could before we were saved (Romans 6:11, 14, 14:23; Acts 26:18). Before Jesus comes, we are putty in the devil's hands. But through Jesus, we have the power to move toward perfection. We should, out of gratitude to Jesus, try to do the good He desires and avoid the sin He hates.

This verse centers around the "faith" that saves us and all that we gain only after "repentance from dead works." We are born trusting in our seemingly good works and our own feeble efforts to get us to heaven, because this is our natural way of thinking (Proverbs 14:12). As this verse tells us, we must repent of trusting in our dead works before we can place our entire trust in Jesus for eternal life. Repentance (sorrow for sin) is linked to salvation in various verses in the Bible (Acts 3:19, etc.). But how can we be saved if we must repent of all our sins, because we probably can't even remember all the sins we committed yesterday, let alone in a lifetime? Even if we could remember all our sins, how much sorrow is enough? Yes, we should be sorry for our sins and we should try to avoid sin when we are saved. But the repentance that is linked to salvation is the repentance that we are taught in this verse; it is to repent of trusting in our dead works in order to gain eternal life, and as this verse indicates, this is a one-time event. If we think that we gain eternal life by trusting in our own works or partly in our works and partly in Jesus, we are telling Jesus that to the extent we are trusting in urselves, it is to that same extent we are saying Jesus is not ufficient. Let us repent of trusting in our works and other things nd place our entire trust, however small it may be, entirely in ₀sus and thereby gain eternal life in heaven!

HEBREWS 6

For it is impossible for those who were once nlightened, and have tasted of the heavenly gift, nd were made partakers of the Holy Ghost, and ₀ave tasted the good word of God, and the powers of ₀e world to come, if they shall fall away, to renew ₀em again unto repentance; seeing they crucify to ₀emselves the Son of God afresh, and put him to an ₀pen shame (Hebrews 6:4–6).

At first glance, these verses would appear to tell us that people who have believed and trusted in Jesus as Savior, and are ₀us saved, could lose that salvation if they "fall away." But is it ₀ossible to be saved by faith (versus good works) and then ₀nsaved by insufficient good works or bad works (sin)? Saved by ₀aith—unsaved by works? That would be back door works ₀alvation, would it not? The Bible teaches that we have everlasting ₀fe (not temporary everlasting life) the moment we believe in ₀sus (John 3:16).

There are, of course, verses in the Bible that superficially ₀eem to conflict with other verses, unless one takes all the verses ₀ealing with a given subject and attempts to reconcile, versus ₀ontradict, these verses. We should seek to reconcile the ₀eemingly odd verse to the central truths of the Bible, as opposed ₀ reconciling the central truths to the odd verse (as the cults and ₀ven a few others are noted for doing). This is a central tenet of ₀ible interpretation and, I might say, common sense as well.

Considering these truths and principles, the key portion ₀f these verses is the phrase "if they shall fall away," with the key ₀ord therein being *if*. When we acknowledge that it is not possible for a Christian who has believed and is thus saved to become unsaved, then these verses make sense in conjunction with all the other salvation verses. The simple answer is that no one falls into the category of a person who is saved and then "shall fall away." These verses are like an argument that would proceed by stating, "If the sun shall rise in the west tomorrow, then here are the things that will happen." These verses tell us the result if the impossible precondition occurred.

If a saved person were to become unsaved, it would then be impossible for such a person to become saved again for the reasons stated in these verses. Since saved people sin, and since all sin is the same to God (James 2:10), if we are saved by faith and then unsaved by sin, no one would be saved. God thus tells us why, in these verses, that He will not allow a saved person to become unsaved. God does not allow the devil or anyone else to pluck any saved person out of Jesus' hand, exactly as the Bible teaches us (John 10:28–29, "shall never perish"). The Savior's grip is good enough for me!

HEBREWS 7

For the law made nothing perfect, but the bringing in of a better hope did; by the which we draw nigh unto God (Hebrews 7:19).

You must be perfect (Matthew 5:48) and righteous (Romans 3:20–26) in order to "draw nigh unto God" or, in other words, to be saved and live with God in heaven forever. How can we become perfect and righteous? The Bible tells us that all have sinned (Romans 3:23) and that none are righteous (Romans 3:10). If we were to keep the entire Law, meaning the Ten Commandments, then we could live with God in heaven forever. **BUT** this verse, and many others, tells us that we cannot become "perfect" by keeping the Law, because none of us keep the entire Law. Yet, the Bible talks much about heaven and it tells us that God wants us to be with Him in heaven forever, but how can we get there?

If we can't get there through the Law, or by being good enough, then there must be some other way, right?

I am not very computer savvy, but the other day I was trying to get a certain printer to work with my computer. I knew that in the past, this very printer had worked on this computer, but now I kept getting the message that the two were incompatible. I knew that the printer and the computer were compatible because they had worked together in the past, but what could I do? I was loading the program for this given printer onto the computer, but it would not run the printer. My mind was telling me that this was how it logically must work. But after repeatedly trying this and failing, I then remembered the computer technician, who had originally caused the printer to work, had loaded a program for an entirely different printer (but one which was compatible with the printer I was attempting to use) and had thus caused the printer to work. When I tried this solution, out came the documents properly printed. In other words, there was another way to the end goal, when the way that seemed logical did not work.

So it is with eternal life. The way that seems right to us, trying to get to heaven by being good enough, is actually the wrong way (Proverbs 14:12) because no one can be good enough to work his way before a holy God. The right way is to simply trust in Jesus and trust that His blood sacrifice on the cross at Calvary takes away our sins (I John 1:7). Then, when God looks at us, He sees Jesus' blood sacrifice and not our sins, which it takes away. Jesus' blood completely covers and removes our sins when we accept and put on Jesus' robe of righteousness. God then looks at us and He sees perfection (Jesus' robe of righteousness) and not the sins that we could never wash away on our own. Jesus' blood is what God Himself calls our "garment of salvation" (Isaiah 61:10). People all over the world today are looking for hope; it is Jesus that is the "better hope." In fact, he is the **BEST** hope of all!

> *Wherefore he is able also to save them to the uttermost that come unto God by him, seeing he ever liveth to make intercession for them. For such an high priest became us, who is holy, harmless, undefiled, separate from sinners, and made higher than the heavens; who needeth not daily, as those high priests, to offer up sacrifice, first for his own sins, and then for the people's; for this he did once, when he offered up himself (Hebrews 7:25–27).*

God is love (I John 4:8) but He is also just (Exodus 34:7). God loves each of us but He hates our sin. If God were only love, everyone would be saved and if God were only just, no one would be saved. Let's say, for example, that I committed a crime, was caught red-handed, and went before a judge who loved me. If this were a just judge, he would have to punish me for my crime even though he loved me. This is the same with God, who is infinitely more perfect than any earthly judge.

The punishment that God requires for our sins is blood —not works, rituals, or anything else (Ephesians 2:8–9; Galatians 5:1–6). God is the judge and He, not you or I, determines the punishment for our sins. In the Old Testament, as a symbol of the coming Lamb of God, Jesus, the priests had to continuously slaughter a lamb and offer its blood as a sacrifice to cover the sins of the people (Hebrews 9:7), so that by trusting in that coming Savior, Jesus, their sins were forgiven.

These verses refer to the "high priest," which means Jesus. Jesus was part man, part God, and He was holy, undefiled, and sinless. These verses also tell us that when Jesus died and shed His blood on the cross, we no longer needed to make daily or yearly sacrifices for sin; Jesus was the once-and-for-all sacrifice for the sins of everyone. By simply believing and trusting in Jesus and His great sacrifice, nothing more and nothing less, our sins are covered and we gain eternal life in heaven forever with God.

Your faith may be very small, but if you will take all of it and place it on Jesus, and none of it on anything else, you have gained God's greatest gift of forgiveness of sins and eternal life. Praise God!

How much more shall the blood of Christ, who through the eternal Spirit offered himself without spot to God, purge your conscience from dead works to serve the living God? And for this cause he is the mediator of the new testament, that by means of death, for the redemption of the transgressions that were under the first testament, they which are called might receive the promise of eternal inheritance (Hebrews 9:14–15).

In Old Testament times, the high priest had to yearly sacrifice the blood of a lamb (the symbol of the coming Savior, Jesus) for the sins of the people, from behind the veil in the temple (Hebrews 9:3, 7). When Jesus died on the cross, that veil in the temple was miraculously torn in two by God (Mark 15:37–39). This was a dramatic statement by God that now people may directly approach God through Jesus.

There have always been those who have attempted to stand between the people and God, thus taking the place of Jesus. This is why the religious priests of Jesus' day so violently opposed Jesus; Jesus was about to destroy their good thing. Are there religious leaders today who are okay with your thinking that they are your mediator with God, that they can forgive your sins, or that they can save you with their ceremonies? Yet, these verses, and the entire ninth chapter of Hebrews, as well as many other parts of the Bible, make abundantly clear that there is only one mediator between God and man, Jesus (I Timothy 2:5). These verses also make it clear that it is only the blood of Jesus that will wash away our sins and allow us to stop trusting in our own pitiful and insufficient dead works for eternal life. Jesus shed His blood on the cross to cover our sins and to save us. Do you regard that blood highly enough to place *all* your trust in that blood for eternal life in heaven? If so, Jesus is now your mediator with God, and I think, based upon what the Bible says, that that is good enough—don't you?

HEBREWS 9

And almost all things are by the law purged with blood; and without shedding of blood is no remission. It was therefore necessary that the patterns of things in the heavens should be purified with these; but the heavenly things themselves with better sacrifices than these. For Christ is not entered into the holy places made with hands, which are the figures of the true; but into heaven itself, now to appear in the presence of God for us: Nor yet that he should offer himself often, as the high priest entereth into the holy place every year with blood of others; (Hebrews 9:22–25).

For some reason that I don't think any of us fully understand, blood is necessary to pay the price for our sins.

In Old Testament times (before Jesus came to earth), symbols like circumcision and the priests' yearly sacrificing the blood of the lamb pointed forward to Christ. In our day, symbols like baptism and communion (with wine or grape juice reminding us of Jesus' blood) point backward to Jesus. The Old Testament told of how a Savior, Jesus, would come to earth (Isaiah 53). The entire New Testament tells of how Jesus, Who is also God, came to earth and willingly died on the cross. Jesus willingly shed His blood for our sins so that if we believe in that great blood sacrifice, then (and only then) Jesus' blood will cover our sins and we can live in heaven with God forever (I John 1:7; John 3:16).

There are those today, as in Jesus' day (Galatians 5:1–6), who tell us that trusting in the symbols will save us. Man can and does create and administer these symbols. When one trusts in the symbol, instead of the One (Jesus) Whom these symbolize, then he also begins to trust in the men who create the symbols. The temptation to subtly shift people from trusting in Jesus alone to trusting in symbols or Jesus plus symbols is obvious. But the truth is that while man can create and administer symbols, only Jesus can create life—eternal life (John 6:35, 11:25, 14:6). When it comes to salvation, Jesus does not operate with partners. Any church is at its very best when it points people to the Savior, Jesus; it is at its very worst when it seeks to become the Savior. In what or whom is your trust?

HEBREWS 9

For then must he often have suffered since the foundation of the world: but now once in the end of the world hath he appeared to put away sin by the sacrifice of himself. And as it is appointed unto men once to die, but after this the judgment: So Christ was once offered to bear the sins of many; and unto them that look for him shall he appear the second time without sin unto salvation (Hebrews 9:26–28).

The one thing in this life that is certain is that life is coming to an end for each of us. Ignoring the "judgment" that is coming for each of us is foolish. The devil's greatest distraction is the items and events that keep us busy each day. Don't you think that the devil is keeping each of us busier than ever? It is important to spend time on things like work, family, recreation, school, school events, and many other good things. But spending all one's time on these temporary earthly matters while not seeking the pathway to eternal life, which God has set forth in the Bible, is like spending all one's time dusting the house but ignoring the termites that will eventually collapse the house.

The few years that we spend on this earth, whether in pleasure or sorrow, are nothing compared to eternity. I heard an analogy once that if a bird came to earth from outer space once every million years and took away one grain of sand, by the time that bird had removed all the sand on earth, eternity will have only begun. I would say that whether we spend eternity in eternal paradise or eternal suffering is an important matter.

These verses, like the many others that we have studied, tell us that Jesus took all our sins upon Himself as He suffered on the cross to pay the penalty for those sins. Jesus sacrificed Himself so that our sins might be "put away." It is incredible but a loving powerful God sacrificed Himself for a sinner such as you or me. The moment that we simply accept and believe this, we have gained God's great gift of eternal life (John 3:16). The bonus is that once we have set this most important issue of life right, a lot of the other things begin to fall into place as well (Matthew 6:33). If you haven't done so before, don't you think that right now you should bow your head and tell God that you are now throwing overboard all those other things that you've been trusting in for eternal life and that you are now trusting in Jesus alone? Shouldn't you **THEN** thank Jesus for His great gift to you and **THEN** try to live the way He wants you to live, not to *earn* eternal life but rather out of gratitude for what He has done for you?

HEBREWS 10

By the which will we are sanctified through the offering of the body of Jesus Christ once for all (Hebrews 10:10).

Have you ever owned something that broke, you would have it fixed, then it would break again, you would have it fixed again, and so on and so forth? Have you ever said, "I wish I could find someone who could fix this thing once and for all?" When you did find a repairman who was reliable and would fix

ngs that stayed fixed, do you remember the relief that this gave
u? You didn't want another repairman then, did you?

The nine verses preceding this verse recount how the
Hebrews yearly sacrificed animals to pay for their sins. Those
ses also tell us that those animal sacrifices, which were just a
cture or symbol of the real Savior (Jesus—the perfect Lamb of
od) to come, did not of themselves "take away sins." Those
cient Hebrews were saved when they regarded the animal
crifice as a **SYMBOL** to look ahead and trust in their coming
vior, Jesus, not by trusting in the animal sacrifice itself. But
hat about today?

We are "sanctified," or made holy or free from sin,
rough the "offering of the body of Jesus Christ once for all."
hose few words give us the greatest truth of the ages. Jesus,
ho was God, did not have to sacrifice Himself on the cross; He
uld have destroyed His captors. But He willingly went to the
oss and shed His blood so that the perfect blood of our perfect
vior would pay the penalty for all of our sins. And He did this
nce for all." There is nothing that we need except to look to
sus in simple childlike trust in His sacrifice (transferring our
ust from our own good works or anything else), thus relying
lely upon Jesus for our salvation. And we need only do it once
cause at that moment, we have gained eternal life in heaven
ohn 3:16). When we set aside everything else and trust in Jesus
one we have no need or desire to trust in self or those other
an-made things again.

Jesus is like a kindly father or mother who will sacrifice
any things to give their child some needed gift. The child need
o nothing but accept it. I guess a child would have to think the
ift was real though in order to accept it. Shouldn't we do the
ame based upon what God tells us in His Bible?

HEBREWS 10

*And every priest standeth daily ministering
and offering oftentimes the same sacrifices, which*

can never take away sins. But this man, after he had offered one sacrifice for sins for ever, sat down on the right hand of God. From henceforth expecting till his enemies be made his footstool. For by one offering he hath perfected forever them that are sanctified (Hebrews 10:11–14).

The priests in the Old Testament offered animal blood sacrifices and the priests and ministers today offer benedictions, but these "can never take away sins." The "man" referenced in these verses, whose "sacrifice" takes away sins "forever" is not a priest or minister—it is Jesus. Deep down, everyone knows that his sin separates him from God. Man tries everything from good works to human intermediaries to religious rituals to get closer to God. These things are always man working his way toward heaven. Then, there is the right way—the way the Bible tells us about (Ephesians 2:8–9). It is God reaching down to sinful undeserving man through Jesus. This "offering" that satisfied God's penalty for our sin was the blood that Jesus shed on the cross at Calvary. There is a song that contains this telling verse: "You may have your religion but, brother, not me—give me the blood from Calvary." It is by trusting solely in Jesus and the blood that He shed to cover our sins that, praise God, we gain eternal life in heaven!

There is a fine but critical line between any religious institution pointing people to the Savior or trying to become the Savior. When a church points its people to itself, it is doing great harm; when it points its people to Jesus, it is doing the greatest good in the world. A pastor or a priest can be doing either the greatest good or the greatest harm on earth; no president or king even comes close. May God bless each of the churches and their leaders who are selflessly and sacrificially pointing people to Jesus and Him alone.

> *This is the covenant that I will make with them*
> *after those days, saith the Lord, I will put my laws*
> *into their hearts, and in their minds will I write*
> *them; and their sins and iniquities will I remember*
> *no more. Now where remission of these is, there is no*
> *more offering for sin. Having therefore, brethren,*
> *boldness to enter into the holiest by the blood of*
> *Jesus (Hebrews 10:16–19).*

It seems that man is always looking for an intermediary to bring him to God. This is because each of us knows, deep down, that we are sinful and that we cannot come into the presence of a holy God with our sins. We try to find someone else to come to God for us. Thus, we think that pastors, priests, saints, or people like Mary or others can go to God for us and pave the way. The bad news is that none of the aforementioned is God's intermediaries. The good news is that there is an intermediary and He is part of God Himself; His name is Jesus. The news gets even better. God Himself tells us here, and in other places in the Bible, that He has made a "covenant" with us, He will wipe away all our sins and iniquities, and He will do all this because of the "blood of Jesus." A covenant is defined in the dictionary as a "binding agreement." The Bible tells us that we can know for sure that we are going to heaven when we die (I John 5:13). The reason is that we have a "binding agreement" with God Himself. If we simply trust in Jesus and the blood that He shed on the cross to pay the full penalty for our sins, we have gained eternal life in heaven. Jesus is our intermediary with God. If God should ask you at the door to heaven why He should let you in, you can with all confidence reply, "Because of your covenant and because I simply trusted in Jesus and His blood as my sole requirement."

It would be hard to imagine a better, more loving God. He established the price for our sins and then He sent His own precious Son to pay that price. Do you really think we should be casting about for shortcuts to heaven when God's way is this plain and this simple?

By a new and living way, which he hath consecrated for us, through the veil, that is to say, his flesh; and having an high priest over the house of God; let us draw near with a true heart in full assurance of faith, having our hearts sprinkled from an evil conscience, and our bodies washed with pure water. Let us hold fast the profession of our faith without wavering; (for he is faithful that promised) (Hebrews 10:20–23).

These verses are full of symbolism that shows us how we might become Christians who might then live eternally in heaven with God. There is a "high priest" (Jesus) over this earthly "house of God" (the true church is comprised of believing Christians, regardless of their denomination). How does one become a member of this "house of God"? The key word here, as in many other places in the Bible, is "faith." By believing and trusting in our "high priest," Jesus, we are admitted to the "house of God."

Please note all the other symbolism. When we are believers, we have that "assurance of faith" and our bodies are then washed with "pure water." There is a similar reference in Revelation 22:1 to pure water and this is the "living water," which is the life-giving living water that comes from Jesus to each believer (John 4:10). Such living water is like the life-giving water that God gives us in the form of rain that gives life to all things on this earth, only Jesus is the living water that gives each Christian life for eternity. This is also why every believer should be baptized with water as a symbol of having trusted the Giver of all life.

Let's not forget that in Old Testament times, God would ~~d~~well within the Ark of the Covenant, and there was a veil in the ~~te~~mple (Exodus chapters 26 and 27) that separated God from ~~m~~an. Only the priests could enter through the veil to the presence ~~of~~ the God (Hebrews 9:6–7). But when Jesus died on the cross, ~~th~~is veil was miraculously torn in two at the moment of His ~~de~~ath (Matthew 27:51). This tearing of the veil symbol showed us ~~t~~hat these verses tell us—we sinners could and should now come ~~di~~rectly to God, through all veils, through Jesus and His flesh. We ~~d~~o not have to find the actual flesh of Jesus and walk through it; ~~it~~ is a symbol. Please note what is most important here. The ~~ce~~nter and substance of all these symbols is Jesus; they all point ~~to~~ Jesus. When we believe and trust in our great Savior as the ~~gi~~ver of life, He does all the rest.

HEBREWS 10

Of how much sorer punishment, suppose ye, ~~s~~hall he be thought worthy, who hath trodden under ~~fo~~ot the Son of God, and hath counted the blood of ~~t~~he covenant, wherewith he was sanctified, an ~~u~~nholy thing, and hath done despite unto the Spirit ~~o~~f grace? For we know him that hath said, ~~V~~engeance belongeth unto me, I will recompense, ~~s~~aith the Lord. And again, the Lord shall judge his ~~p~~eople. It is a fearful thing to fall into the hands of ~~t~~he living God (Hebrews 10:29–31).

In today's "anything goes" world, where our last remaining virtue is tolerance of all things, it seems difficult to believe that ~~G~~od would punish a person simply because he or she did not ~~tr~~ust in Jesus and His sacrifice on the cross as the full pardon for ~~al~~l our sins. What we may think has nothing to do with it; it is ~~w~~hat God does that counts because He will be the final judge. ~~R~~ather than wonder about whether something is fair or not to ~~o~~ur limited way of thinking, maybe our time is better spent considering God's requirements to avoid hell and gain eternal life in heaven.

Maybe you are trusting in something other than Jesus for eternal life. Maybe you are trusting in yourself and your good works for eternal life. Or maybe you trust Jesus only partially along with other things, even good things, to gain eternal life. What is wrong with not trusting in Jesus fully for eternal life? It is because Jesus was God and as God He died for us. Yes, a God dying for a hopeless sinner. God tells us here and elsewhere that Jesus' blood was sufficient to "sanctify" (make us holy by covering our sins with His blood) each of us. How serious is it to tell God and Jesus that Jesus' precious blood was not sufficient to cover our sins? In centuries past, earthly kings had absolute power of life and death over their subjects. Rejecting Jesus would be the equivalent of going up to an earthly king and giving him the greatest insult one could imagine. Your life would be in jeopardy before that earthly king and your eternal life is in jeopardy before God if you reject Him by not trusting Him fully. Would you reject Jesus and His blood as your sole and all-sufficient Savior? Let each of us, in simple childlike faith, forsake our man-made ways to heaven and accept God's love and sacrifice so that we do not become subject to His judgment. As we are told: "It is a fearful thing to fall into the hands of the living God."

HEBREWS 10

Now the just shall live by faith; but if any man draw back, my soul shall have no pleasure in him. But we are not of them who draw back unto perdition; but of them that believe to the saving of the soul (Hebrews 10:38–39).

These verses, like many others, tell us quite clearly that when we "believe" we have saved our souls. In other words, we

ill live (eternally in heaven) by the simple act of "faith." But
ith in what or whom? Everyone has faith—the question is the
bject of that faith. The atheist trusts in himself and the religious
erson may trust in his denomination, ceremonies, or his
:ligious authorities, but the Christian trusts in Jesus. Throughout
1e Bible, you will find Jesus rebuking people for their doubt and
isbelief, and you will find Jesus rebuking religious authorities for
:aching people to trust in themselves and their ceremonies
istead of Jesus. Is this because Jesus was a megalomaniac? No, it
as because Jesus was the Son of God and as such, He knew the
1e and only pathway to heaven, and He knew that it led through
Iimself and through people trusting in His shed blood as a
omplete covering of their sins (John 14:6; Colossians 1:14).

If Jesus was simply a megalomaniac, He probably would
ot have voluntarily died for us, He could not have done all the
irthly miracles He did to prove He was the Son of God, and He
ertainly could not have risen from the dead. This is what
eparates Christianity from all the other false religions of the
orld, most of which are constantly demonstrating themselves
ilse through their crazy and wicked activities. There is no other
eligion that makes the claim of power over death through factual
yewitness (versus vague spiritualized) accounts. We have a book,
1e Bible, given to us by God, and its hundreds of fulfilled
rophecies prove it to be the work of God, right down to the
resent-day prophecy of little Israel being the center of world
ttention at the end of time. The book centers around Jesus Who
erformed miracles and rose from the grave. The book tells us
ow everything we see around us came into being and, no, it
idn't create itself out of nothing. We have such a book, the
iible, and we are told therein how to gain eternal life in heaven
rith God. Don't you think we should study it and then accept its
mple teaching—saved by faith alone in Jesus our Savior?

By faith Abel offered unto God a more excellent sacrifice than Cain, by which he obtained witness that he was righteous, God testifying of his gifts; and by it he being dead yet speaketh (Hebrews 11:4).

It was Abel's "faith" that caused him to be "righteous" in God's eyes and thus gain salvation.

This entire chapter of Hebrews is a good one to read because it is dedicated to faith, and faith is the key that unlocks the door to heaven.

You may recall the well-known story of Cain and Abel in the Bible. When Adam and Eve were evicted from the Garden of Eden because of their sin, thereafter, God required a sacrifice for sin. The sacrifice required by God was a blood sacrifice of an animal. Abel decided to do it God's way and brought some of his sheep to God for a sacrifice. Abel's brother, Cain, had enough religion to bring God a sacrifice, but Cain was going to do it his way; he brought God some fruit as his sacrifice instead of the blood sacrifice of an animal. God accepted Abel's sacrifice and rejected Cain's sacrifice. Compounding the problem, Cain became angry (pride and jealousy) and killed Abel (Genesis 4:1–16).

There are many lessons in this true story and everything in the Bible is there for our benefit. You may think it is unfair that God rejected Cain's sacrifice because, you may think, Cain was at least religious enough to bring a sacrifice, even if it wasn't exactly what God wanted. I believe you can see all the problems that resulted from not doing it **EXACTLY** God's way.

Let's fast forward to today. There are many individuals, churches, and religious authorities today that give us slightly different ways to heaven that aren't exactly the way that God demands. A lot of it is tradition, some of it is self-interest, and you may be assured that all of it, if it is not exactly what God demands, is not only unacceptable to God; it is very offensive to

God. The lesson of Cain should be enough to prove that point. But beyond that, God cared enough for each of us to send His dear Son, Jesus, our Savior, to suffer and die on the cross so that His blood would pay the penalty for all our sins. There is simply nothing more that is required, as we are told over and over again in the Bible. We are saved by faith in Jesus alone. If we are taught something in the Bible, we had better do it. If it is not in the Bible, it is not from God. There are a lot of supposed salvation additions today that are not found anywhere in the Bible. Lest we become like Cain, angry at those trying to do it God's way, let us consider whether we are more devoted to our tradition or to seeking, from the Bible, God's way to heaven. As we consider the lesson of Cain, I am hoping that everyone trusts solely in Jesus and His great sacrifice (John 3:16), thereby gaining God's great GIFT of eternal life in heaven forever.

HEBREWS 11

But without faith, it is impossible to please Him; for he that cometh to God must believe that he is, and that he is a rewarder of them that diligently seek him (Hebrews 11:6).

The Bible tells us, in one verse after another, as we have been learning for weeks, that we gain eternal life by faith in Jesus alone. Because God is just, in addition to loving, a penalty had to be paid for our sins. That price was Jesus' blood. Jesus paid the price of every sin of every one of us, with His blood that He shed on the cross (Matthew 26:28).

This verse, like Isaiah 64:6, tells us that until we come to this faith, there is absolutely nothing that we can do that will please God. Does this mean that a person who is not a Christian believer can do seemingly good things, like helping others, etc., and this will not please God? Yes, that is exactly what this verse means. Why? Because the nonbeliever who does seemingly good things has rejected God's own Son, Jesus, and His precious sacrifice, as being insufficient to cover his sins. This is a direct insult to God. No other good thing that person may do will overcome that one unforgivable sin.

How can this be? Let's say that you had a neighbor who had a son who became severely injured saving your life. But you were so prideful that you went around pretending that you had saved yourself and that your neighbor's son had nothing to do with it, despite the great harm that had been caused to him. Do you think a few little favors that you might do for your neighbor would really please him, when he knows what you are doing to his son? Do you think that God is pleased with the few good things that you may do if you walk around rejecting His Son, Jesus, as your all sufficient Savior? Maybe you are too prideful to admit you need a Savior, maybe someone told you a different way to heaven, or maybe your tradition is different. The reason does not matter. God has given us the roadmap to heaven in the Bible. Why not trust Jesus as your Savior and then do the good things, out of gratitude, that will then please God? Eternity waits in the balance!

HEBREWS 11

By faith Noah, being warned of God of things not seen as yet, moved with fear, prepared an ark to the saving of his house; by the which he condemned the world, and became heir of the righteousness which is by faith (Hebrews 11:7).

We know from the many verses we have studied each week that we gain eternal life in heaven by trusting in Jesus alone and the sacrifice that Jesus made to pay for our sins when He suffered, died, and shed His blood on the cross at Calvary. This verse tells us that the faith we utilize to put our trust in Jesus is like the faith that Noah utilized when God told him to build the ark; Noah simply obeyed. No doubt, Noah did not understand everything or even much about building the ark because there had never been violent floods at any time previous.

Noah was mocked and ridiculed for building that ark. We know that in Noah's day, just like today, there was great wickedness and mockery of God occurring all over the earth (Genesis chapters 6 and 7). Yet, Noah wisely ignored the skeptics, the agnostics, the mockers, and everyone else and built the ark. He saved himself and his family, who had enough faith to get into the ark with him. What are the lessons in all this?

First, the obvious lesson is that when God tells us to do something, like trust Jesus for eternal life, we should simply obey. Second, the true story of Noah's faith and obedience resulting in his earthly salvation is used as a picture of today's Christian securing his eternal salvation by trusting in our ark, Jesus, for eternal life in heaven (I Peter 3:20–21). Noah and his ark are thus a symbol of our salvation and baptism is likewise a symbol of our salvation. Noah actually built his ark and saved his earthly life. Jesus, by His suffering and resurrection, has already built our salvation "ark." Like Noah's family, we need only have enough faith to trust Jesus and board that ark (Jesus), thereby transferring our trust from the world and its methods to Jesus alone. Baptism is a symbol to the world that when we trusted Jesus for eternal life, we buried and crucified our trust in anything except Jesus, and as He rose from the dead we rise with Him. Lastly, we are explicitly told in the Bible (Matthew 24:37) that the days before Jesus comes again will be just like the day of Noah—full of wicked people rejecting God. With all we see around us today, do we really want our trust in anything other than Jesus?

JAMES 1

Blessed is the man that endureth temptation; for when he is tried, he shall receive the crown of life, which the Lord hath promised to them that love him (James 1:12).

This verse tells us that if we "love" Jesus, we shall receive the "crown of life," which means eternal life in heaven with

Jesus. This verse further tells us that Christians and non-Christians alike are tempted. Temptations come from the devil (James 1:13). The Christian can actually be joyful about temptations because, when resisted, they can build patience and godliness (James 1:1–4). Sadly, the Christian may not always resist the temptation. What happens then?

The person who loves Jesus is saved and if that saved person also resists temptation, he will be "blessed." If a person does not resist temptation, he will not be "blessed" in that regard. A Christian, unlike the non-Christian (Acts 26:18), always has the power to resist temptation and sin (I Corinthians 10:13).

Since receiving the "crown of life"—our eternal life—depends upon loving Jesus, how does one do this, and how much love is enough? This means, as we are told in John 3:16 and many other places in the Bible, that we must love Jesus enough to believe and trust in Him alone for eternal life. Let us love and trust Jesus, gain eternal life in heaven, resist temptation, and be blessed on this earth.

JAMES 1

Wherefore lay apart all filthiness and super-fluity of naughtiness, and receive with meekness the engrafted word, which is able to save your souls (James 1:21).

This verse does not tell us explicitly how we might be saved but it does tell us where to look. This verse tells us the "word" is able to save our souls and this, of course, means the Word of God, which is the Bible.

God promises that if we seek Him, we will find Him (Jeremiah 29:13; Psalm 9:10). One way of seeking God would be to read ahead from the passage we are studying each week and see if you can find the next verse that tells you how you might gain eternal life in heaven. When you do this, I encourage you to circle that verse in your Bible and then study it and pray over it.

Ask God to show you what that verse is teaching you. Just as God commended the Bereans for studying their Bibles to see if what the great apostle Paul taught them was true, you should study your own Bible to determine whether what you are taught about the Bible, by anyone, is true (Acts 17:11). If God wanted people to check out what Paul was teaching them from the Bible, I think He wants you to check out what anyone teaches you from the Bible. The people who knew the most about the Bible in Jesus' day—the Pharisees and the Sadducees—were often leading people in the wrong direction for their own purposes. If it happened then, it can happen today. Praise God for Bible teachers and preachers who lead people in the right way, and may we be ready for those who don't. It is essential that searching one's own Bible be a part of finding salvation.

There is only One in the entire universe Who has personal knowledge of the way to heaven—God. He has drawn a road map; it is the Bible. The route to heaven leads through God's Son, Jesus (John 3:16). May each of us find and travel the God-given pathway to heaven, not one of our own or one from someone else's imagination!

JAMES 2

What doth it profit, my brethren, though a man say he hath faith, and have not works? Can faith save him? If a brother or sister be naked, and destitute of daily food, and one of you say unto them, depart in peace, be ye warmed and filled; notwithstanding ye give them not those things which are needful to the body; what doth it profit? Even so faith, if it hath not works, is dead, being alone. Yea, a man may say, thou hast faith, and I have works; shew me thy faith without thy works, and I will shew thee my faith by my works. Thou believest that there is one God; thou doest well; the devils also believe,

and tremble. But wilt thou know, O vain man, that faith without works is dead? (James 2:14–20).

This is the one set of verses in the Bible in which those who teach faith by works or faith plus works for salvation, instead of faith solely in Jesus, will commonly cite. However, as we have repeatedly seen over many weeks, there are literally hundreds of verses in the Bible that tell us that we gain salvation by faith in Jesus alone, nothing else. It is an important rule of Bible construction that when a single verse in the Bible seems to conflict with a multitude of other verses, that one assumes the multitude of verses to be correct and one then proceeds to square the odd verse with the multitude, rather than the reverse. Cults are notorious for taking the odd verse in the Bible and then constructing a theology around the odd verse, thus leaving their teaching at odds with primary messages in the Bible. Since we do not want to do this, let us see if these verses can be reconciled with all the other verses we have been studying.

Using the demons as an example, we are told that the demons "believe," or know that Jesus is real, and thus have an intellectual faith in Jesus, but they are not saved. The problem is that this is merely an intellectual belief or faith, and not real trust in Jesus. When the Bible tells us that "faith" alone in Jesus saves us, it means not mere intellectual knowledge or phony lip service, but actually placing our entire trust in Jesus for salvation.

This is like the story of Charles Blondin, the famous tightrope walker who would push wheelbarrows full of cement across Niagara Falls on a tightrope. When Blondin asked the crowd if they thought he could push a human being across Niagara Falls in the same wheelbarrow, everyone raised their hands. But when asked for a volunteer, no one raised his hand. The crowd had an intellectual faith that Blondin could perform the task, but no one would fully trust him with his life.

If we are fully trusting Jesus for eternal life, it is now possible to resist sin and the good works will follow, not to earn our salvation but as a result of our salvation. If not, we have

een paying mere lip service and intellectual assent to Jesus, but
e are not really trusting in Him alone for eternal life in heaven.
he works are the proof but not the cause of our salvation, just
ke a dead canary will be the proof but not the cause of gas in
he coal mine.

James is not telling us that we must do good works to
arn eternal life in heaven. If that were the case, he would be at
dds with the rest of the Bible. He is telling us to check our faith
o ascertain that we are really trusting Jesus, by the good works
hat should follow. James is telling us how to separate a real
eliever from one who just says he believes. Do you say that you
rust Jesus, but you do not try to resist sin, attend church, read
our Bible, or try to do the things that please God? If so, maybe
t is more talk than trust, and you need to remove the things that
ou really trust in that are other than, or in addition to, Jesus.

I PETER 1

Blessed be the God and Father of our Lord
Jesus Christ, which according to his abundant mercy
hath begotten us again unto a lively hope by the
resurrection of Jesus Christ from the dead. To an
inheritance incorruptible, and undefiled, and that
fadeth not away, reserved in heaven for you. Who
are kept by the power of God through faith unto
salvation ready to be revealed in the last time
(I Peter 1:3–5).

These verses, like many others, tell us that it is "through faith"
that we gain salvation, meaning eternal life with God in
heaven. We are told that this is an "inheritance." Is it the
beneficiary or the grantor who controls or gains the inheritance
and for what reason? It is like that with eternal life. We may have
our own ideas as to what should gain us eternal life in heaven,
whether it be good works or whatever. But it is God, the grantor,
Who determines how we gain eternal life. God has told us here,

and in many other places in the Bible that it is faith, and faith alone, that gains us eternal life in heaven. If that does not coincide with our natural human way of thinking, then maybe we had better change our way of thinking before it is too late.

Each of us is placing our faith in something for eternal life. Our faith might be in ourselves, good works, our church, or any other thing. But here we are told that our "lively hope" of eternal life is to be in the "resurrection of Jesus Christ from the dead." This means Jesus' suffering and death on the cross is the **FULL** payment for our sins, and His resurrection is proof that He is God and thus able to pay the price for our sins. When the day comes that we cast away all the other things that we trust in for our salvation that seem right to our own minds (Proverbs 14:12) and place our faith in Jesus, then, according to God, we instantly gain our "inheritance incorruptible" and our "salvation." Praise God for this great gift! Praise God for the Savior Who paid for this gift!

I PETER 1

Whom having not seen, ye love; in whom, though now ye see him not, yet believing, ye rejoice with joy unspeakable and full of glory. Receiving the end of your faith, even the salvation of your souls (I Peter 1:8–9).

This verse, like hundreds of others that we have studied, tells us that we receive the salvation of our souls, meaning eternal life with God in heaven, as a result of "faith." The first part of these verses is referring to Jesus, making plain that our "faith" is to be in Jesus, even though we do not see Him. Some might ask how they can trust in someone or something they cannot see. We can't see electricity, yet we trust it to accomplish its function. We cannot see air and the wind speed that lifts the airplane off the ground, yet we trust it to accomplish its purpose. We have that trust because we have seen the results.

With Jesus, we cannot see Him now, but we see the results everywhere. We can see the results in the nations where Jesus is or has been honored, glorified, and worshiped, and we can see the results in nations where He is not. We can see the results in our nation when Jesus is honored, glorified, and worshiped, and we can see the results when He is not. We can see the results in lives where Jesus reigns as Savior, and we can see the results in lives where He is not. We can look around us and see a world of plants, trees, animals, and people that God has created, or we can choose to believe that it all created itself. We can read the Bible and the hundreds of prophecies that have already been fulfilled to the letter, which would be impossible if there were no God. We can see that today the entire world has its focus upon Israel—a little nation with a relative handful of people—just as the Bible foretold two thousand years ago. No, we can't visibly see Jesus yet. But ignoring Him would be like ignoring the love that we cannot visibly see from a parent, spouse, or family; it would be very self-destructive.

You might say, "Couldn't Jesus make it easier for us by just simply physically appearing?" I doubt it. The last time Jesus physically appeared on this earth, He was crucified. Jesus is real and I think that deep down most of us know this. The problem is not in the head or the seeing; the problem is in the heart. The real question is whether we'll trust our own man-made devices for eternal life in heaven or trust in Jesus. As we near the end of this search in the Bible, what is your decision?

I PETER 1

Because it is written, be ye holy; for I am holy. And if ye call on the Father, who without respect of persons judgeth according to every man's work, pass the time of your sojourning here in fear. Forasmuch as ye know that ye were not redeemed with corruptible things, as silver and gold, from your vain conversation received by tradition from your fathers. But with the precious blood of Christ, as of a lamb without blemish and without spot (I Peter 1:16-19).

At first glance, the first part of these verses seem to conflict with the second part, because the first part seems to imply that we must be holy like God and that God will judge us according to our works. But then God goes on to tell us we are redeemed (meaning saved) by Jesus' blood. The rule is to interpret Bible verses so that they coincide and not conflict with each other when there are various interpretations available. Here is what these verses are telling us.

Each of us has a natural way of thinking that we can work our way to heaven and that we will be saved if we are good enough and do enough good works (Proverbs 14:12). How good would be good enough? God tells us in these verses. He tells us that if we are working our way to heaven, we must become as holy as God is. This would be rather difficult because God is perfect and we are not. In fact, by comparison, the best righteousness of the best man who ever lived, whoever that may be, is as filthy rags compared to God (Isaiah 64:6). Furthermore, God tells us that our works will be judged by God without respect for our status in life or how good we might think we are (Acts 10:34). As if it needs saying, God tells us then that we should live in "fear," and so we should if we think we can be good enough in our own righteousness to pass God's judgment.

God then goes on to say that we are not "redeemed" (or saved) with corruptible things, meaning the things of this earth, even things as precious as silver or gold. In other words, we can spend our lifetime working for silver and gold and then give it all to God, but that would not save us. The greatest good works that we can do will not save us. God further tells us that our "vain conversation" that we receive "by tradition" from our "fathers" (or ancestors) will not save us either. In other words, all the works, rituals, and dos and don'ts that our ancestors or religious authorities may dream up will not save us. What then *will* save us?

's very simple—the "blood" of Jesus. We are told many places the Bible that Jesus came to earth to suffer and die on the oss and shed His blood as the full penalty for our sins. When e place all our trust not in our works (you'd have to be as holy God to work your way to heaven) or our traditions, but rather clusively in Jesus and His shed blood, then, praise God, we are deemed, or saved.

Shouldn't we do the good works that God wants us to do 1d tells us to do in the Bible? Yes, of course. Just as we are rateful to any person who does some great deed for us, we ould also be grateful to Jesus Who suffered and died for us and o as many good works as we can out of gratitude for our lvation. But we should never do this with the foolish idea that e can earn salvation with those good works. The blood of Jesus more precious than silver, gold, or anything that we can earn or o. Let us just place our trust in that blood and then do the good at we should!

I PETER 3

For Christ also hath once suffered for sins, the ust for the unjust, that he might bring us to God, eing put to death in the flesh, but quickened by the pirit (I Peter 3:18).

There are several great truths in this verse. First, this verse tells us that Jesus suffered "once" for our sins. In the Old estament, the priests had to continuously sacrifice lambs for the ins of the people because that sacrifice was not perfect. That vould be like making payments on a mortgage—each payment loes not pay off the mortgage, but rather prevents foreclosure or another month. Today we can trust and believe in Jesus and His sacrifice for our sins. When we do so "once," all of our sins re forgiven. Past, present, and future sins are instantly forgiven, nd we are saved forever (John 3:16). That would be like paying he mortgage in full. Jesus' blood is so powerful that His one sacrifice wiped away all the sins of the entire world for everyone who has just enough faith to believe in Jesus and His sacrifice alone, leaving all of man's other devices behind.

Second, this was the "just" (Jesus) sacrificing for the "unjust" (ourselves). This would be like owing a great debt that we could never repay and then along comes a great, kind, and loving friend who pays that debt for us. The word *love* has become cheapened today but that, my friend, is real love.

Lastly, this verse tells us that Jesus died on the cross so that He might "bring us to God" or, in other words, give us eternal life in heaven when we die. Since Jesus' sacrifice has already paid the full price of our sins, we do not need to worry or wonder whether our sacrifices, works, efforts, or religious rituals are good enough. The price has already been paid and that payment is perfect, all sufficient, and the payor is named Jesus!

I PETER 3

Which sometime were disobedient, when once the longsuffering of God waited in the days of Noah, while the ark was a preparing, wherein few, that is, eight souls were saved by water. The like figure whereunto even baptism doth also now save us (not the putting away of the filth of the flesh, but the answer of good conscience toward God,) by the resurrection of Jesus Christ (I Peter 3:20–21).

Our salvation is compared to the ark, which saved Noah and his family. Our ark is Jesus and His blood sacrifice for our sins on the cross.

These verses tell us that "baptism" saves us. This is one of a handful of verses from which some people conclude that the physical act of water baptism will save a person. However, it is important to remember that in the Bible, there are two kinds of baptism—one is water baptism (a physical baptism) and the other is the baptism of the Holy Spirit (a spiritual baptism), ich occurs when the Holy Spirit enters a person. The Holy irit is there to convict us of our sins prior to salvation and to well permanently after salvation. This always occurs *before* water ptism (Acts 10:47). Water baptism is a symbol, not a cause, of r salvation; salvation always includes the spiritual baptism of e Holy Spirit. These verses tell us that the baptism referenced re is not water baptism but rather the spiritual baptism that mes at salvation. As the verse declares, it is a conscience, not a sh, baptism.

The Holy Spirit works in us prior to and at the time of lvation so that we can understand and accept the great truth of e Bible—that Jesus is the Savior to all who believe and trust in im for forgiveness of sins and eternal life in heaven. The ark is symbol of our salvation just as water baptism is likewise a mbol of our salvation. If we could actually find Noah's ark and op onto it, that act would not save us, although that ark is a mbol of our salvation. Just as Noah actually built his ark and ved his earthly life, Jesus, by His suffering and resurrection, has ready built our ark (Himself) and, like Noah's family, we need nly have enough faith to trust Jesus and board that ark, thereby jecting the world and its methods. Water baptism symbolizes ur conscious decision to leave behind the world and its devices, d rising out of the water symbolizes a new creature trusting nly in Jesus. Our spiritual baptism of the Holy Spirit helps ffectuate that which our water baptism symbolizes.

I PETER 5

But the God of all grace, who hath called us nto his eternal glory by Christ Jesus, after that ye ave suffered a while, make you perfect, stablish, trengthen, settle you (I Peter 5:10).

e are told here that God calls us to "eternal glory," meaning eternal life in heaven with God. And how do we gain this "eternal glory"? We gain this place in paradise "by Christ Jesus."

Our sins separate us from God (Isaiah 59:2). But when Jesus died on the cross, His shed blood paid the full price for our sins; it covers all our sins and gives us the forgiveness of all our sins (Ephesians 1:7). Thus, it is "by Christ Jesus" that we gain eternal life in heaven with God. Jesus asks only one thing in return. Jesus demands that our trust and faith for eternal life must be in Him and that blood (Romans 3:25). If not, Jesus' sacrifice for our sins will do us no good.

You might have a terrible disease and a skilled doctor may be able to cure that disease by operating on you. But if you do not have enough faith and trust in that doctor to allow him to operate, his ability to cure your disease will do you no good. It is like that with Jesus and the blood that He shed to cover our sins. It is only after we decide to take our faith and trust and place it in Jesus and His shed blood that we gain the great blessing of eternal life for which Jesus has already paid the price.

I JOHN 1

But if we walk in the light, as he is in the light, we have fellowship one with another, and the blood of Jesus Christ his Son cleanseth us from all sin. If we say that we have no sin, we deceive ourselves, and the truth is not in us (I John 1:7–8).

These verses teach us that if we think we have no sin, we will never come to the knowledge of the truth. We have all sinned (Romans 3:23). However, some of us deceive ourselves into thinking, "My sin is not as bad as that terrible criminal I read about in the newspaper." Or maybe we think, "Since I do some things that are good, God will condemn the other fellow but not me." The Bible teaches that even a seemingly innocent little sin, like maybe telling a little lie, is just as bad as murder (James 2:10). It is not that murder is acceptable but the truth is that God is so bly that even a seemingly innocent little sin is terribly offensive to Him.

In order to gain eternal life in heaven, we must first admit that we are terrible sinners in the eyes of God, and we can do nothing to help ourselves. In an age where self-esteem is a lot more highly valued than truth, this is hard to understand. But you and I are terrible sinners, and until we diagnose the problem correctly, we will never come to the cure.

Once we realize what sinners we are, the cure is obvious and it is stated, once again, in these verses. The cure is Jesus and the blood that He shed on the cross at Calvary. Jesus' blood is the penalty that God demanded for the sins of you, me, and everyone else in this world. I don't know why this was the price, but it is the price that God demanded and you and I should rejoice that Jesus willingly paid this price. And, yes, there is one further step. We must place our trust in Jesus and His blood to cover our sins. When we do, at that moment, we have gained eternal life in heaven. Let's accept this great gift and then live our lives, in gratitude to Jesus, to do the things in the Bible that Jesus tells us we should do.

I JOHN 2

My little children, these things write I unto you, that ye sin not. And if any man sin, we have an advocate with the Father, Jesus Christ the righteous; and he is the propitiation for our sins and not for ours only, but also for the sins of the whole world (I John 2:1–2).

If you were on trial for your life and the best attorney in the world was available as your advocate with the judge, would that not be whom you would retain? When your eternal life is at stake, with God as the judge, would you not want the advocate whom God recommends? That would be Jesus. Whom you choose as your advocate with God is up to you. You can choose yourself, another person, a dead saint, a religious system, or you can choose Jesus. Since Jesus alone died to pay the price for our sins, wouldn't we want the One Who has paid the price to wipe away our sins (i.e. the "propitiation" for our sins) be the One telling God why our sins cannot be held against us? This would be like retaining as an advocate the man who had already paid for and given to you the goods that you are accused of stealing; that would be an open and shut case, right? We gain Jesus as our advocate much like we gain an earthly attorney or advocate—by simply placing our belief and trust in Him so He can advocate for us. But Jesus is not an ambulance chaser; He won't represent you if you don't ask Him to do so. When our sins are forgiven, we have eternal life in heaven with God. Jesus will certainly be the greatest advocate you could ever have!

I JOHN 2

I write unto you, little children, because your sins are forgiven you for his name's sake (I John 2:12).

This verse is talking about Jesus and telling us that our sins— past, present, and future—are forgiven for Jesus' name's sake. This is great news because when our sins are forgiven, we have eternal life in heaven with God. But how can this be? Let's say that a man walked into a car dealership, bought every car on the lot, and told the dealer to keep the cars there until he came to possess them. That man could take some or all of the cars home today, or anyone he designates could walk into that dealership at any time in the future and drive any of those cars away. The cars have been paid for and can thus be taken freely at any time.

It is somewhat like that with Jesus and His having paid for all of our sins with His suffering on the cross at Calvary. Jesus grants the forgiveness sins that He has already paid for to whomsoever He chooses. And God tells us whom Jesus will choose. God tells us in the Bible that Jesus will give that forgiveness to everyone who believes in Jesus and the sacrifice He made for our sins (Acts 16:31). May we always praise our great Savior and, out of gratitude for His great gift, seek to do the things that He tells us in the Bible we should do.

I JOHN 2

Whosoever denieth the Son, the same hath not the Father; but he that acknowledgeth the Son hath the Father also. Let that therefore abide in you, which ye have heard from the beginning. If that which ye have heard from the beginning shall remain in you, ye also shall continue in the Son, and in the Father. And this is the promise that he hath promised us, even eternal life (I John 2:23–25).

The "Son" referred to here is Jesus, and the Father is of course God, the Father. If we "continue in the Son," we have eternal life in heaven. As we have learned in many previous verses, when we place all our trust for eternal life in Jesus and His blood sacrifice on the cross at Calvary, which paid the full penalty for each of our sins, we are thereby continuing in the Son.

Have you ever noticed how the devil many times plays upon something that is good to try to get you to sin? Maybe you are a kind person, and kindness is a wonderful virtue. The devil may use that kindness to cause you overlook, or maybe even help another person in their sin, because you do not want to offend that person. Or if you are a morally upright person, maybe the devil will tempt you to be harsh with other people who do not meet your standards. The devil can use even our strengths to cause us to sin if we are not careful.

In these verses, we are taught that Jesus is the way to God and God is the way to heaven. Maybe you already know this and still you want to add other conditions, maybe even seemingly good conditions, to God's plan of getting to heaven. What would

God say to this? I think God would and does say "continue in the Son"!

And this is his commandment, that we should believe on the name of his Son Jesus Christ, and love one another, as he gave us commandment. And he that keepeth his commandments dwelleth in him, and he in him. And hereby we know that he abideth in us, by the Spirit which he hath given us (I John 3:23–24).

Each of us is a sinner who has broken God's commandments (Romans 3:23). God sent Jesus to this earth to die on the cross so that His blood would pay the penalty for our sins. A new commandment (coming after the Ten Commandments) that God gives us is to "believe on the name of His son Jesus Christ," which will then allow us to love one another. We could not keep the Law, the Ten Commandments, so God had to send His Son, Jesus, to pay the price for our sins. Why?

God is love (I John 4:8), but God is also just (Exodus 34:7). If God were only love, everyone would be saved and if God were only just, no one would be saved. God loves me, but He hates my sin. God wants you and me to live in heaven with Him forever, but He is also just, so our sin must be punished. How could God solve this seemingly unsolvable problem?

God is like an earthly judge who must sentence a criminal (even if the criminal is a person he might like) because that is justice. To carry the analogy further, the judge would then send his own son to serve the sentence that he had given the criminal so that the criminal might go free. That is exactly what God did for us when He sent Jesus to pay the price for our sins. No earthly judge would do this for us, but God did—God is real love! With God and Jesus as our example, in gratitude for the great sacrificial gift of eternal life that God has given us, we should do our best to love one another to please God. Once we believe in Jesus, we not only gain eternal life in heaven, but God sends His Holy Spirit to live within us (Ephesians 1:13; John 7:39) to help us gain a deeper understanding of what He tells us in His Bible. God gives us His blessings on this earth as well as in heaven to come!

I JOHN 4

Beloved, believe not every spirit, but try the spirits whether they are of God; because many false prophets are gone out into the world. Hereby know ye the Spirit of God; every spirit that confesseth that Jesus Christ is come in the flesh is of God; and every spirit that confesseth not that Jesus Christ is come in the flesh, is not of God; and this is that spirit of antichrist, whereof ye have heard that it should come; and even now already is it in the world (I John 4:1–3).

This is not a salvation verse but it is an important verse because it tells us how we can separate the gems from the phonies. We know the devil masquerades as an "angel of light." And the place he loves most to put his helpers is in a pulpit (II Corinthians 11:13–15). When the devil seeks to deceive you, do you think he is going to use the town grouch to do it? No, he will use the man standing behind your pulpit to do it if he can possibly do so. That is why God commanded the Bereans in Paul's day to check what even with the great apostle Paul taught them against the Bible, and I don't think he expects any less of us today (Acts 17:11). I praise God for the many great men of God who stand behind their pulpits and clearly deliver God's messages. This is the most critical and important job on earth, more important than that of any king or president. May God have mercy upon the souls of those who use their pulpits to deceive their followers through the gates of hell.

In these verses, we are given one test to separate a real preacher from a phony preacher. Does he believe that Jesus came in the flesh and that he was both man and God? There are many purported preachers today who think that the Bible is a pack of fairy tales and that they are smarter than God. They think that they can choose which parts of the Bible they will follow or not. Many spiritual leaders today do not believe that Jesus came in the flesh and died on the cross as sufficient and full payment for our sins and then rose again from the dead, proving He is also God. For your spiritual well-being and the spiritual well-being of your children and grandchildren, you would not want to stay in such an environment.

I JOHN 4

In this was manifested the love of God toward us, because that God sent his only begotten Son into the world, that we might live through him (I John 4:9).

Today we hear a lot of talk of love. And most of it is just that —talk. In fact, the world, apart from Jesus, is the devil's playground (Ephesians 2:2–3). The devil has so perverted the meaning of the word *love* that it has become the exact opposite— one person taking advantage of another. And much of it is in the name of love. As the old saying goes: "Many a deception is hidden behind a smile." As with all things, the Bible defines the issue perfectly.

If you want to know if someone really loves you, what do you do? You observe their actions more closely than their talk, do you not? It is of course good to hear verbal assurances that you are loved, but nothing takes the place of action and especially action involving self-sacrifice. How do we know that our parents or our family members really care for us? We see them day after day and week after week and year after year sacrificing of themselves to help us. That is love.

How do we know that God loves us, as we are told in John 3:16 and elsewhere? We know because, for some reason, there was only one price that God could accept for the full payment for our sins and that was the blood of a perfect person. There is only one person Who ever was or ever will be perfect and that is God's own son, Jesus. Did God say that price is too great? No, God sent Jesus to die on the cross to shed His blood so that His blood would be the payment for all our sins and that we might gain forgiveness of sins and eternal life by simply believing and trusting in Jesus and His shed blood.

I would call that love, wouldn't you? Now, here's the key question. Will you accept that great love and that great gift of eternal life in heaven by believing and trusting in Jesus alone? Or do you take that great love, turn your back upon it, and try to do it your own way?

I JOHN 4

Herein is love, not that we loved God, but that he loved us, and sent his Son to be the propitiation for our sins (I John 4:10).

John Wesley said, "If you show me a worm who can understand a man, then I will show you a man who can understand God." In our humanist world, sometimes we think that God is at the level of man or maybe just a little bit higher. We think that we'll construct our own devices to work and earn our way to heaven. The truth is that God is as far above man as man is above a worm and even much higher. Do you know any man who would die for a worm? Yet, through the Bible, we know that God (Jesus) came to earth to die for man, specifically you and me. There is no reason, other than love, that Jesus had to do this, yet He did it.

Why did Jesus come to earth to die on the cross for you and me? This verse tells us that it was so that Jesus could be the "propitiation" for our sins. We know from other verses in the Bible that we have studied, that as many good works, rituals, or other efforts that we might make, none of this will take away our sins. Only the blood of a perfect person, Jesus, could take away our sins (Ephesians 1:7). According to the dictionary, *propitiate* means to "regain the good will" or "appease." Jesus paid the price of our sins to "appease" God for us.

When Jesus died on the cross and rose from the dead proving that He is God, He paid the price for all of our sins (past, present, and future), thereby giving us eternal life in heaven, if only we will believe and trust in Jesus and His great sacrifice. But like the airplane that will do us no good if we do not have the confidence to board it, Jesus' sacrifice will do us no good if we do not have enough faith to place our faith in Him and His sacrifice. A great gift is waiting for us. Will we simply, in childlike faith, humble ourselves enough to set aside self and claim it?

I JOHN 4

Whosoever shall confess that Jesus is the Son of God, God dwelleth in him, and he in God (I John 4:15).

Here, we are told that if we "confess" Jesus, God will dwell in us and we will dwell in God, which means that we will live with and have eternal life with God in heaven forever. But what does it mean to "confess" Jesus? Does it mean mere lip service? I don't think so, because that is called hypocrisy. A confession that leads to salvation is described in Romans 10:9–10, and it tells us that it must be preceded by belief in Jesus, which means trusting solely in Jesus for eternal life. By doing so, we gain the imputed righteousness of Jesus (i.e. when God looks at us, He sees us covered with the blood of Jesus, which covers our sins and gives us the righteousness of Jesus). This belief is the foundation for the confession of Jesus that we can then properly make with our mouths (I John 4:2–3). It is true that a person can confess Jesus with his mouth without believing or trusting in sus, but that would be the sort of lip-service Christianity that ill yield no fruit and that James condemns (James 2:14–26).

The final question that one might ask is how much faith is enough? I am sure that as with Peter, none of us has a faith that is perfect. But, like Peter, whose faith failed him at times, our entire faith for salvation must rest upon Jesus and His blood sacrifice for our sins on the cross. We come to this point of saving faith when we repent of our unpardonable sin of not having trusted in Jesus alone; toss aside all the other things that we cling to like good works, man-made rituals, ceremonies, and traditions; acknowledge that we cannot save ourselves; and transfer our entire trust for salvation to Jesus. All Jesus asks is that we leave self and its man-made devices behind and trust Him alone and then, praise God, He saves us. What a Savior!

I JOHN 5

Whosoever believeth that Jesus is the Christ is born of God; and every one that loveth him that begat loveth him also that is begotten of him (I John 5:1).

The Bible tells us that when we are "born of God" or "born again" we are saved and will spend eternity with God in heaven forever. Everyone trusts in something for when they leave this earth. The atheist and the secularist trust that there is nothing beyond the grave. The religious person trusts in his church, pastor, priest, or their rituals to save him. The self-righteous person trusts in his good works to save him. But the Christian trusts in Jesus, alone, to save him, because the Bible tells him so. As this verse and many others tell us, a person must believe that Jesus is the Christ and then, as simple as it may be, that person is saved.

For many, this is too simple, so the human mind wants to conjure up all sorts of other requirements for eternal life and substitute or add to believing in Jesus. There are many today, as always, who are all too willing to pretend to be the intermediary between God and man. Why do you think they might do that? That would be the wrong way, which leads to death (Proverbs 14:12). So, like the electricity that we perhaps cannot explain, but know is real because of its effects, everyone who tosses aside all the other means of gaining eternal life in heaven and trusts in Jesus alone, knows that Jesus is real because of the peace with God that He gives us. The doubts about where we will spend eternity vanish because we have done what God has told us to do to gain eternal life in heaven (I John 5:13). So, will you choose one of those other ways and keep the doubts or choose Jesus and gain peace? Praise God for the peace that He gives us through Jesus in this life and eternal life in the next!

I JOHN 5

And this is the record, that God hath given to us eternal life, and this life is in his Son. He that hath the Son hath life; and he that hath not the Son of God hath not life. These things have I written unto you that believe on the name of the Son of God; that ye may know that ye have eternal life, and that ye may believe on the name of the Son of God (I John 5:11–13).

These verses tell us that we can "know" that we have eternal life. How can anyone know this? We can know this because of what God tells us and promises to us in His Bible.

When you die and appear before God, if He should ask you, "Why should I let you into heaven?" what would you say? If you tell God that it is because you've done good things, how could you ever know that you have done enough good things? If you tell God that it is because you have not sinned very much, how could you ever know how little sin is acceptable? If you tell God that it is because you attended the right church, how would you know that, except for your church telling you that of course? If you tell God that it is because you did the things your church told you to do, how would you know if your church got it right?

f you tell God that it is because you trusted partly in Jesus and partly in these other things, where does the Bible teach you that?

But if you tell God that it is because you "believe on the name of the Son of God," not in part but in whole, since this is exactly what God said would gain you eternal life, wouldn't you know that this is the answer that God requires? God tells you what you need to do to gain eternal life in heaven, as He does here and in many other places. I guess it boils down to whether you will trust man (and his institutions), self (and its good works), or God for your salvation. Will you trust Jesus enough to allow Him to save you? When you toss aside all the other crutches and devices and believe in Jesus alone for eternal life, can't you then tell God, "Because I have done exactly what You told me to do"?

REVELATION 1

And from Jesus Christ, who is the faithful witness, and the first begotten of the dead, and the prince of the kings of the earth. Unto him that loved us, and washed us from our sins in his own blood (Revelation 1:5).

We learn, once again, that the blood of Jesus washes us from our sins. When our sins are gone, we can live with God in heaven forever. As we have learned in many other verses, this blood will wash you and me of all our sins (past, present, and future) the moment that we believe and trust in that blood and the One who shed it, Jesus. All the sins that we ever have or ever shall commit are paid in full. Neither you nor I paid the price for our sins because the price that God demands for our sins is much more than any of us on this earth could ever pay.

This would be like a wealthy judge sentencing someone to pay a fine of one million dollars or spend ten years in jail for a crime that that person committed. To complete the analogy, after issuing the sentence, the judge would then step down from the bench, take off his robe, and write a check for one million dollars to pay the fine on behalf of the person who was just sentenced. This is exactly what God, through Jesus, did for us. He demands the price for our sins because He is holy and just, but Jesus then paid that price because He loves us. God hates sin but He loves you and through Jesus, the price for sin is paid and you are saved.

However, as with the kindly, benevolent judge in this hypothetical example, you can choose not to accept Jesus or His blood. You can do this by outright refusing Him, or you can do this by turning to other forms of payment instead of or in addition to Jesus. I am sure you can think of many things that we could trust in instead of or in addition to Jesus. That won't work because the Bible tells us that we gain eternal life by trusting solely in Jesus, and nothing else. If you don't trust Jesus enough to trust Him fully, then you do not really trust Him at all. Each of us must humble ourselves and admit that we are great sinners, but Jesus is a greater Savior!

REVELATION 5

And when he had taken the book, the four beasts and four and twenty elders fell down before the Lamb, having every one of them harps, and golden vials full of odours, which are the prayers of saints. And they sung a new song, saying, thou art worthy to take the book, and to open the seals thereof; for thou wast slain, and hast redeemed us to God by thy blood out of every kindred, and tongue, and people, and nation (Revelation 5:8–9).

We are now coming very close to the end of the verses that tell us how we might be saved. The book of Revelation tells us that there is a wonderful future awaiting every saved person, but there is an eternity of torment awaiting every person who is not saved. Wouldn't you agree that the most important thing that any of us can do on this earth is to find the way to ternal life? "For what is a man profited, if he shall gain the whole world and lose his own soul?" (Matthew 16:26). And then, would not the next most important thing to do on this earth be to help others find that same pathway to eternal life in heaven?

Throughout this examination of each salvation verse in the New Testament, it has been my prayer that you would take your own Bible, read ahead from the verse we are studying, and see if you could find the next salvation verse on your own. When that verse is found, you should study it, pray over it, and ask God what He is teaching you in that verse. I suggest circling the verse so you can come back to it. In doing this search, you are obeying God in searching your own Bible to insure that whatever anyone (myself included) tells you about spiritual matters is true. God commended the Bereans for double checking what even the great apostle Paul told them about spiritual matters, and I doubt He expects any less today (Acts 17:11). In doing so, you are seeking God and eternal life in heaven, and God promises you will find it (Jeremiah 29:13; I Chronicles 28:9; Proverbs 8:17). Do not think you can gain God's greatest truths and blessings without seeking Him on your own, as opposed to just listening to what others say about Him.

These verses tell us that God "redeems" each Christian by Jesus' blood. Jesus died on the cross to shed His precious blood as full payment for our sins. But even though the payment has been made, your sins are not forgiven until you put aside everything else that you are trusting in, and trust in that blood and the Savior Who gave it as your One and only Savior. Then, praise God, you are saved and your name will be found in that Book of Life—what a glorious day that will be!

REVELATION 7

And I said unto him, Sir, thou knowest. And he said to me, these are they which came out of great tribulation, and have washed their robes, and made them white in the blood of the Lamb. Therefore are they before the throne of God, and serve him day and night in his temple; and he that sitteth on the throne shall dwell among them (Revelation 7:14–15).

The robes here are a metaphor for us—stained with our sin. But God tells us how these metaphorical robes can become "white," or without sin, so that we can come before and stay with God in heaven. God tells us that we can become "white" or sinless in God's eyes by washing "in the blood of the Lamb," meaning in Jesus' blood. Baptism is a picture, or a symbol, of our washing our sin away. How do we do this? Do we have to find some remnant of Jesus' blood and wash ourselves in that blood? Will water wash that sin away? No, God is speaking symbolically.

A price had to be paid for our sins and that price was the sinless blood of Jesus, which He willingly shed for us on the cross. When we trust in that blood, and the Savior Who gave it, all our sins are forgiven (because the price is paid) and we have eternal life in heaven with God (Ephesians 1:7; Romans 5:9).

Yet, like the miracle cleanser that can take the stain out of our carpet if we only trust it enough to use it, this blood, the price that Jesus paid for our sins, will do us no good if we do not have enough faith to trust in that blood and the Savior Who gave it. My friend, will you lay aside all the other things that you might be trusting in, from self to ceremonies, and trust in that blood and the great Savior Who gave it and thereby gain eternal life in heaven?

REVELATION 12

And I heard a loud voice saying in heaven, now is come salvation, and strength, and the kingdom of our God, and the power of his Christ; for the accuser of our brethren is cast down, which accused them before our God day and night. And they overcame him by the blood of the Lamb, and by the word of their testimony; and they loved not their lives unto death (Revelation 12:10–11).

The "accuser" here is the devil, but God tells us in the Bible that we overcome the devil by "the blood of the Lamb" and "the word of (our) testimony." By these means, we gain eternal life in heaven with God. Jesus shed His blood on the cross at Calvary to pay the price for our sins so that we would be forgiven (Romans 5:9; Ephesians 1:7). The "word of (our) testimony" is the ability of each believer to truthfully tell God that he or she trusts in Jesus and His shed blood, thereby gaining eternal life by faith in Jesus alone and His blood.

The "Lamb" referenced is to remind us of the time when God sent the death angel to Egypt after Pharaoh stubbornly refused to let the Israelites go free, despite one warning and miracle after another. This would be like the rebel who refuses to follow God's instructions despite one warning after another. The Israelites were instructed to take a lamb without blemish and kill and put the blood of that lamb on the doorposts of their houses. When the death angel saw that blood, he would pass over that house (Exodus 12:1–30). But the houses without the blood suffered death. Salvation is just that simple. When we figuratively take Jesus' blood, by trusting in that blood and claiming it as the full payment for our sins, then eternal death will pass us by and we shall live in heaven forever. The accuser, who is the devil, will try to accuse us of our sins before God, but God will see only the perfectly righteous blood of Jesus covering our sins in full payment thereof. As believers, we then need worry no more about our salvation, because the blood of Jesus is more powerful than the accusations of the devil (I John 5:13). The "word of (our) testimony" is our declaration to God, Who can easily separate fact from fiction, that we only trust in Jesus and His shed blood for eternal life—that is the sort of belief that will produce good works out of gratitude to Jesus for what He has done to save us (James 2:14–26). A real belief in Jesus is the belief that tosses aside all the other man-made gimmicks, believes that Jesus alone can save, and relies upon Jesus alone for eternal life.

Here is the patience of the saints; here are they that keep the commandments of God, and the faith of Jesus. And I heard a voice from heaven saying unto me, write, blessed are the dead which die in the Lord from henceforth; yea, saith the Spirit, that they may rest from their labours; and their works do follow them (Revelation 14:12–13).

Blessed are they that do his commandments, that they may have right to the tree of life, and may enter in through the gates into the city. For without are dogs, and sorcerers, and whoremongers, and murderers, and idolaters, and whosoever loveth and maketh a lie. I Jesus have sent mine angel to testify unto you these things in the churches. I am the root and the offspring of David, and the bright and morning star. And the Spirit and the bride say, Come. And let him that heareth say, Come. And let him that is athirst come. And whosoever will, let him take the water of life freely (Revelation 22:14–17).

These are a few of a handful of verses that, taken alone, would indicate that we gain eternal life by both works (keeping the commandments) and faith in Jesus. However, we know from the hundreds of other verses we have studied that the vast multitude of these verses tell us that it is faith in Jesus alone that saves us. So, how do we reconcile these seemingly odd verses with the multitude of others?

Maybe a little mathematical exercise in logic will illustrate part of what I am about to say. We know that 1=1. If we also

ve a formula 1+x=1, what is the value of x? We know that x is
Similarly, if (faith in Jesus=salvation) and (faith in
us+works=salvation), and both statements are true, what does
rks contribute to salvation? The answer is obviously zero. But
y state the latter? It is because works are important, but as
VIDENCE of salvation and not as a **CAUSE** of salvation.
u could substitute the word baptism for works and you would
ve the same situation. Just as works are an **EVIDENCE** of
lvation, baptism is important because it is a **SYMBOL** of
lvation but neither is a **CAUSE** of salvation. The **CAUSE** is
ith in Jesus.

Jesus told us, "By their fruits ye shall know them"
Matthew 7:20). It is important that the Christian do his best to
llow the commandments, both out of gratitude to Jesus for
hat He has done for us, and to be a good witness to people
ound us. If your stockbroker told you to buy stock in company
and you learned that your stockbroker at the same time was
lling stock in company X, what would you think? That
ockbroker would not likely influence you to buy that stock,
ould he? So too with the backsliding Christian who disobeys
od's commandments. Each Christian should try to help his
llow man find eternal life in heaven and perhaps the best way to
o this is to live a life that will influence others toward, and not
way from, our great Savior.

REVELATION 21

*He that overcometh shall inherit all things;
nd I will be his God, and he shall be my son. But the
earful, and unbelieving, and the abominable, and
murders, and whoremongers, and sorcerers, and
dolaters, and all liars, shall have their part in the
ake which burneth with fire and brimstone; which is
he second death (Revelation 21:7–8).*

These verses would seem to indicate that good works, or leas
avoidance of sin, play some part in salvation, while the othe
verses we have been examining teach us that we gain eternal life
by trust and belief in Jesus alone and the blood He shed as the
full payment for our sins (Ephesians 2:8–9). The answer to thi
seeming discrepancy is found in I John 5:5, which tells us, "Who
is he that overcometh the world, but he that believeth that Jesus
is the Son of God?" In other words, when we believe in Jesus, we
thereby become the overcomers that these verses talk about.

Unfortunately, the saved believer will sin from time to
time. This does not mean that when the believer sins he becomes
lost. The believer has everlasting life (John 3:16), and
"everlasting" life does not last only until the next time the
believer sins; it lasts forever. A believer has overcome sin by
trusting in Jesus Christ, at which moment Jesus' blood has
covered *all* the believer's sins.

Does this mean that the believer can feel free to sin? No,
the person who believes is instantly freed from sin and has the
power to resist sin (Romans 6:11–15). Why would the Christian,
who now understands what Jesus has done for him, desire to
harm his great Savior? A Christian resists sin not in order to gain
the salvation that he already has but out of gratitude to Jesus for
what He has done.

CONCLUSION

We have studied over two hundred verses (or cluster of
verses) that tell us how we might be saved. These verses
tell us that we are saved by faith solely in Jesus and the blood that
He shed on the cross as the all-sufficient penalty for the sins that
each of us has committed. But this precious gift does us no good
until we accept it. We are told that at the moment we trust in
Jesus as our all-sufficient resurrected Savior, all our sins (past and
present and future sins) are forgiven and we have gained eternal
(not temporary) life in heaven. Yes, we certainly should try and
keep the commandments and we should try to do the good

igs the Bible tells us to do, but never for a moment thinking
t any of this will earn us eternal life. We should do these
igs out of gratitude to Jesus for what He has done for us. If
try to do good works to earn (as opposed to gratitude for) our
 vation, it would be like trying to repay a loved one for a
time worth of love and sacrifice with a few coins. It would be
insult! And what kind of a people would we be if we spent
r lifetime hurting, rather than trying to thank and obey the
at God Who suffered to save us? There's a great old
andinavian hymn that many believers through the ages have
ntified with (many choose it as a final hymn to summarize
eir lives). It so well summarizes how a person comes to be
ved; I cannot say it any better:

He the Pearly Gates Will Open*

Love divine, so great and wondrous,
Deep and mighty, pure, sublime!
Coming from the heart of Jesus,
Just the same through tests of time.

Like a dove when hunted, frightened,
As a wounded fawn was I;
Brokenhearted, yet He healed me,
He will heed the sinner's cry.

Love divine so great and wondrous,
All my sins He then forgave!
I will sing His praise forever,
For His blood, His power to save.

In life's eventide, at twilight,
At His door I'll knock and wait;
By the precious love of Jesus
I shall enter Heaven's gate.

He the pearly gates will open,
So that I may enter in;
For He purchased my redemption
And forgave me all my sin.

Written by Fredrick A. Blom in 1917 and translated to English by Nathaniel
arlson in 1935. The music was written by Alfred O. Duhlin and arranged by
sie R. Ahlwen in 1930.

INDEX

James 1:21.....................247
James 2:14–20.........................248
John 1:12......................26
John 1:29......................27
John 3:3......................28
John 3:14–16......................30
John 3:17–18......................31
John 3:36......................32
John 4: 41–42......................34
John 5: 22–24......................35
John 5:29......................37
John 5:37–44......................38
John 6:26–29......................40
John 6:30–35......................41
John 6:37......................42
John 6:40–41......................43
John 6:47–58......................45
John 6:63......................46
John 7:38–39......................47
John 8:24......................49
John 10:9......................50
John 10:10......................51
John 10:26–30......................52
John 11:25......................52
John 12:25......................53
John 12:32......................54
John 12:37......................55
John 12:46......................56
John 14:6......................58
John 17:3......................59
John 20:31......................60

Luke 7:50......................21
Luke 8:12......................22
Luke 18:42......................23
Luke 19:9–10......................24
Luke 23:42–43......................25

Mark 2:5......................19

Mark 16:16......................2(

Matthew 1:21......................
Matthew 5: 3, 8, 10, 20, 48.......(
Matthew 7: 21–23......................1
Matthew 9:2......................1.
Matthew 18:3......................1.
Matthew 19:21......................1(
Matthew 19:29......................1.
Matthew 26, 28......................1.
Matthew 26:19......................1.
Matthew 27:51–54......................1(

Philippians 3:8–11......................18.

Revelation 1:5......................26(
Revelation 5:8–9......................27(
Revelation 7:14–15......................27.
Revelation 12:10–11......................27.
Revelation 14:12–13......................27.
Revelation 21:7–8......................27(
Revelation 22:14–17......................27.

Romans 1:3–5......................8(
Romans 1:16–17......................8.
Romans 3:20–22......................8.
Romans 3:22......................8.
Romans 3:23–24......................84
Romans 3:25......................85
Romans 3:26......................86
Romans 3:28......................88
Romans 3:30......................89
Romans 4:2–3......................90
Romans 4:20–22......................95
Romans 4:24–25......................97
Romans 4:4–5......................91
Romans 4:6–13......................92
Romans 5:1......................98
Romans 5:2......................99